DEC 0 5 2013

D0678005

MARVEL ADVENTURES SUPER HEROES #6
WRITER: **PAUL TOBIN**
PENCILER: **RONAN CLIQUET**
INKER: **AMILTON SANTOS**
COLORIST: **SOTOCOLOR**
LETTERER: **DAVE SHARPE**
COVER ARTISTS: **CLAYTON HENRY & SOTOCOLOR**
ASSISTANT EDITOR: **MICHAEL HORWITZ**
EDITOR: **NATHAN COSBY**

MARVEL ADVENTURES SUPER HEROES #13
WRITER: **PAUL TOBIN**
PENCILER: **RONAN CLIQUET**
INKER: **AMILTON SANTOS**
COLORIST: **SOTOCOLOR**
LETTERER: **DAVE SHARPE**
COVER ARTIST: **STEPHEN SEGOVIA**
ASSISTANT EDITORS: **RACHEL PINNELAS & STEPHEN WACKER**
EDITORS: **MICHAEL HORWITZ & BILL ROSEMANN**

MARVEL ADVENTURES SUPER HEROES #8
WRITER: **PAUL TOBIN**
ARTIST: **SCOTT KOBLISH**
COLOR ARTIST: **SOTOCOLOR**
LETTERER: **DAVE SHARPE**
COVER ARTISTS: **CLAYTON HENRY & CHRIS SOTOMAYOR**
ASSISTANT EDITORS: **MICHAEL HORWITZ & JOHN DENNING**
EDITOR: **NATHAN COSBY**

"IF HE BE WORTHY"
FROM *MARVEL ADVENTURES SUPER HEROES #19*
WRITER: **JOE CARAMAGNA**
PENCILER: **KEVIN SHARPE**
INKER: **TERRY PALLOT**
COLORIST: **CHRIS SOTOMAYOR**
LETTERER: **DAVE SHARPE**
COVER ARTIST: **STEPHEN SEGOVIA**
ASSISTANT EDITOR: **ELLIE PYLE**
EDITOR: **RACHEL PINNELAS**
CONTRIBUTING EDITOR: **TOM BRENNAN**
SENIOR EDITOR: **STEPHEN WACKER**

COLLECTION EDITOR & DESIGN: CORY LEVINE • ASSISTANT EDITORS: ALEX STARBUCK & NELSON RIBEIRO
EDITORS, SPECIAL PROJECTS: JENNIFER GRÜNWALD & MARK D. BEAZLEY
SENIOR EDITOR, SPECIAL PROJECTS: JEFF YOUNGQUIST • SVP OF PRINT & DIGITAL PUBLISHING SALES: DAVID GABRIEL
EDITOR IN CHIEF: AXEL ALONSO • CHIEF CREATIVE OFFICER: JOE QUESADA
PUBLISHER: DAN BUCKLEY • EXECUTIVE PRODUCER: ALAN FINE

MARVEL UNIVERSE THOR. Contains material originally published in magazine form as MARVEL ADVENTURES SUPER HEROES #6, #8, #13 and #19; and JOURNEY INTO MYSTERY #83. First printing 2013. ISBN# 978-0-7851-8505-5. Published by MARVEL WORLDWIDE, INC., a subsidiary of MARVEL ENTERTAINMENT, LLC. OFFICE OF PUBLICATION: 135 West 50th Street, New York, NY 10020. Copyright © 1962, 2010, 2011 and 2013 Marvel Characters, Inc. All rights reserved. All characters featured in this issue and the distinctive names and likenesses thereof, and all related indicia are trademarks of Marvel Characters, Inc. No similarity between any of the names, characters, persons, and/or institutions in this magazine with those of any living or dead person or institution is intended, and any such similarity which may exist is purely coincidental. **Printed in the U.S.A.** ALAN FINE, EVP - Office of the President, Marvel Worldwide, Inc. and EVP & CMO Marvel Characters B.V.; DAN BUCKLEY, Publisher & President - Print, Animation & Digital Divisions; JOE QUESADA, Chief Creative Officer; TOM BREVOORT, SVP of Publishing; DAVID BOGART, SVP of Operations & Procurement, Publishing; C.B. CEBULSKI, SVP of Creator & Content Development; DAVID GABRIEL, SVP of Print & Digital Publishing Sales; JIM O'KEEFE, VP of Operations & Logistics; DAN CARR, Executive Director of Publishing Technology; SUSAN CRESPI, Editorial Operations Manager; ALEX MORALES, Publishing Operations Manager; STAN LEE, Chairman Emeritus. For information regarding advertising in Marvel Comics or on Marvel.com, please contact Niza Disla, Director of Marvel Partnerships, at ndisla@marvel.com. For Marvel subscription inquiries, please call 800-217-9158. **Manufactured between 9/6/2013 and 10/14/2013** by SHERIDAN BOOKS, INC., CHELSEA, MI, USA.

10 9 8 7 6 5 4 3 2 1

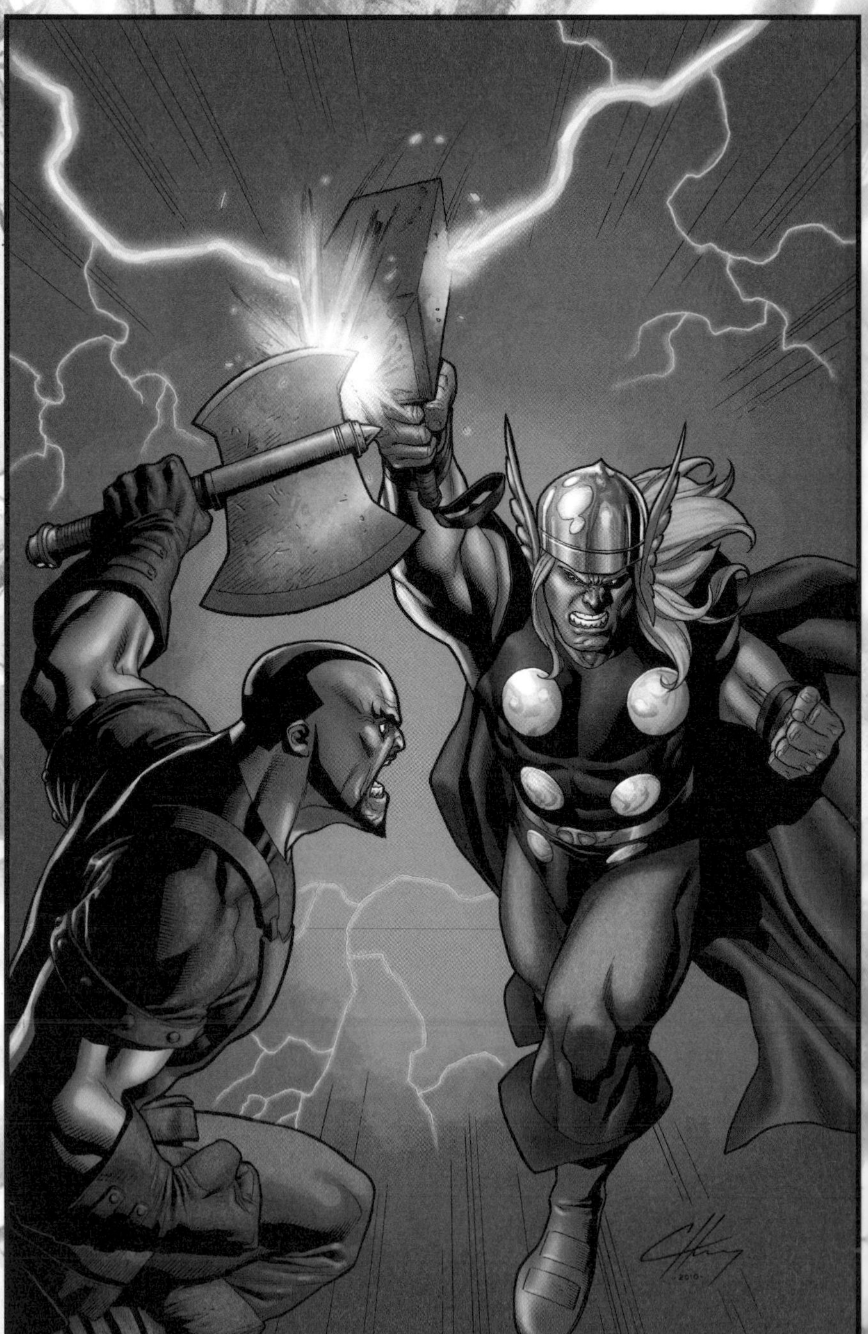

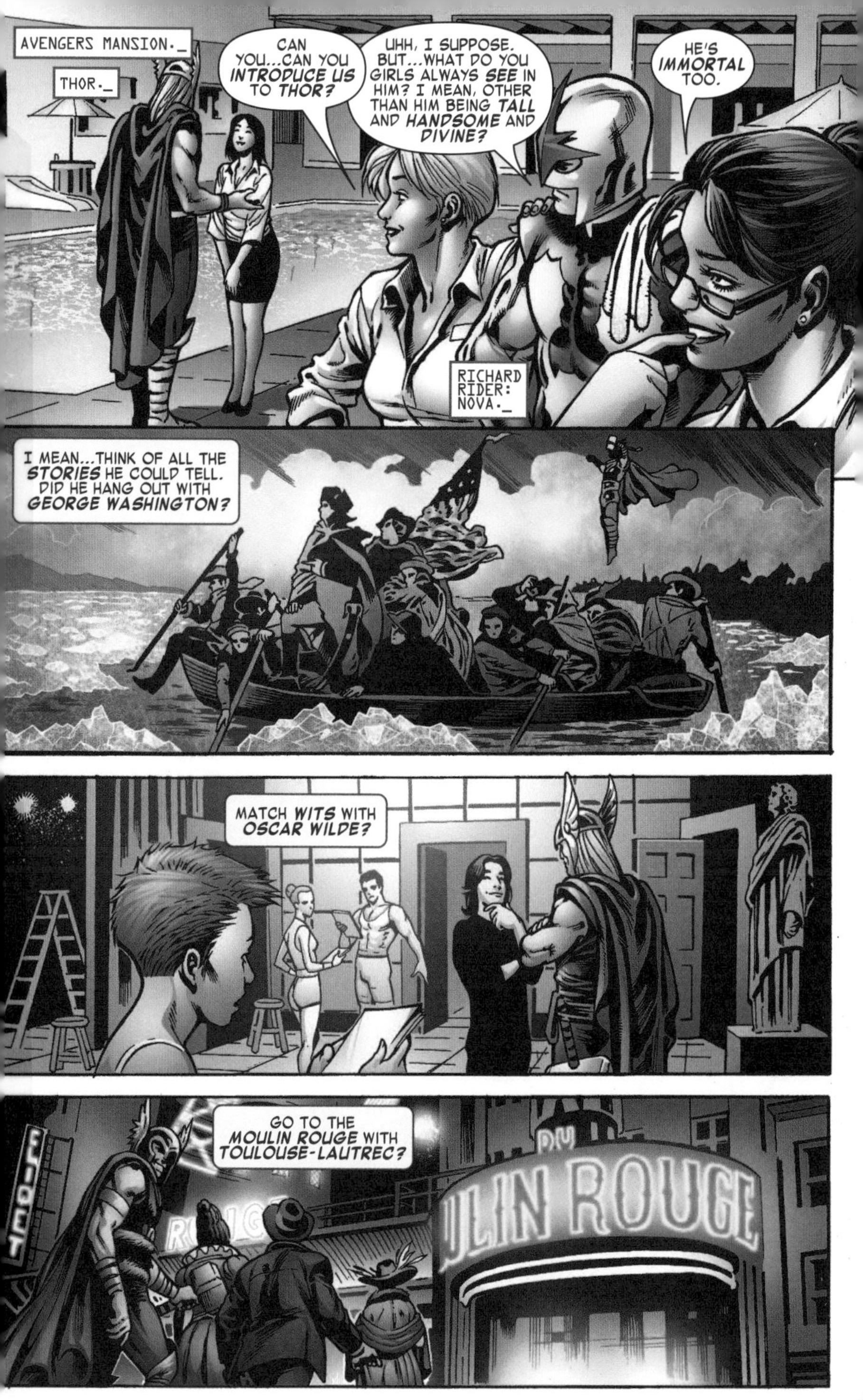
AVENGERS MANSION._
THOR._
CAN YOU...CAN YOU INTRODUCE US TO THOR?
UHH, I SUPPOSE. BUT...WHAT DO YOU GIRLS ALWAYS SEE IN HIM? I MEAN, OTHER THAN HIM BEING TALL AND HANDSOME AND DIVINE?
HE'S IMMORTAL TOO.
RICHARD RIDER: NOVA._
I MEAN...THINK OF ALL THE STORIES HE COULD TELL. DID HE HANG OUT WITH GEORGE WASHINGTON?
MATCH WITS WITH OSCAR WILDE?
GO TO THE MOULIN ROUGE WITH TOULOUSE-LAUTREC?

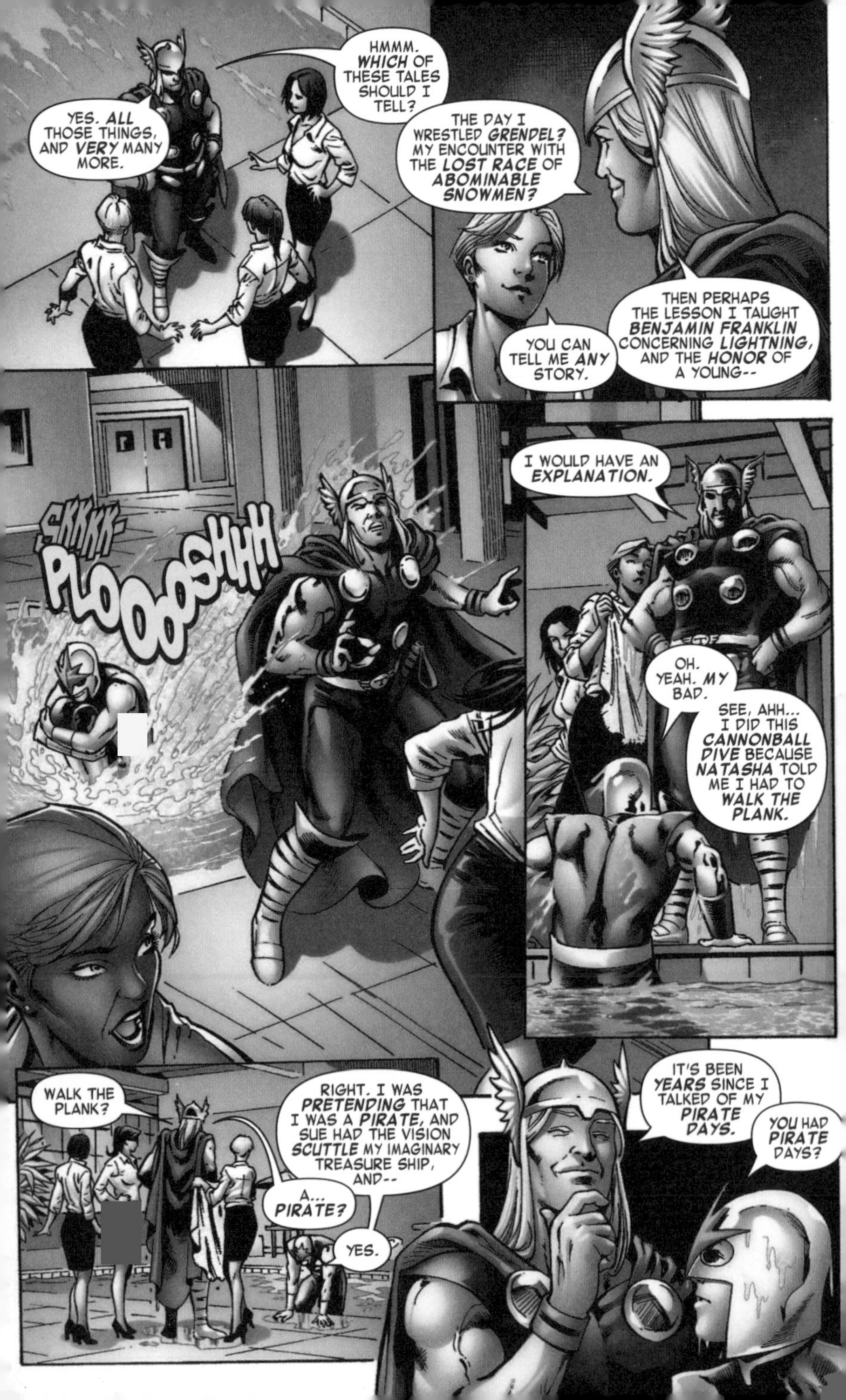

YES. ALL THOSE THINGS, AND VERY MANY MORE.
HMMM. WHICH OF THESE TALES SHOULD I TELL?
THE DAY I WRESTLED GRENDEL? MY ENCOUNTER WITH THE LOST RACE OF ABOMINABLE SNOWMEN?
YOU CAN TELL ME ANY STORY.
THEN PERHAPS THE LESSON I TAUGHT BENJAMIN FRANKLIN CONCERNING LIGHTNING, AND THE HONOR OF A YOUNG--
SKKKK-PLOOOOSHHH
I WOULD HAVE AN EXPLANATION.
OH. YEAH. MY BAD.
SEE, AHH... I DID THIS CANNONBALL DIVE BECAUSE NATASHA TOLD ME I HAD TO WALK THE PLANK.
WALK THE PLANK?
RIGHT. I WAS PRETENDING THAT I WAS A PIRATE, AND SUE HAD THE VISION SCUTTLE MY IMAGINARY TREASURE SHIP, AND--
A... PIRATE?
YES.
IT'S BEEN YEARS SINCE I TALKED OF MY PIRATE DAYS.
YOU HAD PIRATE DAYS?

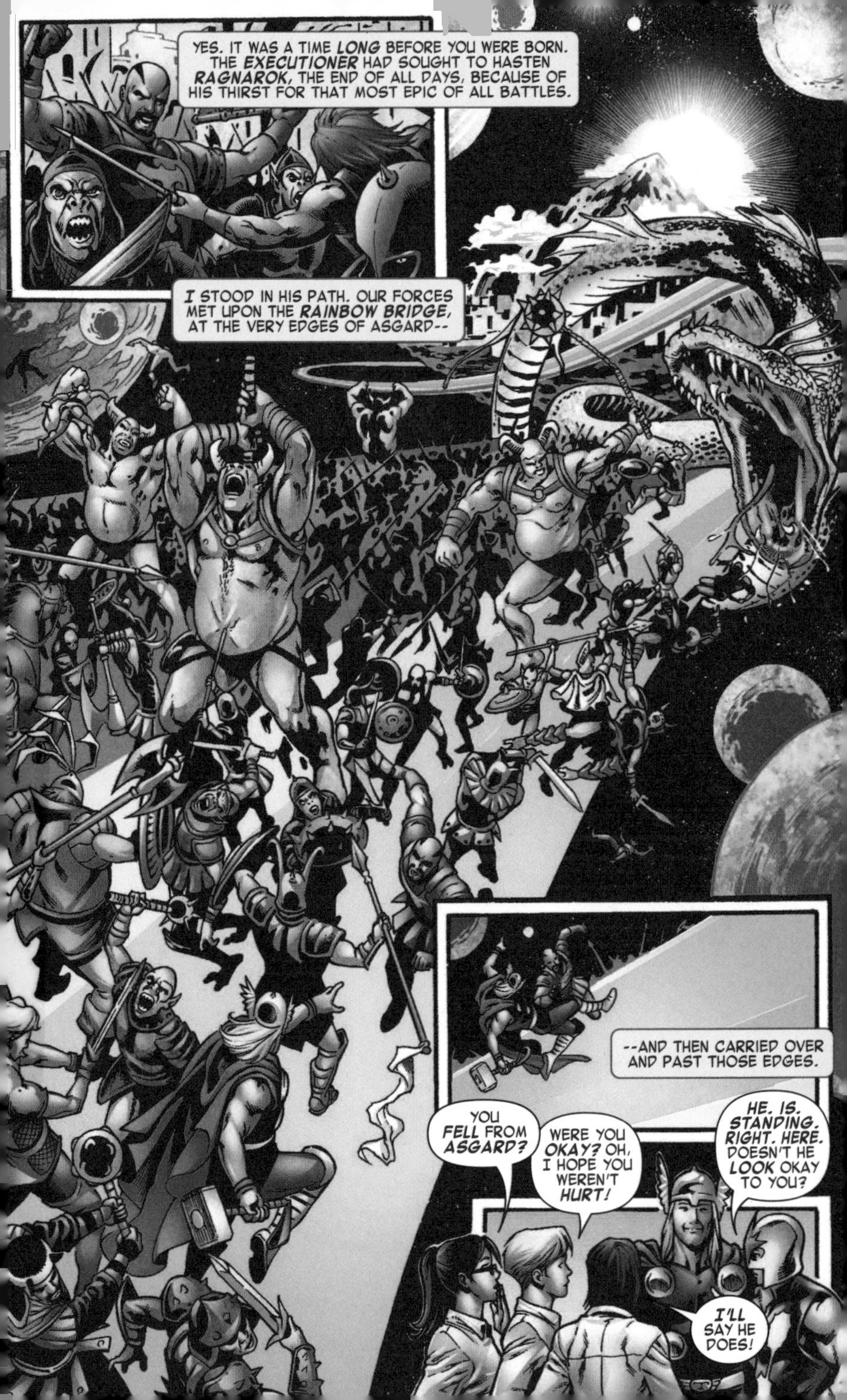
YES. IT WAS A TIME LONG BEFORE YOU WERE BORN. THE EXECUTIONER HAD SOUGHT TO HASTEN RAGNAROK, THE END OF ALL DAYS, BECAUSE OF HIS THIRST FOR THAT MOST EPIC OF ALL BATTLES.
I STOOD IN HIS PATH. OUR FORCES MET UPON THE RAINBOW BRIDGE, AT THE VERY EDGES OF ASGARD--
--AND THEN CARRIED OVER AND PAST THOSE EDGES.
YOU FELL FROM ASGARD?
WERE YOU OKAY? OH, I HOPE YOU WEREN'T HURT!
HE. IS. STANDING. RIGHT. HERE. DOESN'T HE LOOK OKAY TO YOU?
I'LL SAY HE DOES!

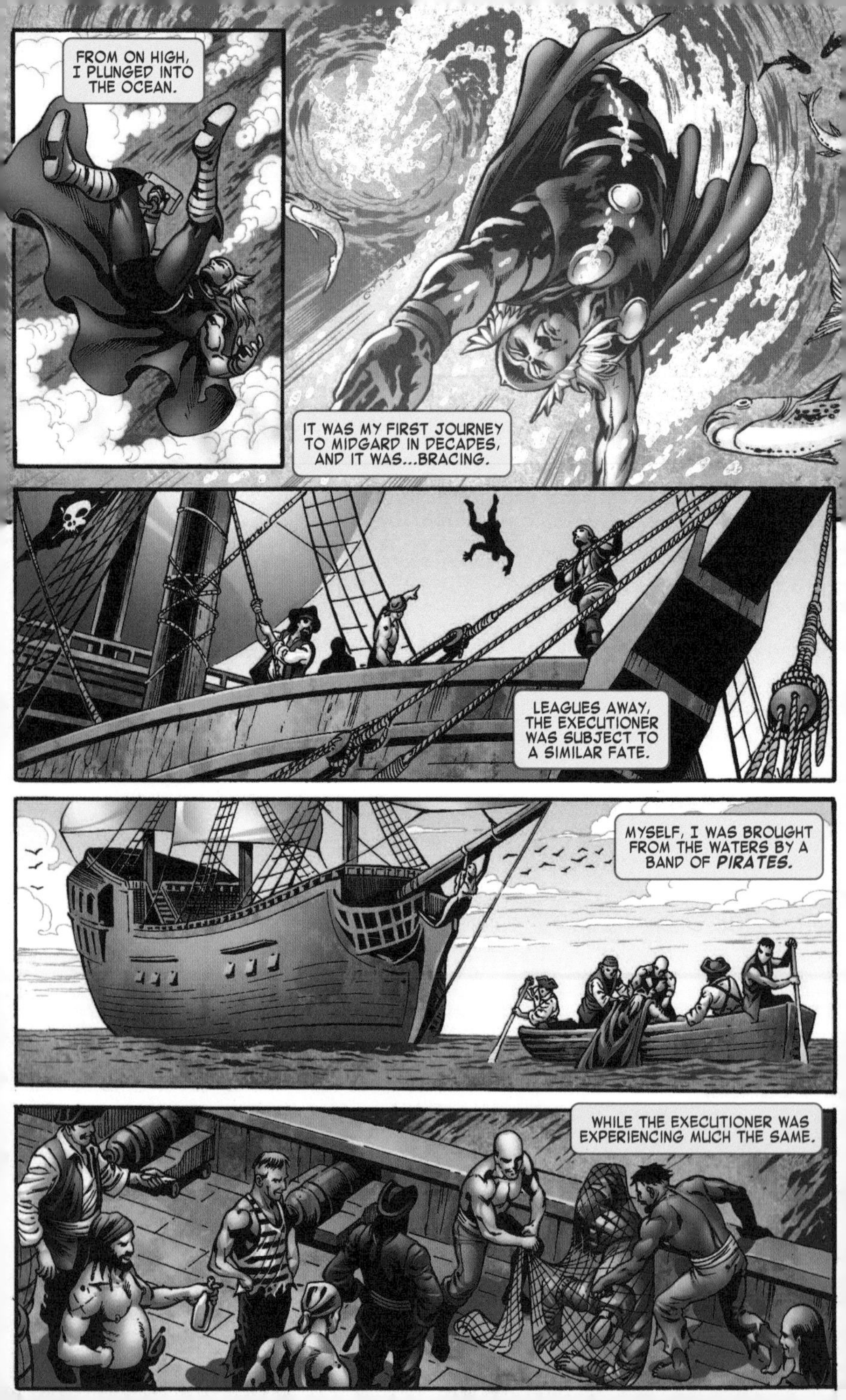

FROM ON HIGH, I PLUNGED INTO THE OCEAN.
IT WAS MY FIRST JOURNEY TO MIDGARD IN DECADES, AND IT WAS...BRACING.
LEAGUES AWAY, THE EXECUTIONER WAS SUBJECT TO A SIMILAR FATE.
MYSELF, I WAS BROUGHT FROM THE WATERS BY A BAND OF *PIRATES.*
WHILE THE EXECUTIONER WAS EXPERIENCING MUCH THE SAME.

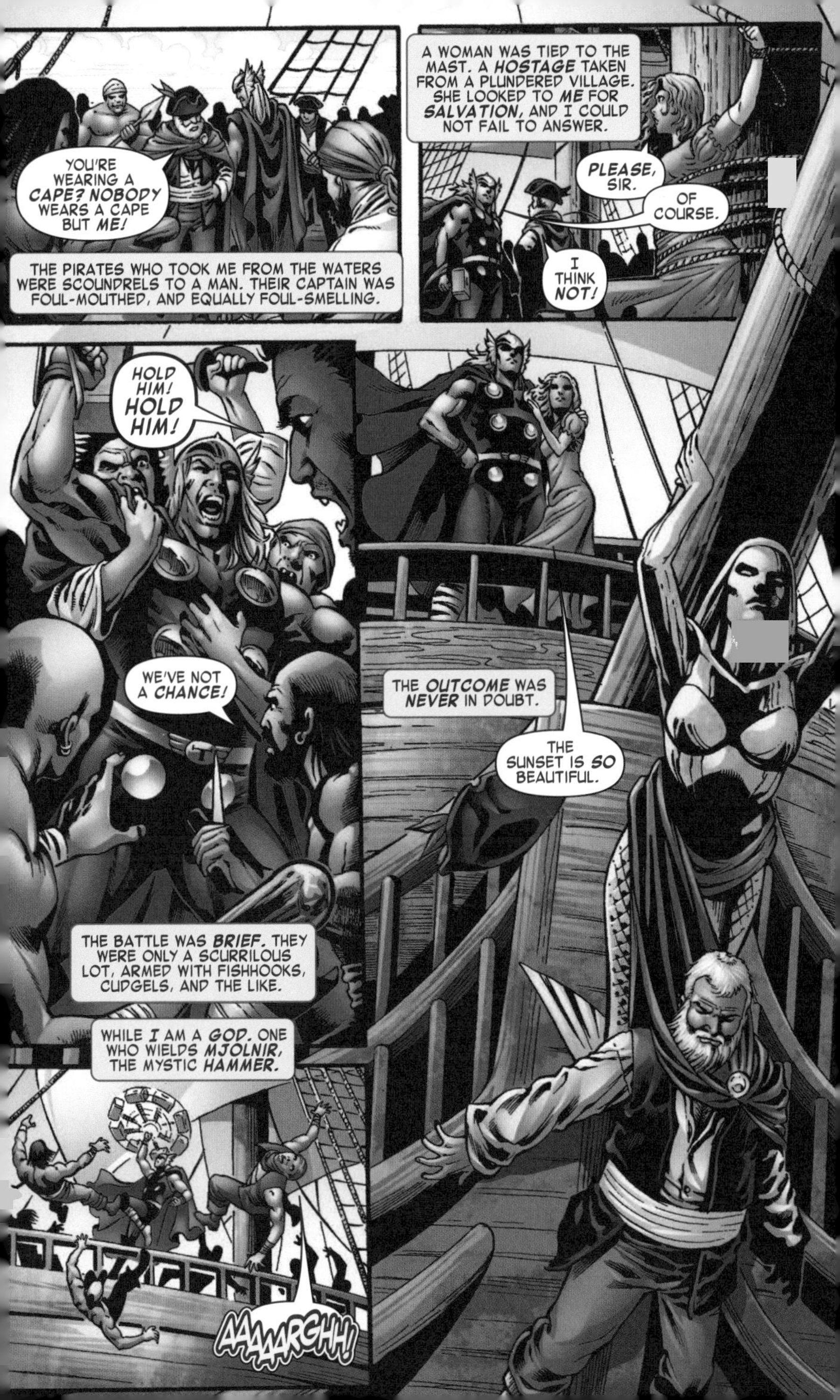
YOU'RE WEARING A CAPE? NOBODY WEARS A CAPE BUT ME!
THE PIRATES WHO TOOK ME FROM THE WATERS WERE SCOUNDRELS TO A MAN. THEIR CAPTAIN WAS FOUL-MOUTHED, AND EQUALLY FOUL-SMELLING.
A WOMAN WAS TIED TO THE MAST. A HOSTAGE TAKEN FROM A PLUNDERED VILLAGE. SHE LOOKED TO ME FOR SALVATION, AND I COULD NOT FAIL TO ANSWER.
PLEASE, SIR.
OF COURSE.
I THINK NOT!
HOLD HIM! HOLD HIM!
WE'VE NOT A CHANCE!
THE BATTLE WAS BRIEF. THEY WERE ONLY A SCURRILOUS LOT, ARMED WITH FISHHOOKS, CUDGELS, AND THE LIKE.
WHILE I AM A GOD. ONE WHO WIELDS MJOLNIR, THE MYSTIC HAMMER.
AAAAARGHH!
THE OUTCOME WAS NEVER IN DOUBT.
THE SUNSET IS SO BEAUTIFUL.

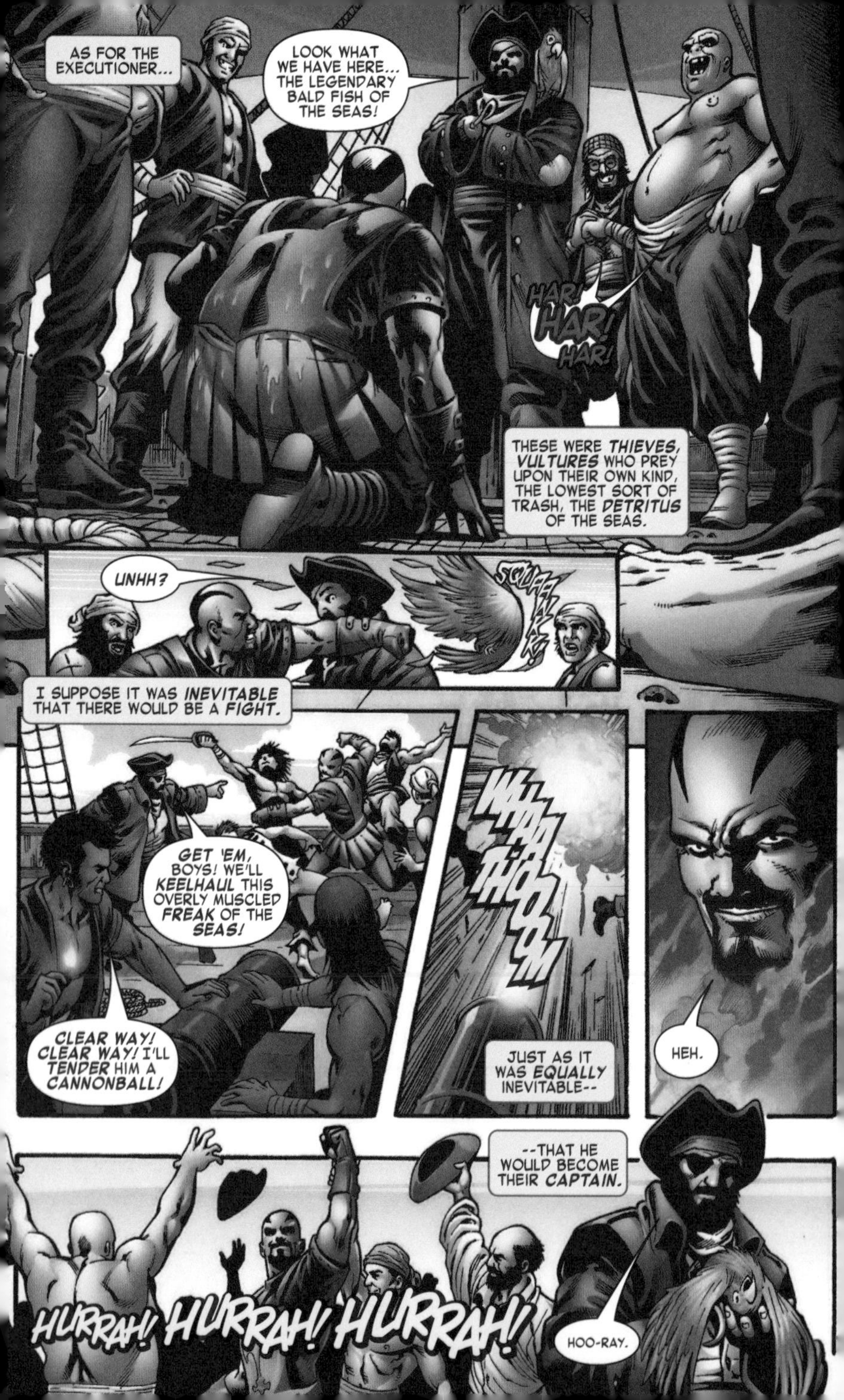
AS FOR THE EXECUTIONER...
LOOK WHAT WE HAVE HERE... THE LEGENDARY BALD FISH OF THE SEAS!
HAR! HAR! HAR!
THESE WERE THIEVES, VULTURES WHO PREY UPON THEIR OWN KIND, THE LOWEST SORT OF TRASH, THE DETRITUS OF THE SEAS.
UNHH?
I SUPPOSE IT WAS INEVITABLE THAT THERE WOULD BE A FIGHT.
GET 'EM, BOYS! WE'LL KEELHAUL THIS OVERLY MUSCLED FREAK OF THE SEAS!
CLEAR WAY! CLEAR WAY! I'LL TENDER HIM A CANNONBALL!
JUST AS IT WAS EQUALLY INEVITABLE--
HEH.
--THAT HE WOULD BECOME THEIR CAPTAIN.
HURRAH! HURRAH! HURRAH!
HOO-RAY.

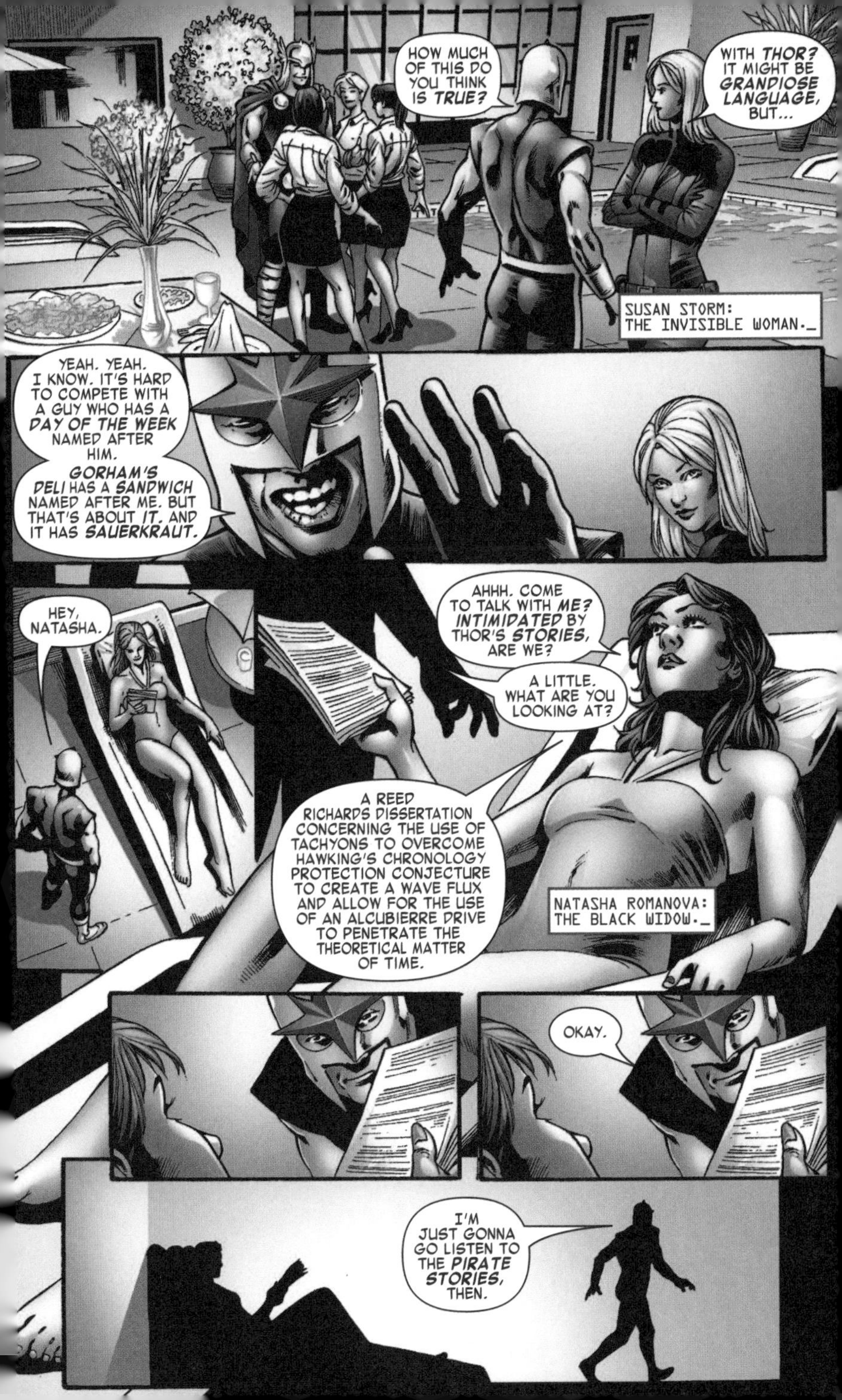

HOW MUCH OF THIS DO YOU THINK IS TRUE?
WITH THOR? IT MIGHT BE GRANDIOSE LANGUAGE, BUT...
SUSAN STORM: THE INVISIBLE WOMAN._
YEAH. YEAH. I KNOW. IT'S HARD TO COMPETE WITH A GUY WHO HAS A DAY OF THE WEEK NAMED AFTER HIM.
GORHAM'S DELI HAS A SANDWICH NAMED AFTER ME. BUT THAT'S ABOUT IT. AND IT HAS SAUERKRAUT.
HEY, NATASHA.
AHHH. COME TO TALK WITH ME? INTIMIDATED BY THOR'S STORIES, ARE WE?
A LITTLE. WHAT ARE YOU LOOKING AT?
A REED RICHARDS DISSERTATION CONCERNING THE USE OF TACHYONS TO OVERCOME HAWKING'S CHRONOLOGY PROTECTION CONJECTURE TO CREATE A WAVE FLUX AND ALLOW FOR THE USE OF AN ALCUBIERRE DRIVE TO PENETRATE THE THEORETICAL MATTER OF TIME.
NATASHA ROMANOVA: THE BLACK WIDOW._
OKAY.
I'M JUST GONNA GO LISTEN TO THE PIRATE STORIES, THEN.

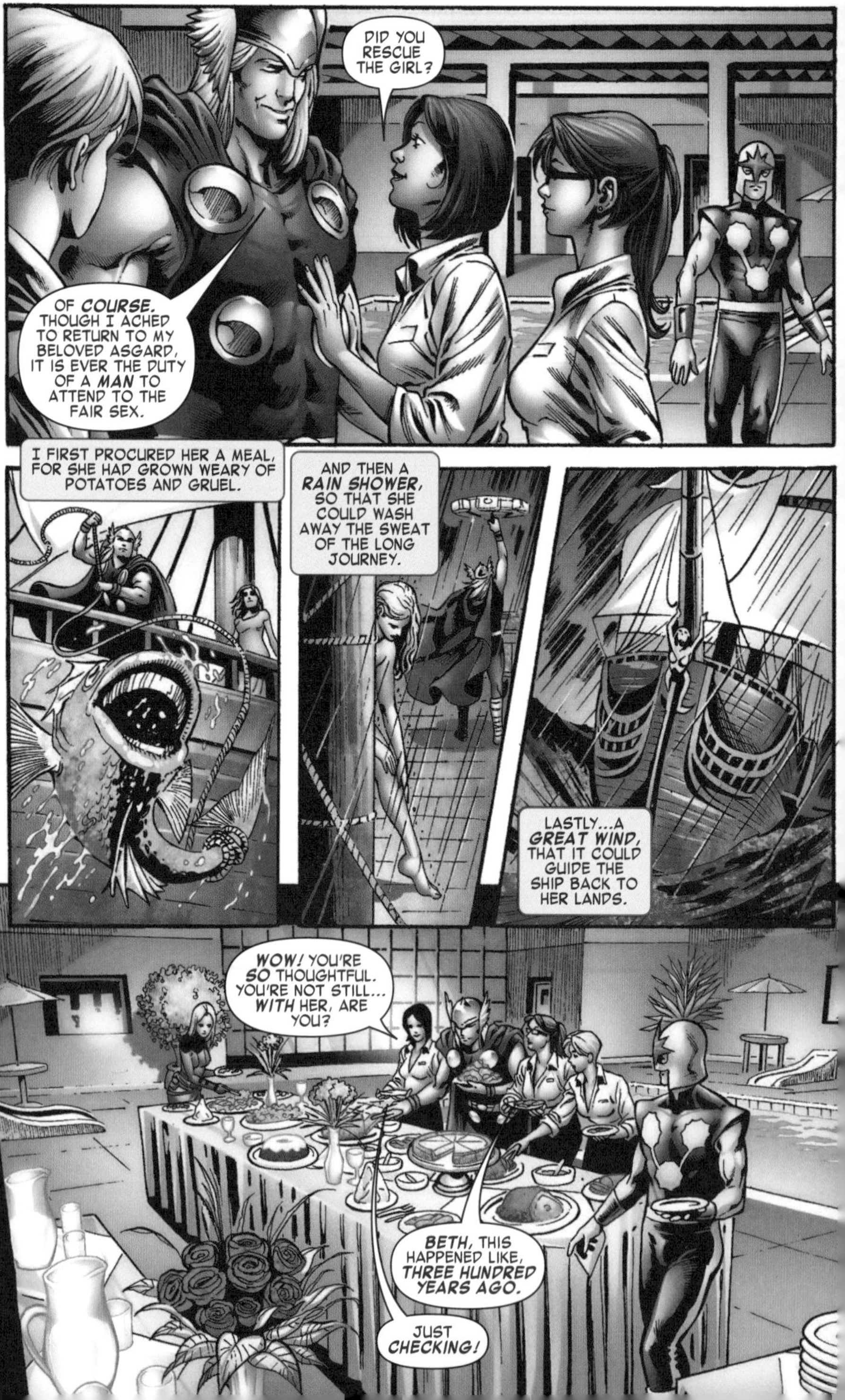

DID YOU RESCUE THE GIRL?
OF COURSE. THOUGH I ACHED TO RETURN TO MY BELOVED ASGARD, IT IS EVER THE DUTY OF A MAN TO ATTEND TO THE FAIR SEX.
I FIRST PROCURED HER A MEAL, FOR SHE HAD GROWN WEARY OF POTATOES AND GRUEL.
AND THEN A RAIN SHOWER, SO THAT SHE COULD WASH AWAY THE SWEAT OF THE LONG JOURNEY.
LASTLY...A GREAT WIND, THAT IT COULD GUIDE THE SHIP BACK TO HER LANDS.
WOW! YOU'RE SO THOUGHTFUL. YOU'RE NOT STILL... WITH HER, ARE YOU?
BETH, THIS HAPPENED LIKE, THREE HUNDRED YEARS AGO.
JUST CHECKING!

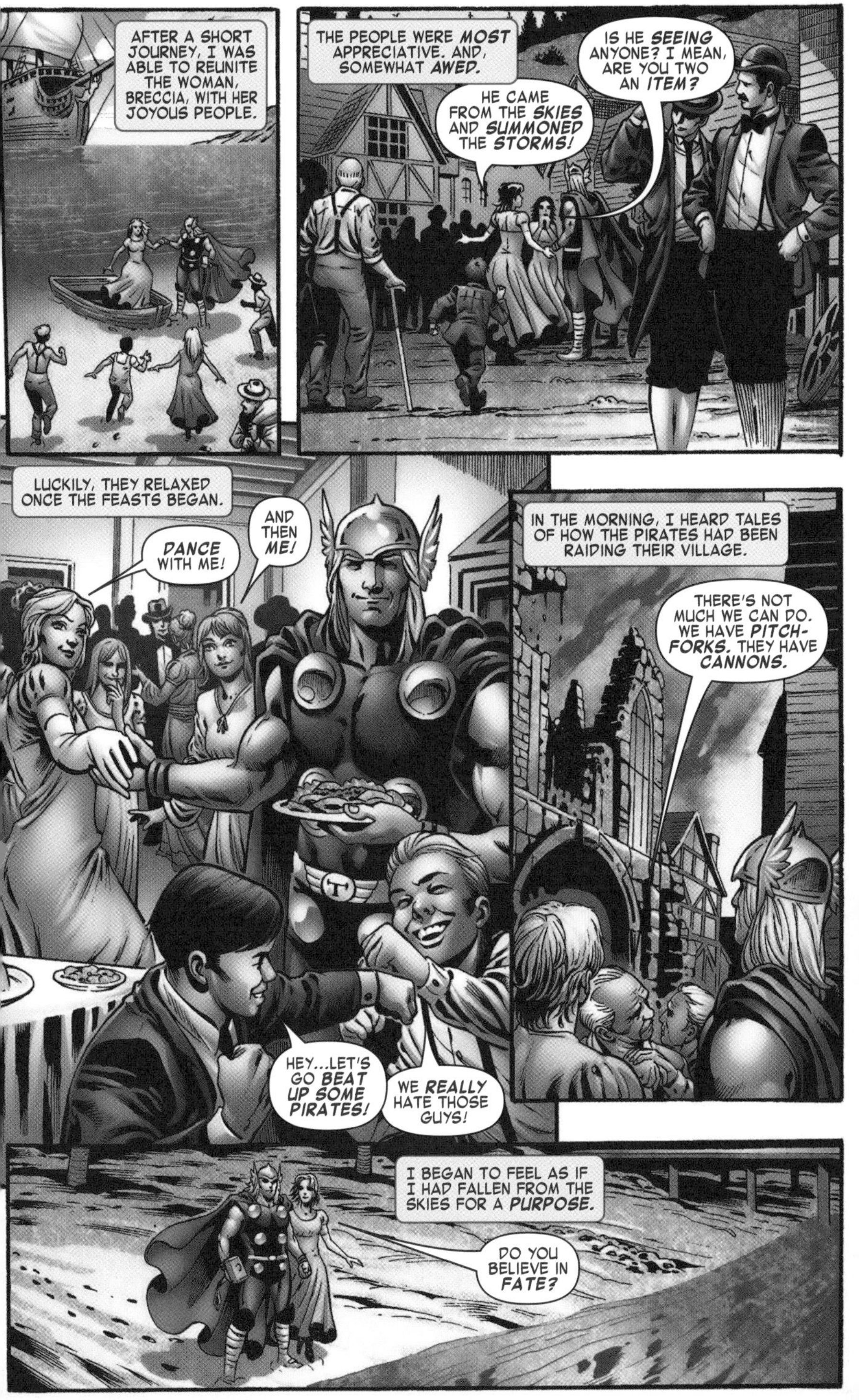

AFTER A SHORT JOURNEY, I WAS ABLE TO REUNITE THE WOMAN, BRECCIA, WITH HER JOYOUS PEOPLE.
THE PEOPLE WERE *MOST* APPRECIATIVE. AND, SOMEWHAT *AWED.*
HE CAME FROM THE *SKIES* AND *SUMMONED* THE *STORMS!*
IS HE *SEEING* ANYONE? I MEAN, ARE YOU TWO AN *ITEM?*
LUCKILY, THEY RELAXED ONCE THE FEASTS BEGAN.
DANCE WITH ME!
AND THEN *ME!*
HEY...LET'S GO *BEAT UP SOME PIRATES!*
WE *REALLY* HATE THOSE GUYS!
IN THE MORNING, I HEARD TALES OF HOW THE PIRATES HAD BEEN RAIDING THEIR VILLAGE.
THERE'S NOT MUCH WE CAN DO. WE HAVE *PITCH-FORKS.* THEY HAVE *CANNONS.*
I BEGAN TO FEEL AS IF I HAD FALLEN FROM THE SKIES FOR A *PURPOSE.*
DO YOU BELIEVE IN *FATE?*

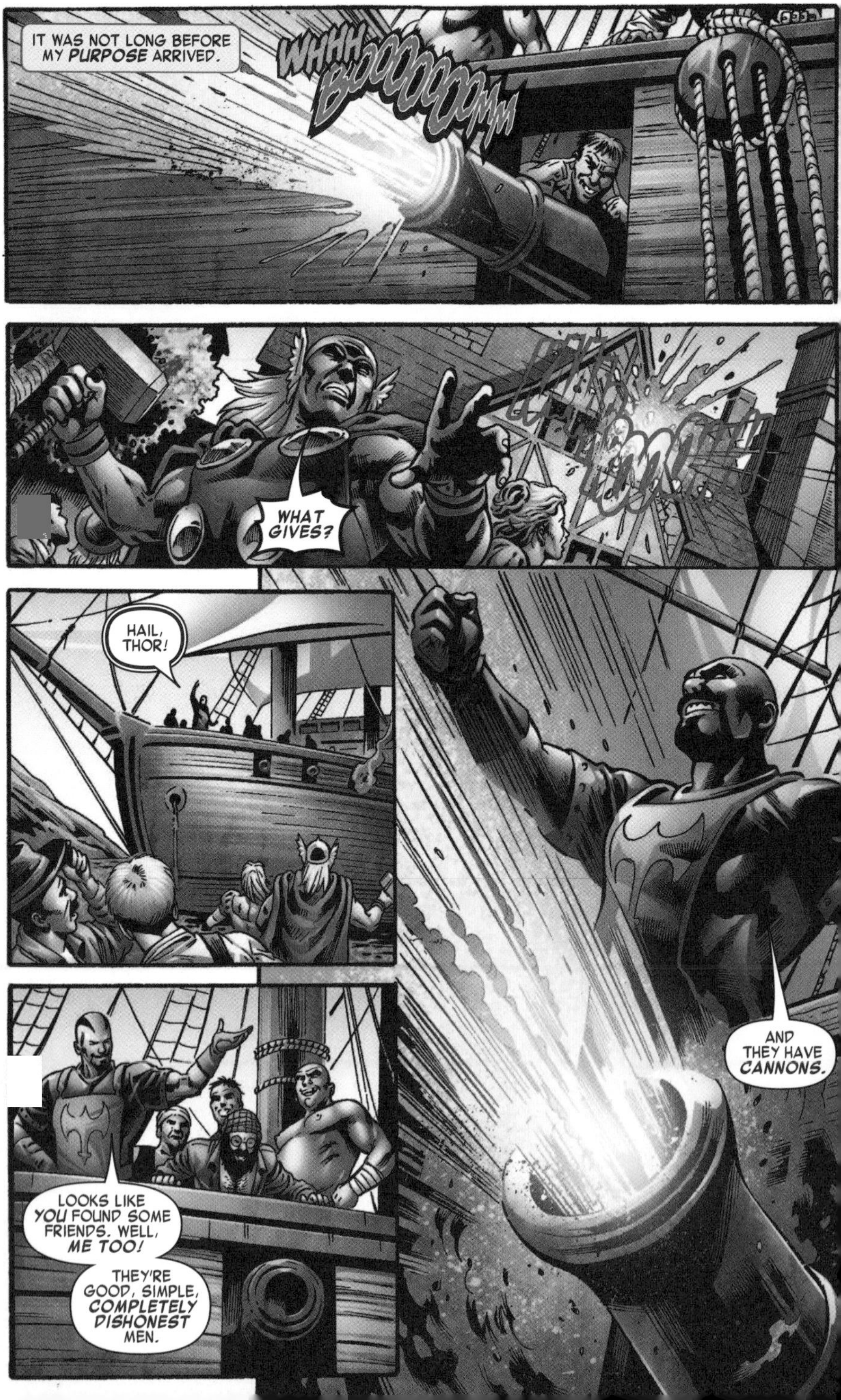
IT WAS NOT LONG BEFORE MY PURPOSE ARRIVED.
WHHH BOOOOOOOMM
WHAT GIVES?
HAIL, THOR!
LOOKS LIKE YOU FOUND SOME FRIENDS. WELL, ME TOO!
THEY'RE GOOD, SIMPLE, COMPLETELY DISHONEST MEN.
AND THEY HAVE CANNONS.

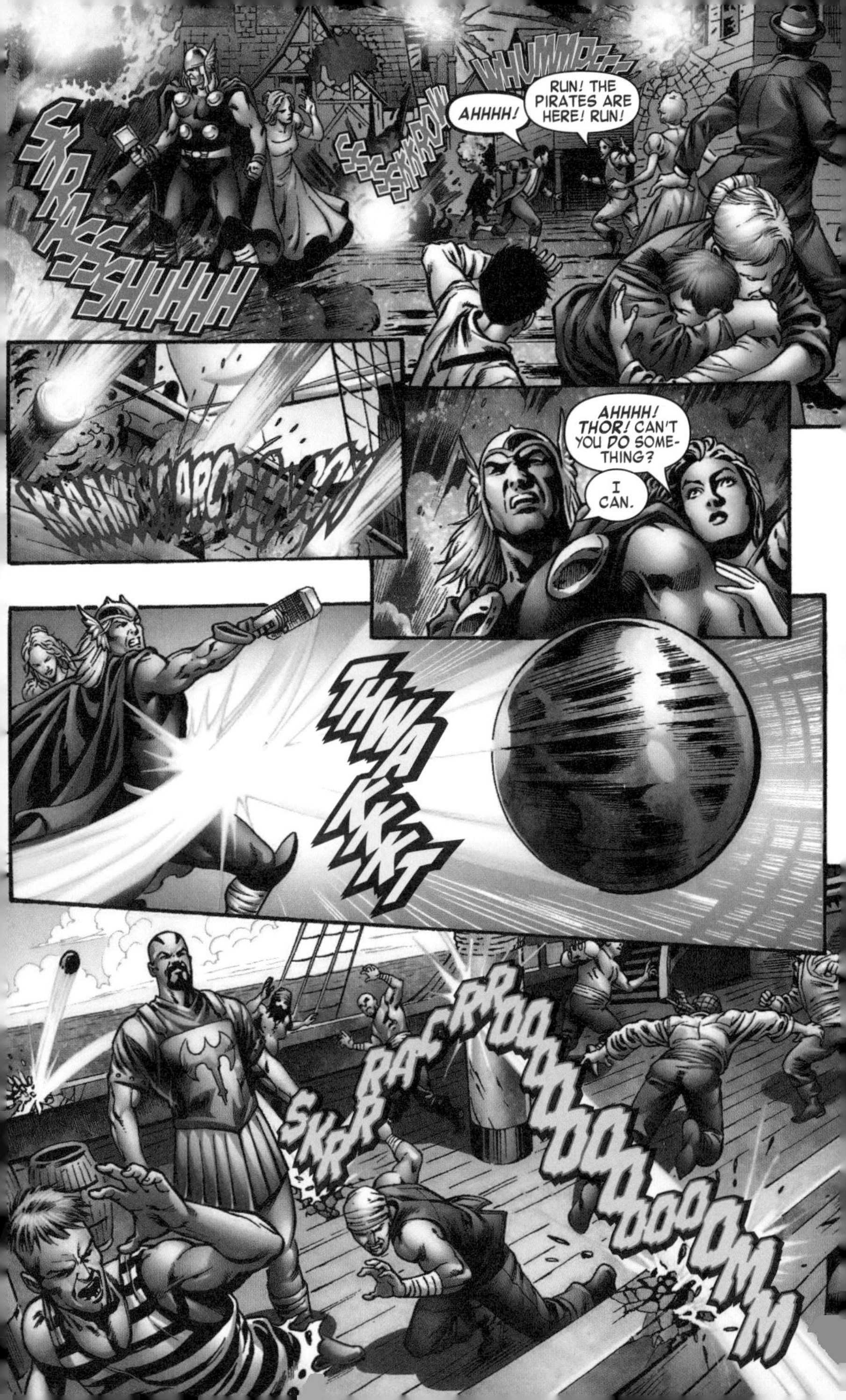
AHHHH!
RUN! THE PIRATES ARE HERE! RUN!
AHHHH! THOR! CAN'T YOU DO SOME-THING?
I CAN.
THWAKKKT

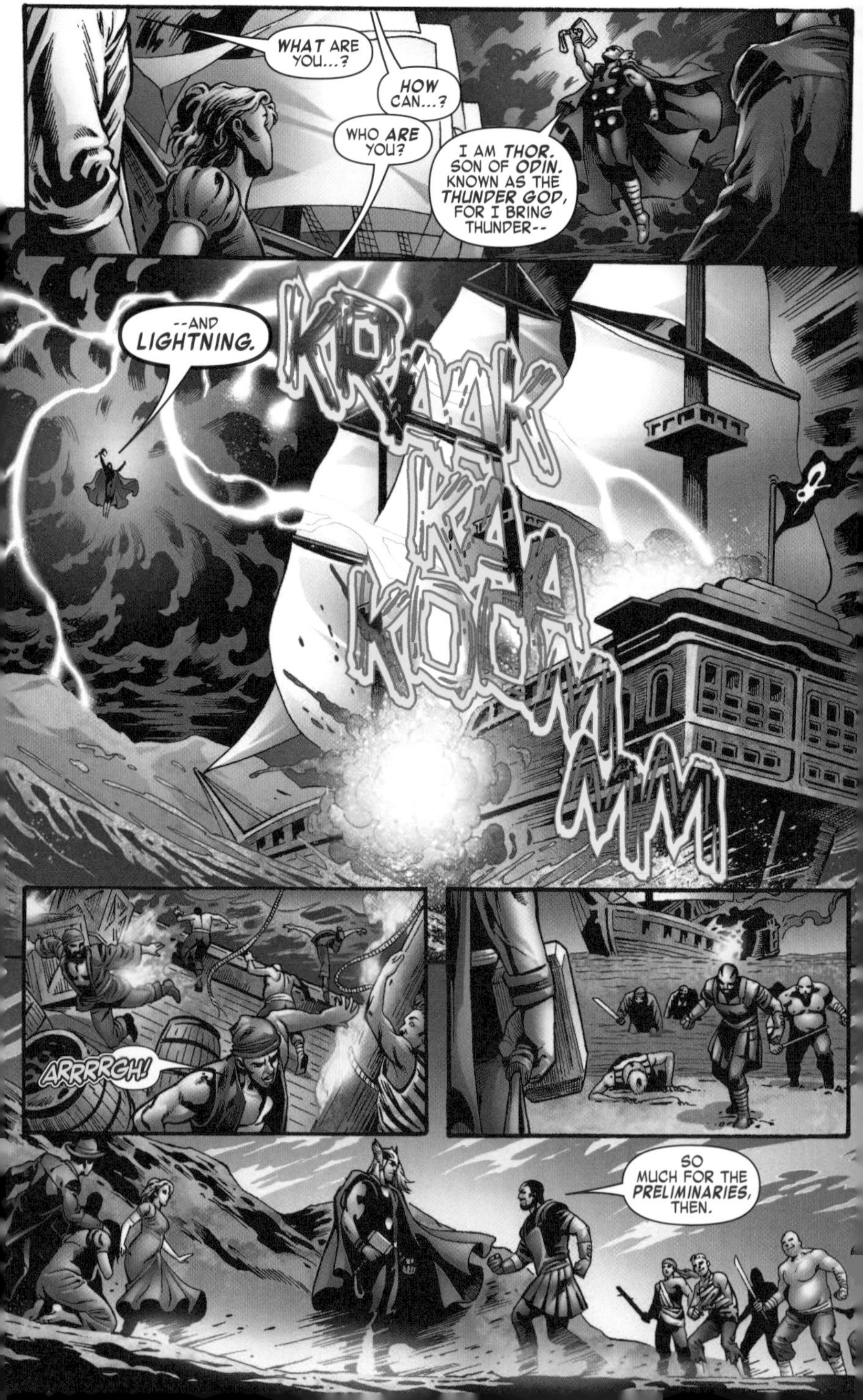
WHAT ARE YOU...?
HOW CAN...?
WHO ARE YOU?
I AM THOR. SON OF ODIN. KNOWN AS THE THUNDER GOD, FOR I BRING THUNDER--
--AND LIGHTNING.
KRAKAKOOM
ARRRRGH!
SO MUCH FOR THE PRELIMINARIES, THEN.

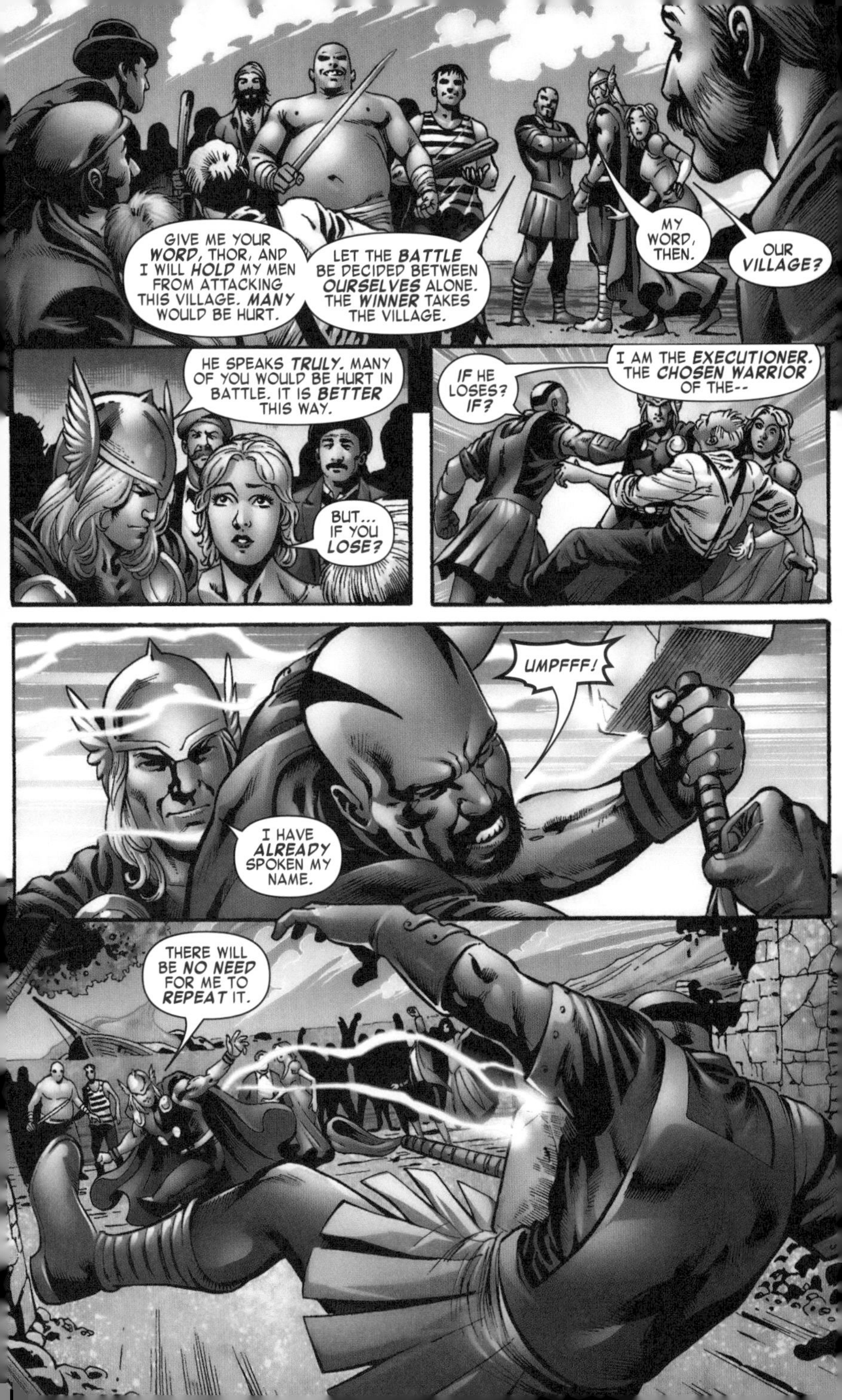
GIVE ME YOUR WORD, THOR, AND I WILL HOLD MY MEN FROM ATTACKING THIS VILLAGE. MANY WOULD BE HURT.
LET THE BATTLE BE DECIDED BETWEEN OURSELVES ALONE. THE WINNER TAKES THE VILLAGE.
MY WORD, THEN.
OUR VILLAGE?
HE SPEAKS TRULY. MANY OF YOU WOULD BE HURT IN BATTLE. IT IS BETTER THIS WAY.
BUT... IF YOU LOSE?
I AM THE EXECUTIONER. THE CHOSEN WARRIOR OF THE--
IF HE LOSES? IF?
UMPFFF!
I HAVE ALREADY SPOKEN MY NAME.
THERE WILL BE NO NEED FOR ME TO REPEAT IT.

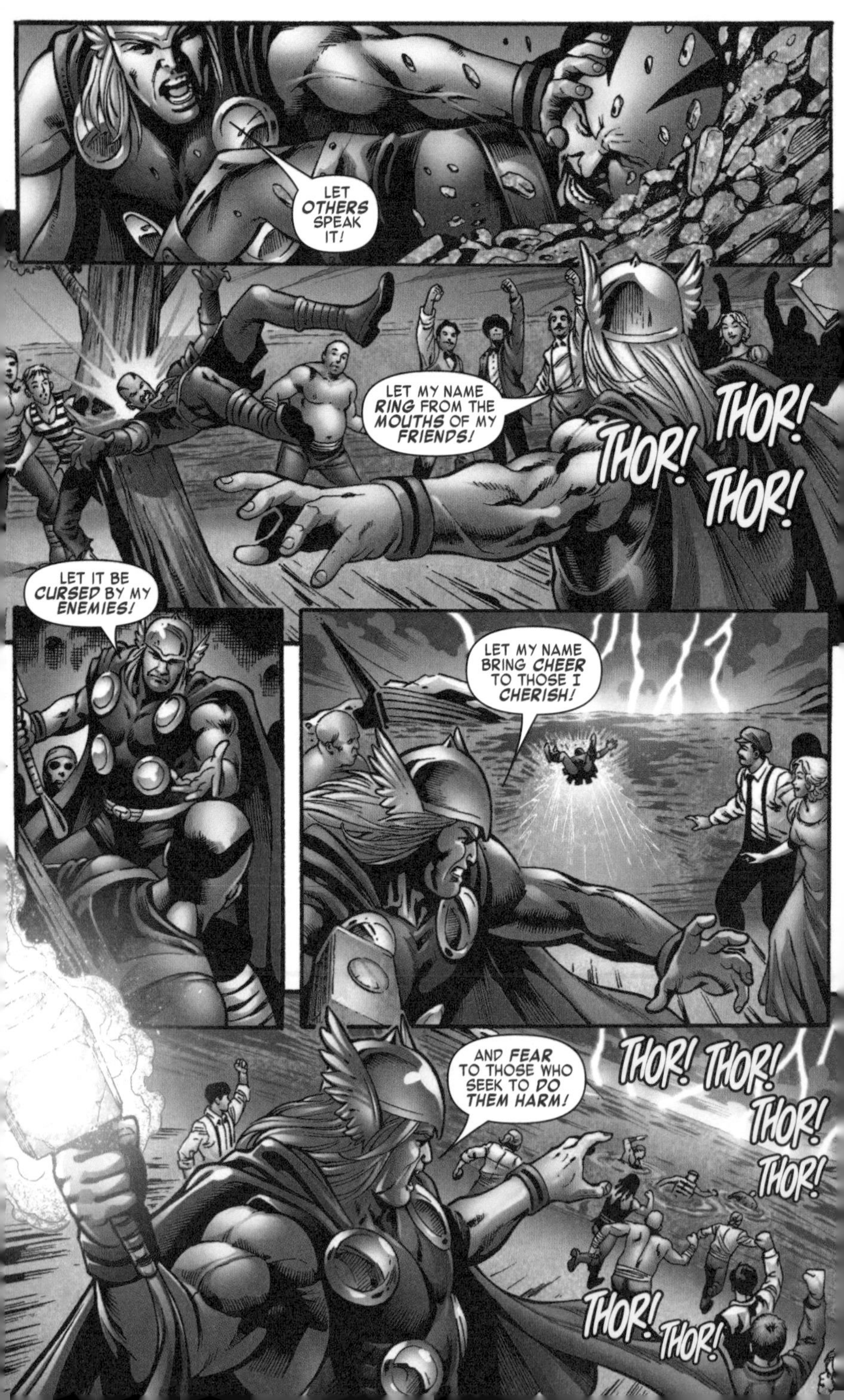
LET OTHERS SPEAK IT!
LET MY NAME RING FROM THE MOUTHS OF MY FRIENDS!
THOR! THOR! THOR!
LET IT BE CURSED BY MY ENEMIES!
LET MY NAME BRING CHEER TO THOSE I CHERISH!
AND FEAR TO THOSE WHO SEEK TO DO THEM HARM!
THOR! THOR! THOR! THOR!
THOR! THOR!

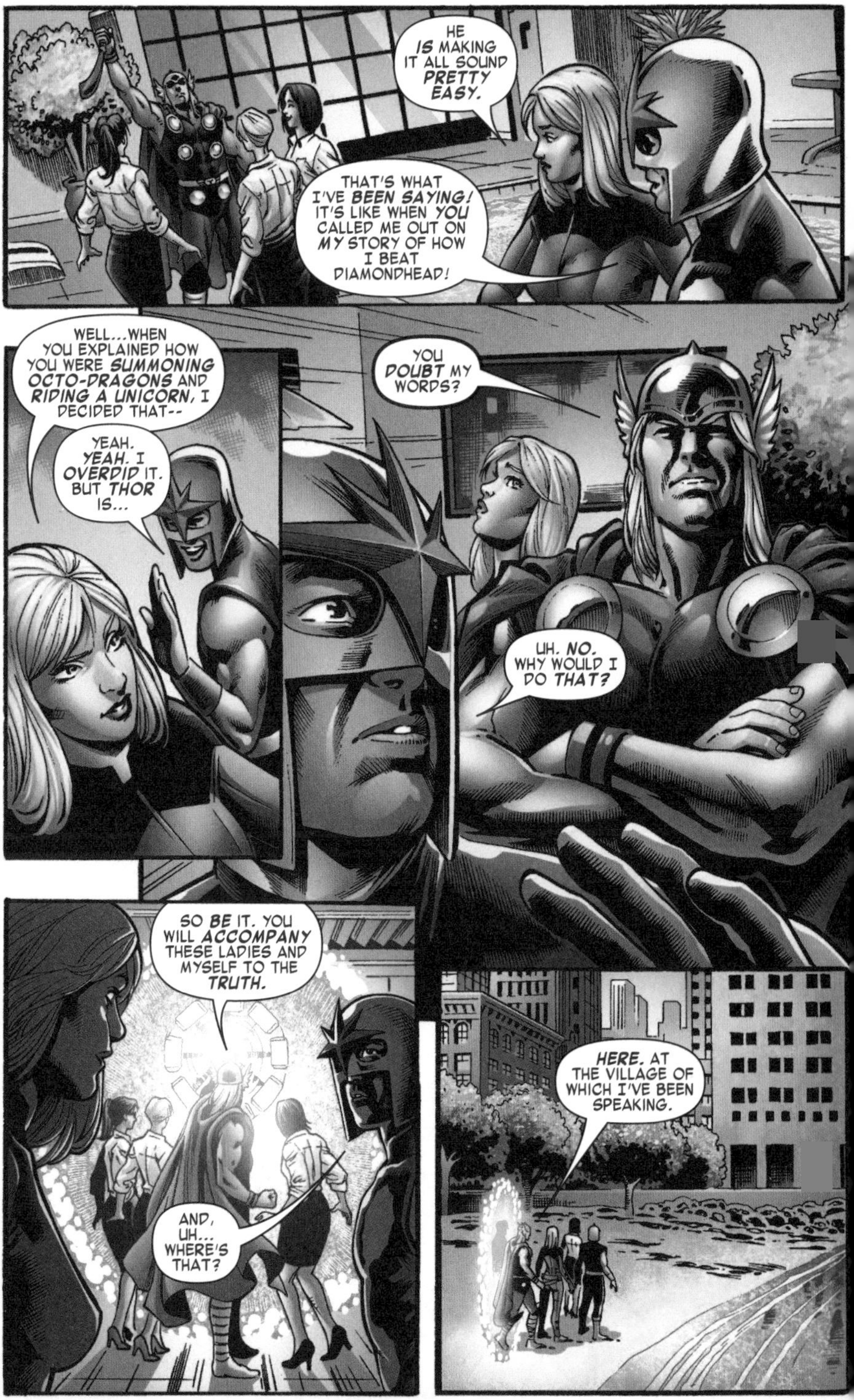

HE IS MAKING IT ALL SOUND PRETTY EASY.
THAT'S WHAT I'VE BEEN SAYING! IT'S LIKE WHEN YOU CALLED ME OUT ON MY STORY OF HOW I BEAT DIAMONDHEAD!
WELL...WHEN YOU EXPLAINED HOW YOU WERE SUMMONING OCTO-DRAGONS AND RIDING A UNICORN, I DECIDED THAT--
YEAH. YEAH. I OVERDID IT. BUT THOR IS...
YOU DOUBT MY WORDS?
UH. NO. WHY WOULD I DO THAT?
SO BE IT. YOU WILL ACCOMPANY THESE LADIES AND MYSELF TO THE TRUTH.
AND, UH... WHERE'S THAT?
HERE. AT THE VILLAGE OF WHICH I'VE BEEN SPEAKING.

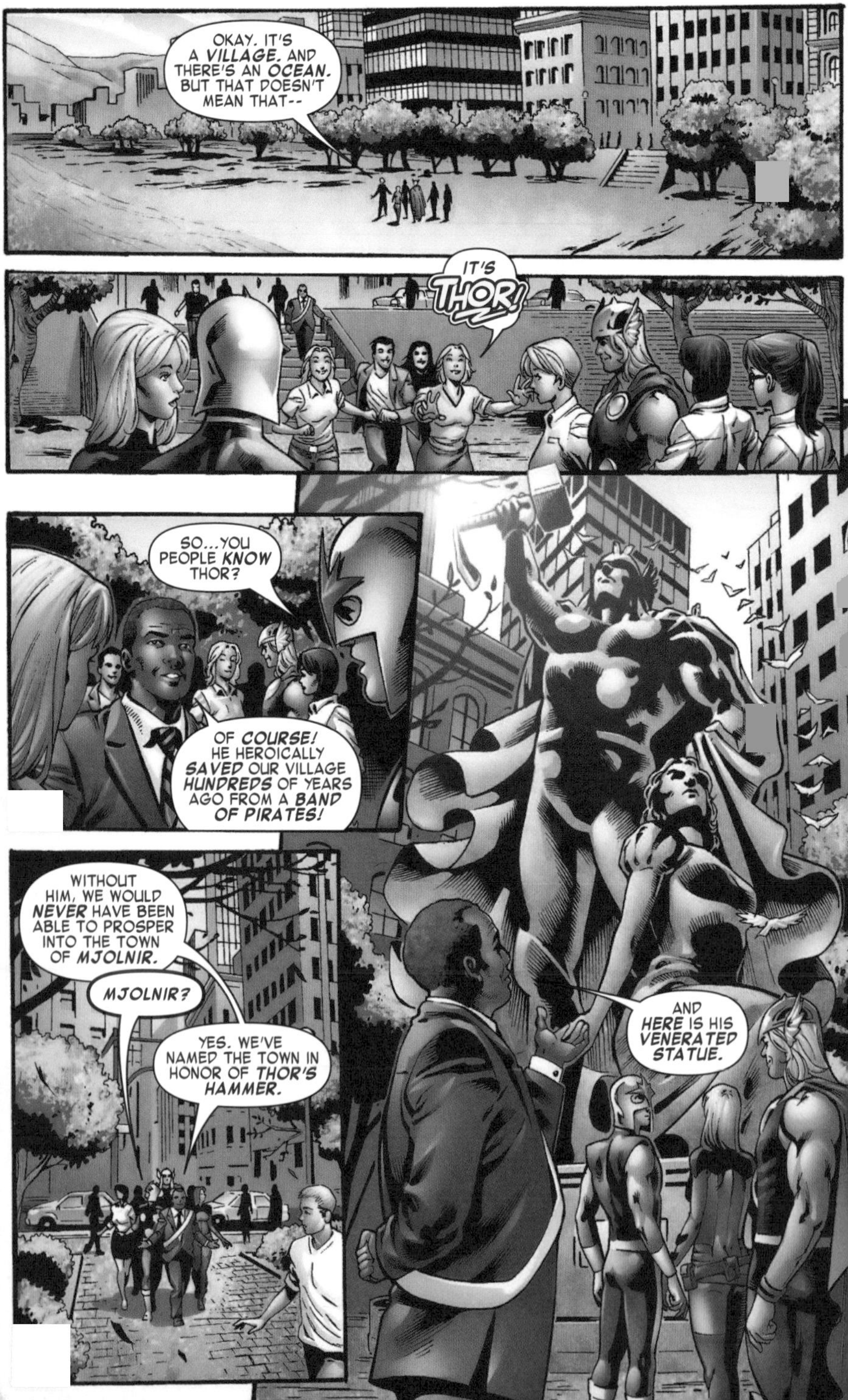
OKAY. IT'S A VILLAGE. AND THERE'S AN OCEAN. BUT THAT DOESN'T MEAN THAT--
IT'S THOR!
SO...YOU PEOPLE KNOW THOR?
OF COURSE! HE HEROICALLY SAVED OUR VILLAGE HUNDREDS OF YEARS AGO FROM A BAND OF PIRATES!
WITHOUT HIM, WE WOULD NEVER HAVE BEEN ABLE TO PROSPER INTO THE TOWN OF MJOLNIR.
MJOLNIR?
YES. WE'VE NAMED THE TOWN IN HONOR OF THOR'S HAMMER.
AND HERE IS HIS VENERATED STATUE.

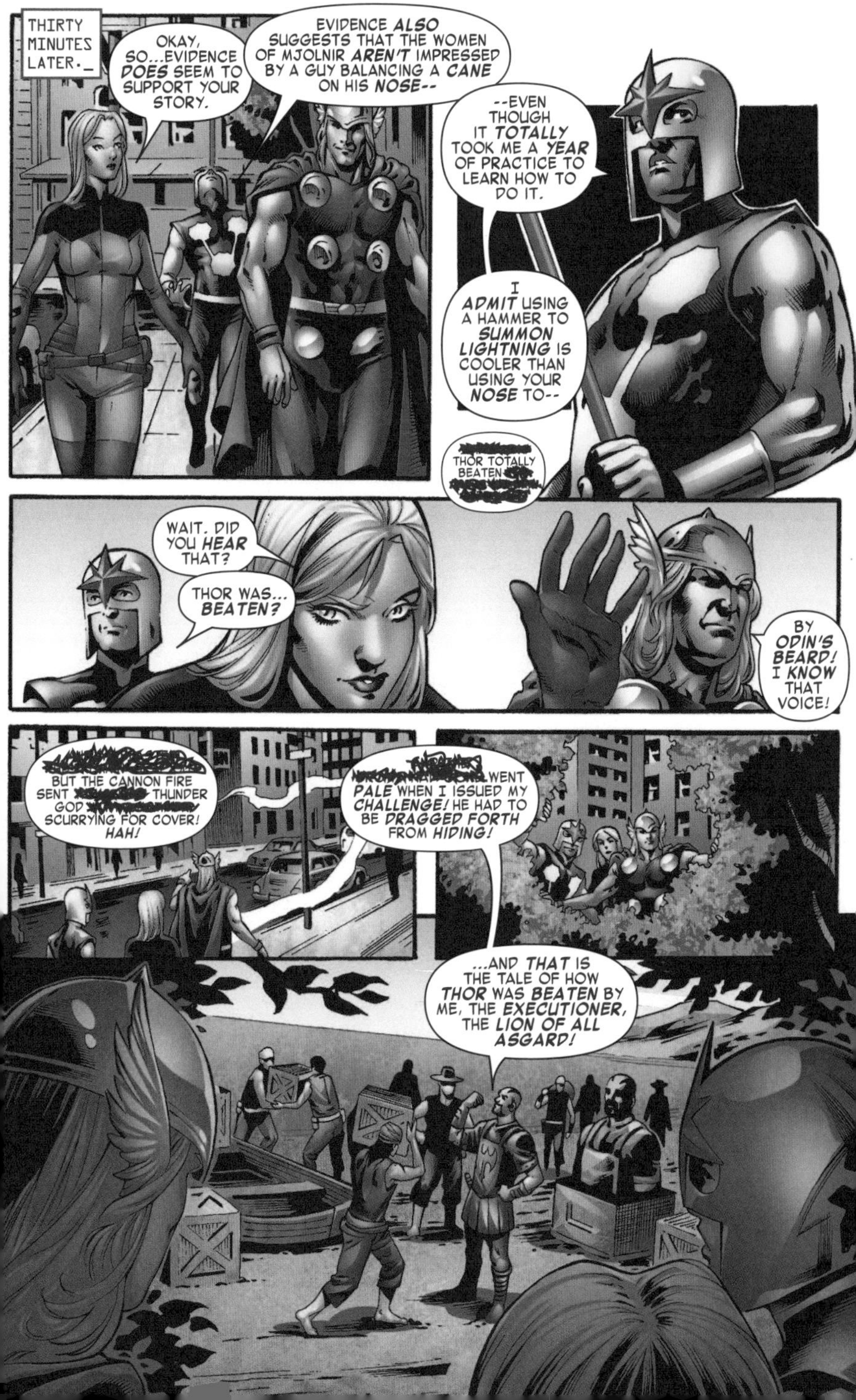
THIRTY MINUTES LATER._
OKAY, SO...EVIDENCE DOES SEEM TO SUPPORT YOUR STORY.
EVIDENCE ALSO SUGGESTS THAT THE WOMEN OF MJOLNIR AREN'T IMPRESSED BY A GUY BALANCING A CANE ON HIS NOSE--
--EVEN THOUGH IT TOTALLY TOOK ME A YEAR OF PRACTICE TO LEARN HOW TO DO IT.
I ADMIT USING A HAMMER TO SUMMON LIGHTNING IS COOLER THAN USING YOUR NOSE TO--
[redacted] THOR TOTALLY BEATEN [redacted]
WAIT. DID YOU HEAR THAT?
THOR WAS... BEATEN?
BY ODIN'S BEARD! I KNOW THAT VOICE!
[redacted] BUT THE CANNON FIRE SENT [redacted] THUNDER GOD [redacted] SCURRYING FOR COVER! HAH!
[redacted] WENT PALE WHEN I ISSUED MY CHALLENGE! HE HAD TO BE DRAGGED FORTH FROM HIDING!
...AND THAT IS THE TALE OF HOW THOR WAS BEATEN BY ME, THE EXECUTIONER, THE LION OF ALL ASGARD!

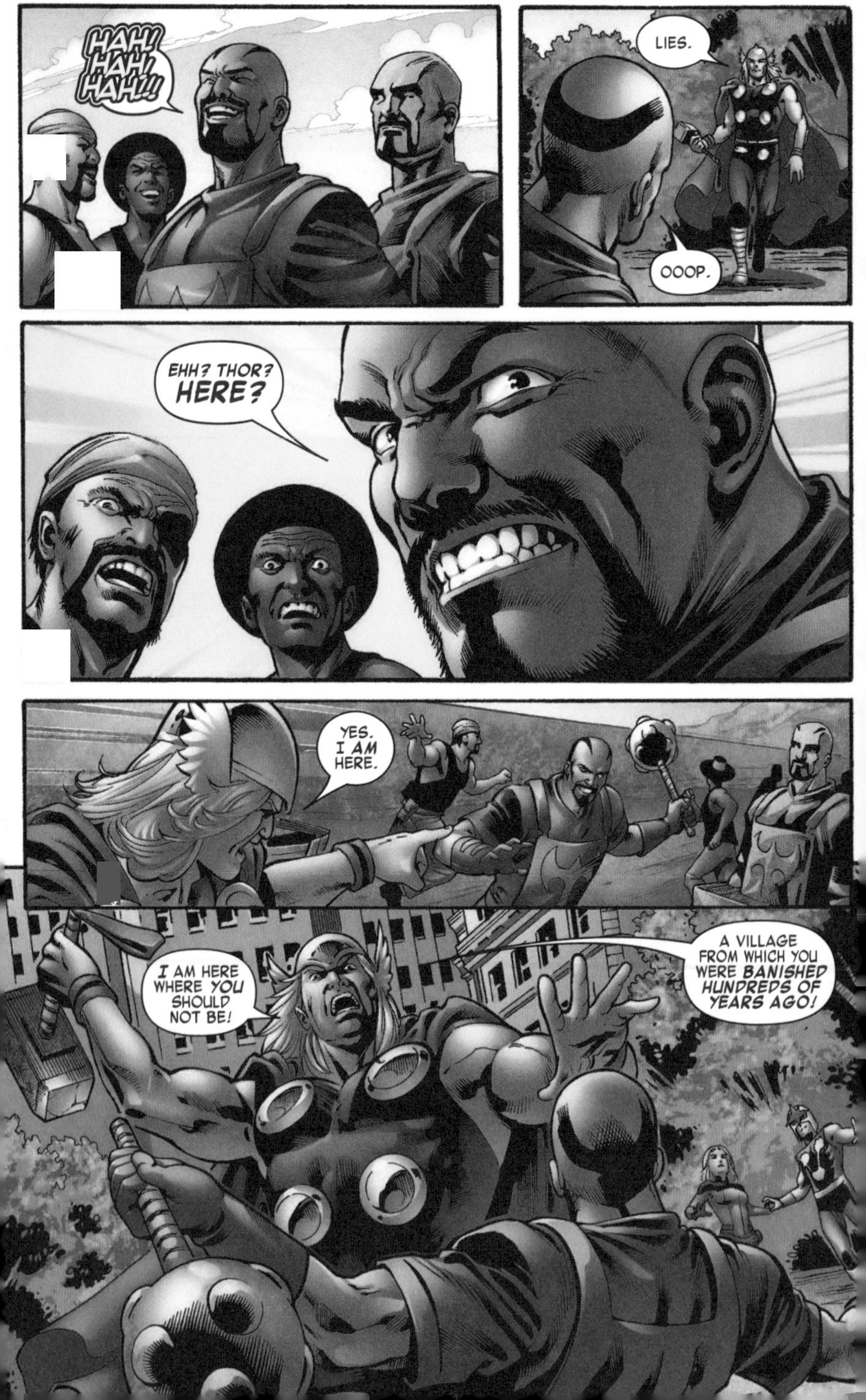
HAH! HAH! HAH!!!
LIES.
OOOP.
EHH? THOR? HERE?
YES. I AM HERE.
I AM HERE WHERE YOU SHOULD NOT BE!
A VILLAGE FROM WHICH YOU WERE BANISHED HUNDREDS OF YEARS AGO!

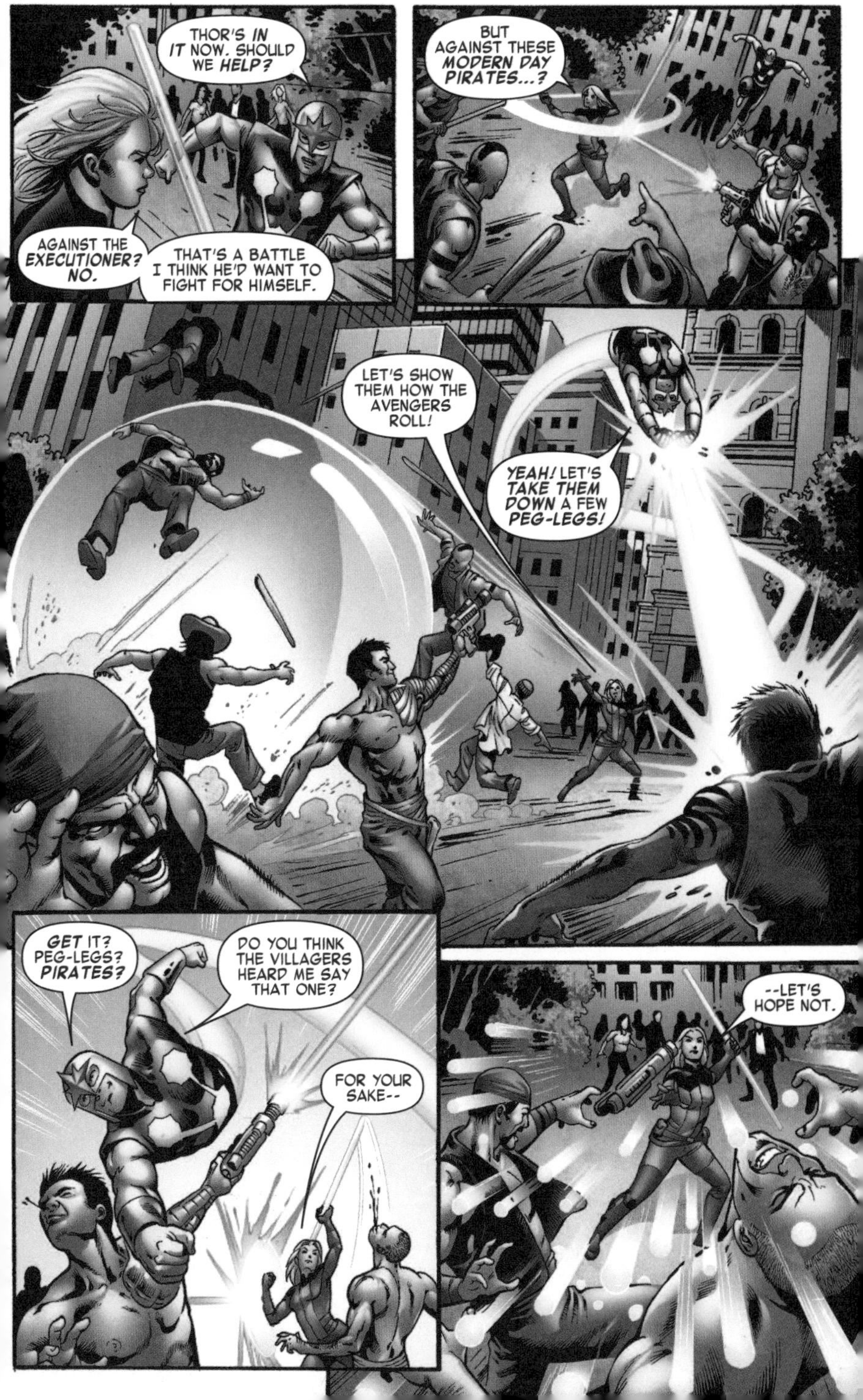
THOR'S IN IT NOW. SHOULD WE HELP?
AGAINST THE EXECUTIONER? NO.
THAT'S A BATTLE I THINK HE'D WANT TO FIGHT FOR HIMSELF.
BUT AGAINST THESE MODERN DAY PIRATES...?
LET'S SHOW THEM HOW THE AVENGERS ROLL!
YEAH! LET'S TAKE THEM DOWN A FEW PEG-LEGS!
GET IT? PEG-LEGS? PIRATES?
DO YOU THINK THE VILLAGERS HEARD ME SAY THAT ONE?
FOR YOUR SAKE--
--LET'S HOPE NOT.

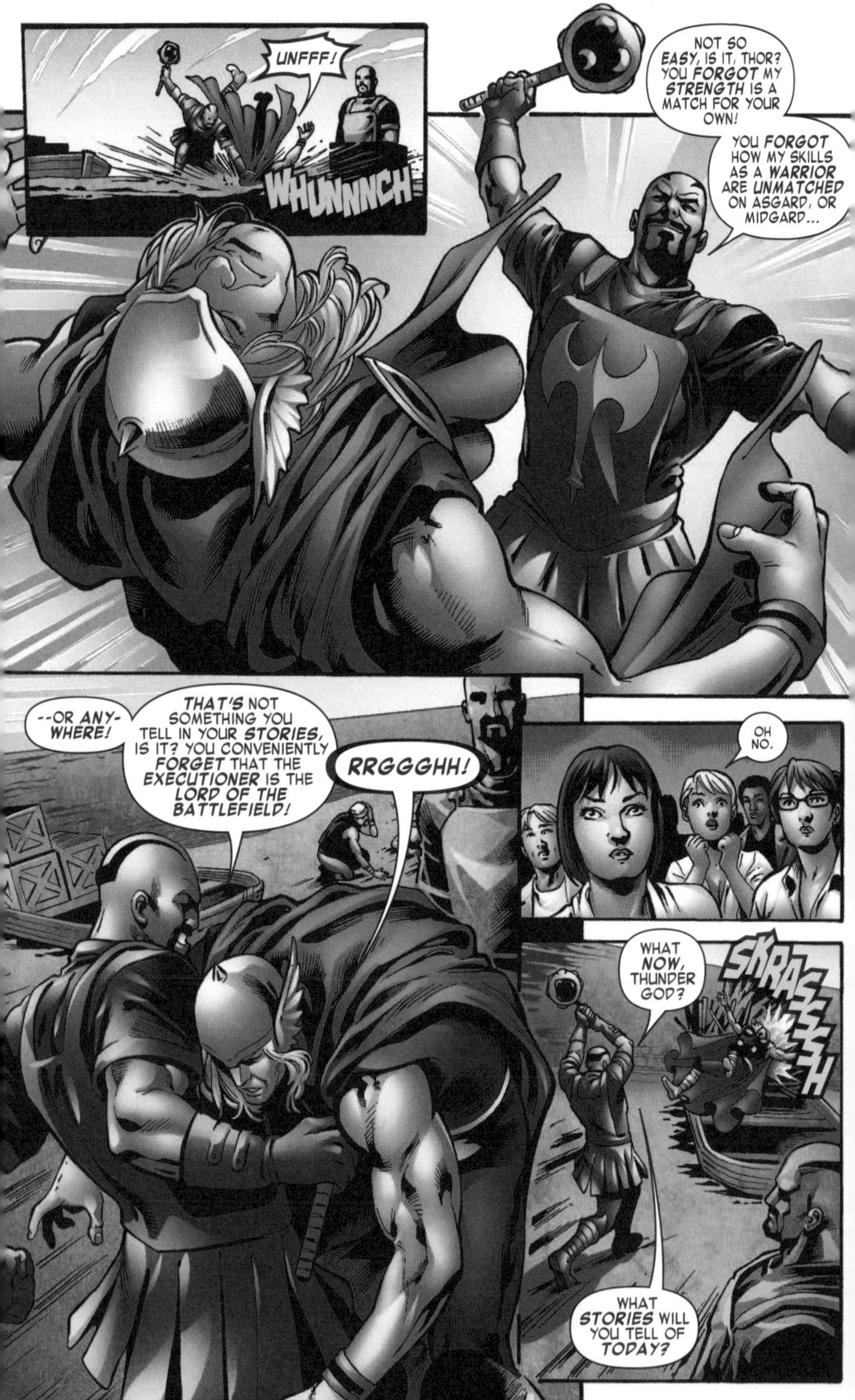
UNFFF!
WHUNNNCH
NOT SO EASY, IS IT, THOR? YOU FORGOT MY STRENGTH IS A MATCH FOR YOUR OWN!
YOU FORGOT HOW MY SKILLS AS A WARRIOR ARE UNMATCHED ON ASGARD, OR MIDGARD...
--OR ANY-WHERE!
THAT'S NOT SOMETHING YOU TELL IN YOUR STORIES, IS IT? YOU CONVENIENTLY FORGET THAT THE EXECUTIONER IS THE LORD OF THE BATTLEFIELD!
RRGGGHH!
OH NO.
WHAT NOW, THUNDER GOD?
SKRASSSH
WHAT STORIES WILL YOU TELL OF TODAY?

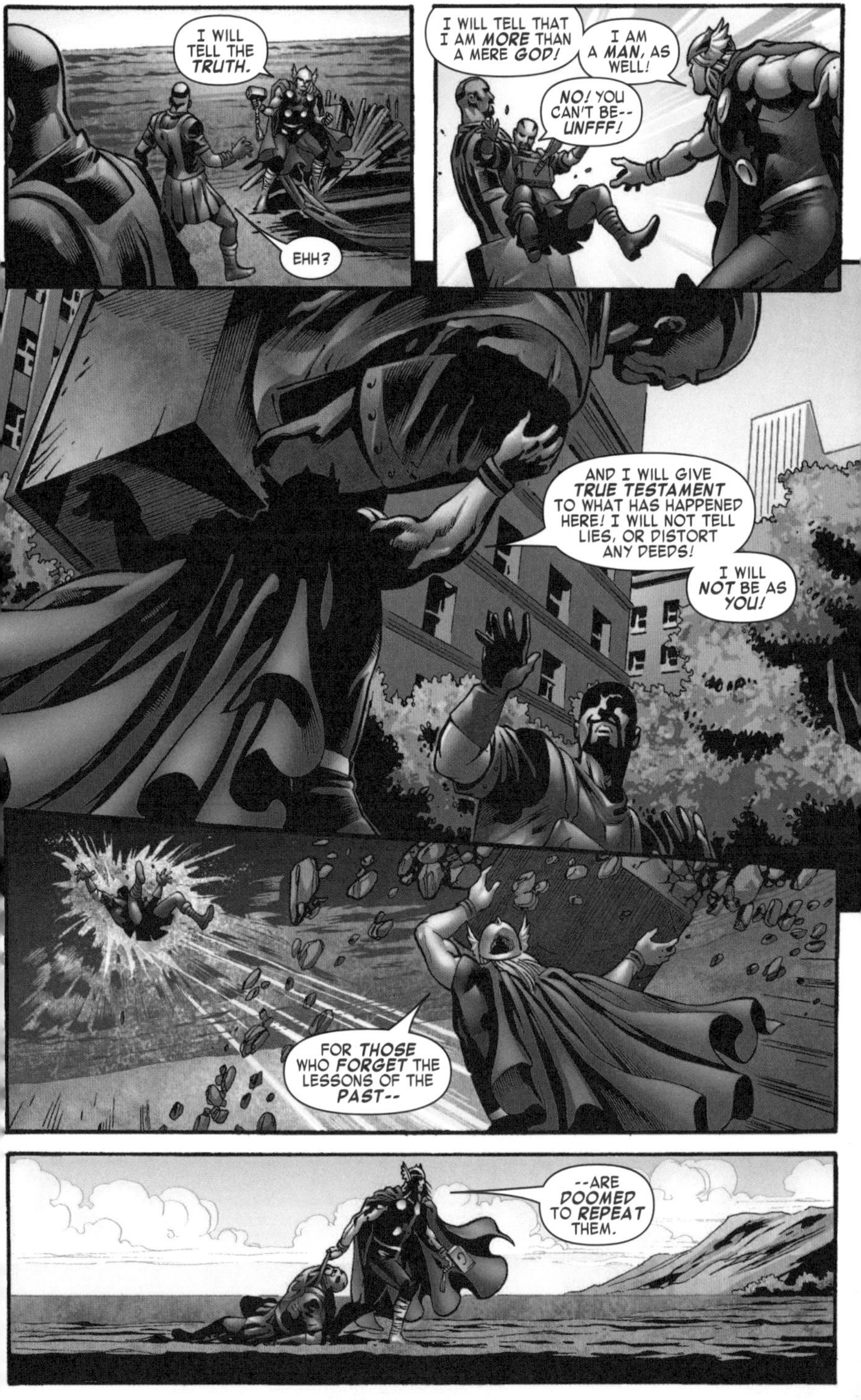
I WILL TELL THE TRUTH.
EHH?
I WILL TELL THAT I AM MORE THAN A MERE GOD!
I AM A MAN, AS WELL!
NO! YOU CAN'T BE-- UNFFF!
AND I WILL GIVE TRUE TESTAMENT TO WHAT HAS HAPPENED HERE! I WILL NOT TELL LIES, OR DISTORT ANY DEEDS!
I WILL NOT BE AS YOU!
FOR THOSE WHO FORGET THE LESSONS OF THE PAST--
--ARE DOOMED TO REPEAT THEM.

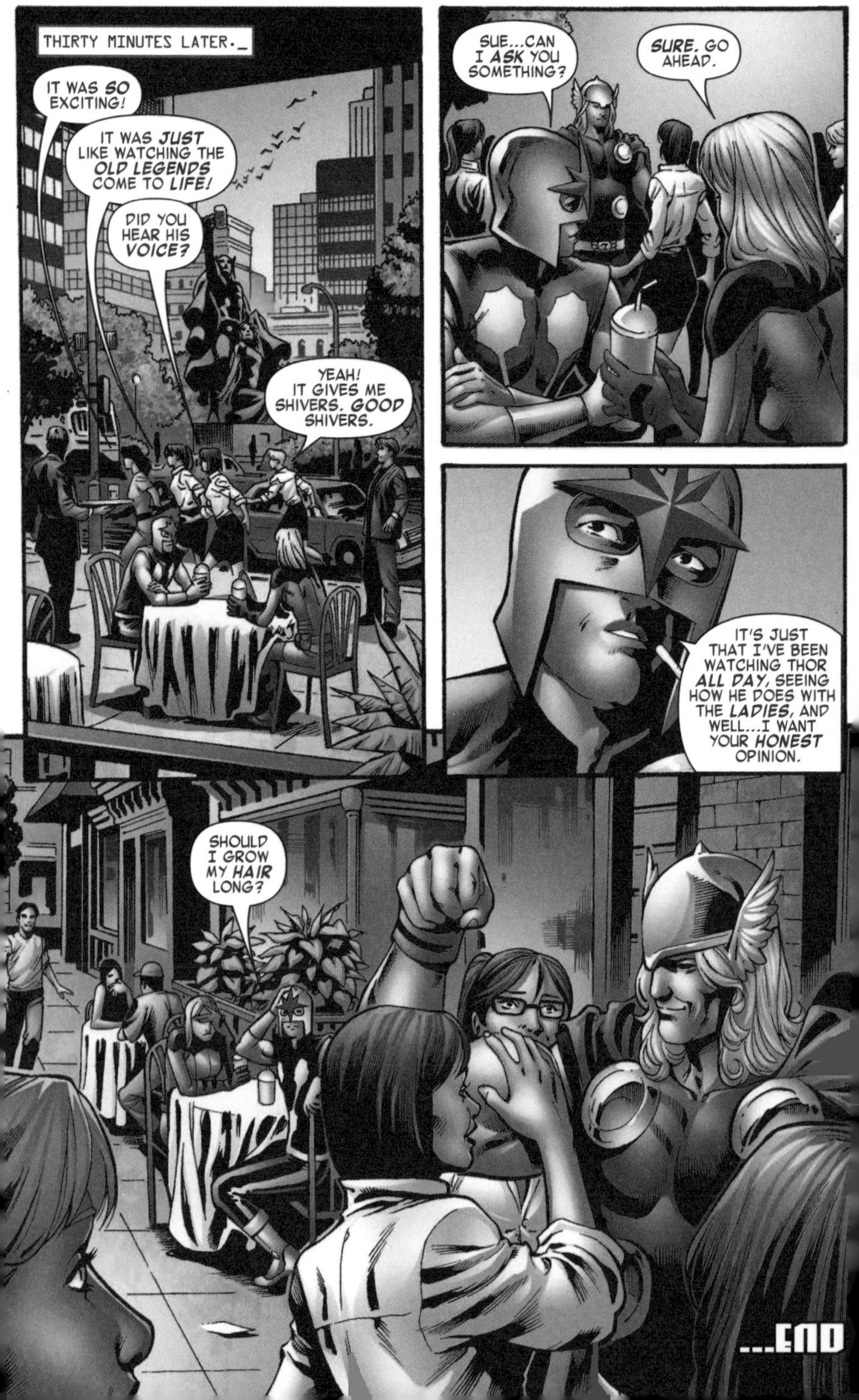
THIRTY MINUTES LATER._
IT WAS SO EXCITING!
IT WAS JUST LIKE WATCHING THE OLD LEGENDS COME TO LIFE!
DID YOU HEAR HIS VOICE?
YEAH! IT GIVES ME SHIVERS. GOOD SHIVERS.
SUE...CAN I ASK YOU SOMETHING?
SURE. GO AHEAD.
IT'S JUST THAT I'VE BEEN WATCHING THOR ALL DAY, SEEING HOW HE DOES WITH THE LADIES, AND WELL...I WANT YOUR HONEST OPINION.
SHOULD I GROW MY HAIR LONG?
...END

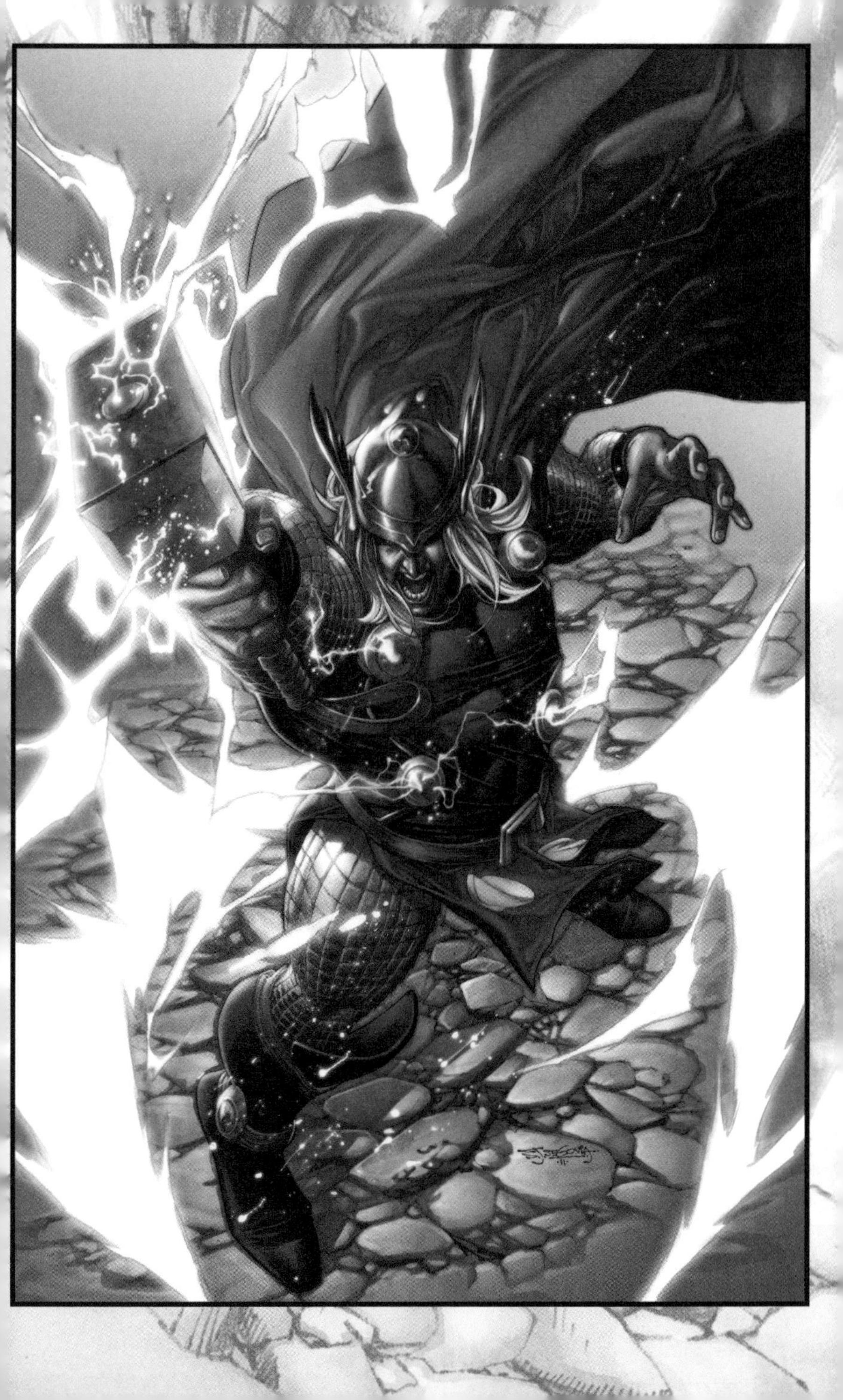

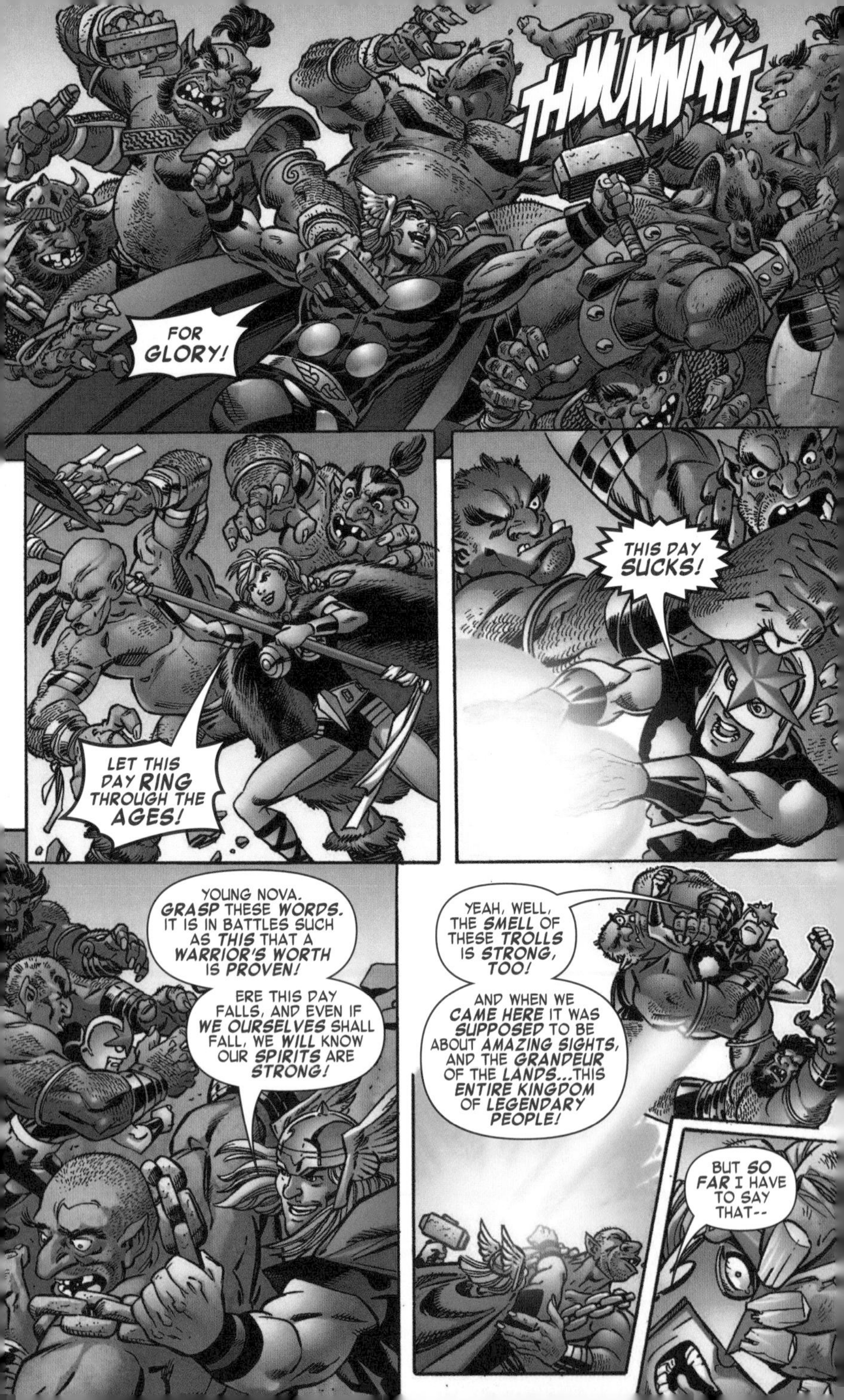
THWUNNKKT
FOR GLORY!
LET THIS DAY RING THROUGH THE AGES!
THIS DAY SUCKS!
YOUNG NOVA. GRASP THESE WORDS. IT IS IN BATTLES SUCH AS THIS THAT A WARRIOR'S WORTH IS PROVEN!
ERE THIS DAY FALLS, AND EVEN IF WE OURSELVES SHALL FALL, WE WILL KNOW OUR SPIRITS ARE STRONG!
YEAH, WELL, THE SMELL OF THESE TROLLS IS STRONG, TOO!
AND WHEN WE CAME HERE IT WAS SUPPOSED TO BE ABOUT AMAZING SIGHTS, AND THE GRANDEUR OF THE LANDS...THIS ENTIRE KINGDOM OF LEGENDARY PEOPLE!
BUT SO FAR I HAVE TO SAY THAT--

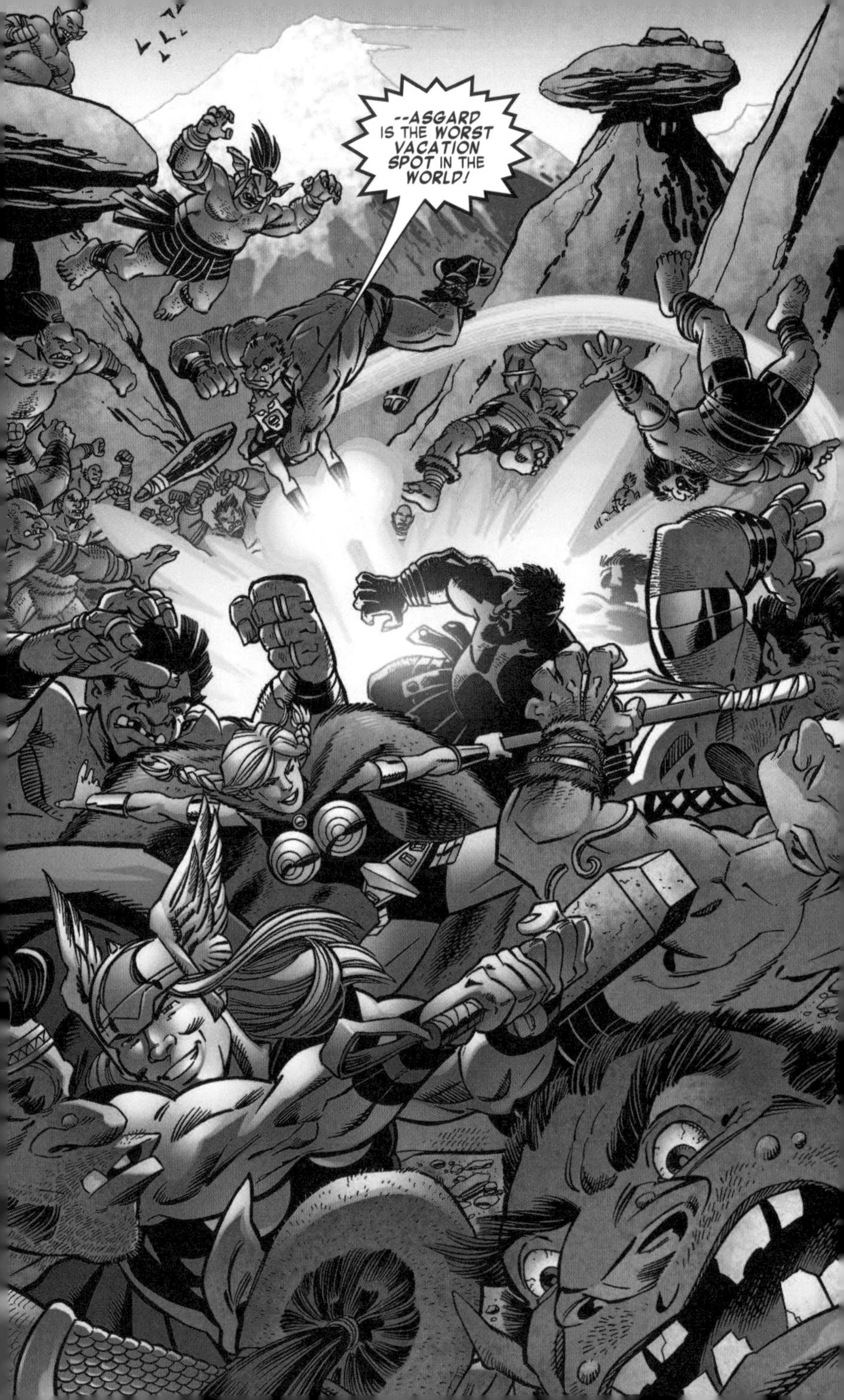
--ASGARD IS THE WORST VACATION SPOT IN THE WORLD!

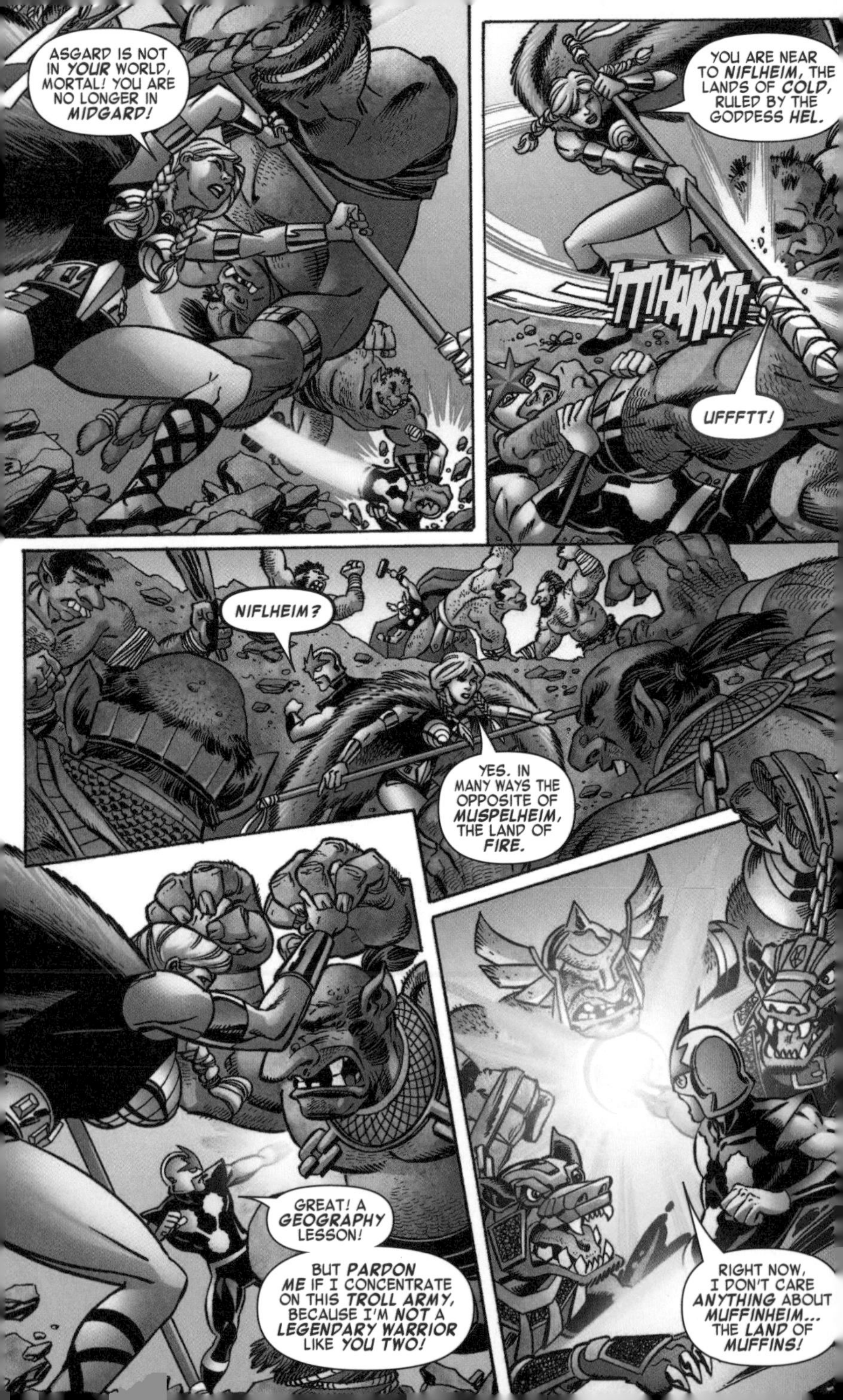
ASGARD IS NOT IN YOUR WORLD, MORTAL! YOU ARE NO LONGER IN MIDGARD!
YOU ARE NEAR TO NIFLHEIM, THE LANDS OF COLD, RULED BY THE GODDESS HEL.
TTTHAKKTT
UFFFTT!
NIFLHEIM?
YES. IN MANY WAYS THE OPPOSITE OF MUSPELHEIM, THE LAND OF FIRE.
GREAT! A GEOGRAPHY LESSON!
BUT PARDON ME IF I CONCENTRATE ON THIS TROLL ARMY, BECAUSE I'M NOT A LEGENDARY WARRIOR LIKE YOU TWO!
RIGHT NOW, I DON'T CARE ANYTHING ABOUT MUFFINHEIM... THE LAND OF MUFFINS!

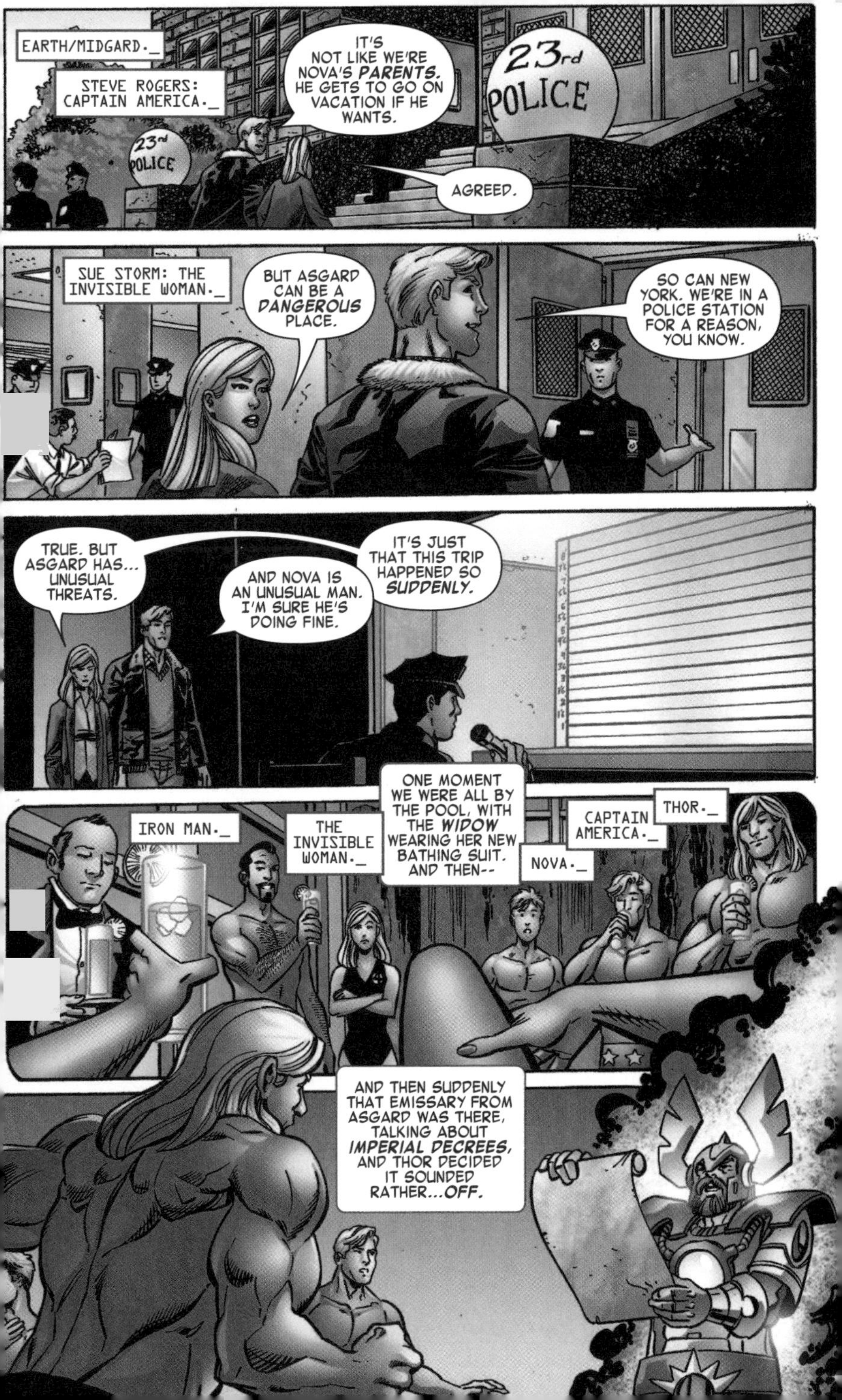
EARTH/MIDGARD._
STEVE ROGERS: CAPTAIN AMERICA._
IT'S NOT LIKE WE'RE NOVA'S PARENTS. HE GETS TO GO ON VACATION IF HE WANTS.
23rd POLICE
23rd POLICE
AGREED.
SUE STORM: THE INVISIBLE WOMAN._
BUT ASGARD CAN BE A DANGEROUS PLACE.
SO CAN NEW YORK. WE'RE IN A POLICE STATION FOR A REASON, YOU KNOW.
TRUE. BUT ASGARD HAS... UNUSUAL THREATS.
IT'S JUST THAT THIS TRIP HAPPENED SO SUDDENLY.
AND NOVA IS AN UNUSUAL MAN. I'M SURE HE'S DOING FINE.
IRON MAN._
THE INVISIBLE WOMAN._
ONE MOMENT WE WERE ALL BY THE POOL, WITH THE WIDOW WEARING HER NEW BATHING SUIT. AND THEN--
NOVA._
CAPTAIN AMERICA._
THOR._
AND THEN SUDDENLY THAT EMISSARY FROM ASGARD WAS THERE, TALKING ABOUT IMPERIAL DECREES, AND THOR DECIDED IT SOUNDED RATHER...OFF.

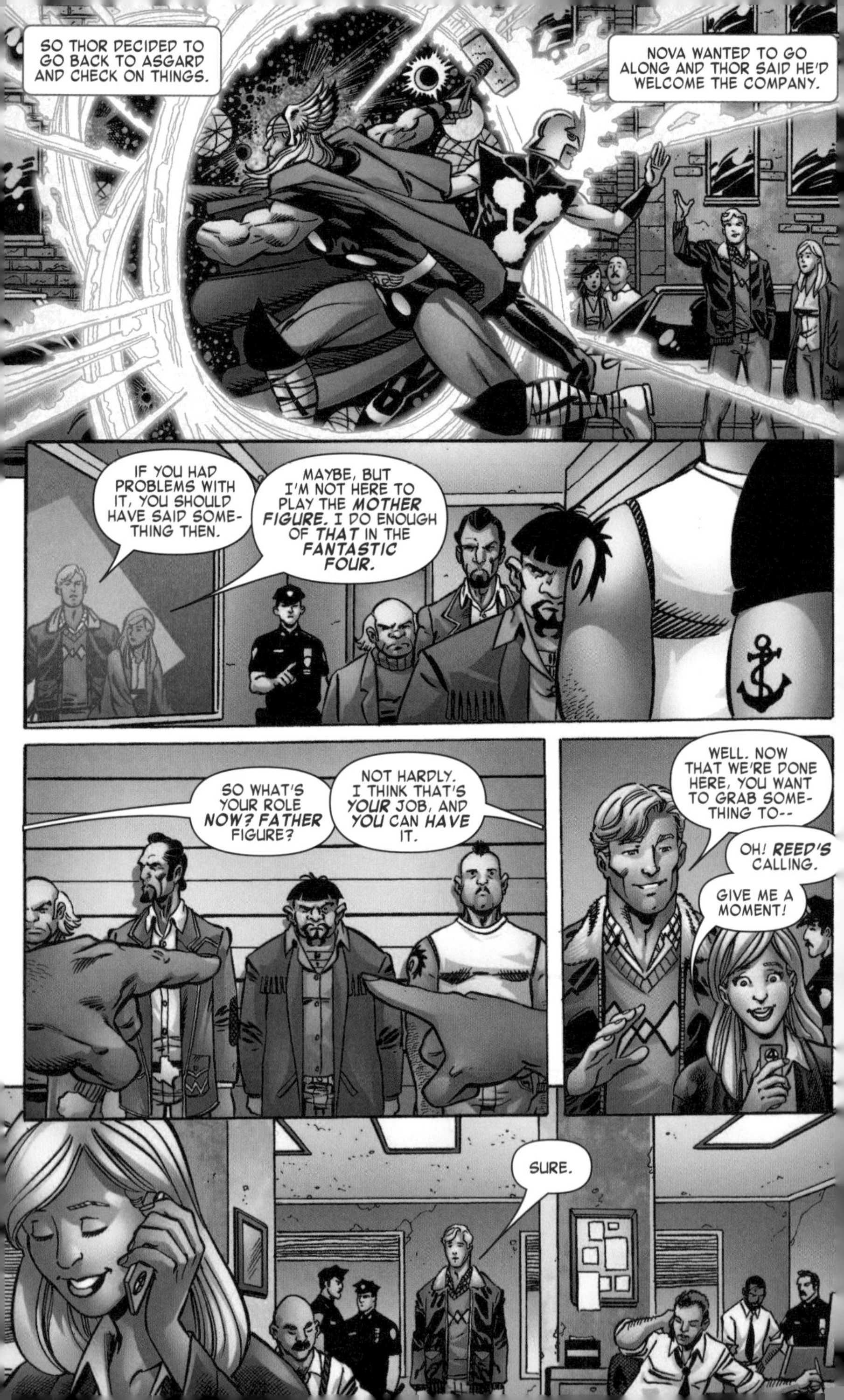
SO THOR DECIDED TO GO BACK TO ASGARD AND CHECK ON THINGS.
NOVA WANTED TO GO ALONG AND THOR SAID HE'D WELCOME THE COMPANY.
IF YOU HAD PROBLEMS WITH IT, YOU SHOULD HAVE SAID SOMETHING THEN.
MAYBE, BUT I'M NOT HERE TO PLAY THE MOTHER FIGURE. I DO ENOUGH OF THAT IN THE FANTASTIC FOUR.
SO WHAT'S YOUR ROLE NOW? FATHER FIGURE?
NOT HARDLY. I THINK THAT'S YOUR JOB, AND YOU CAN HAVE IT.
WELL. NOW THAT WE'RE DONE HERE, YOU WANT TO GRAB SOMETHING TO--
OH! REED'S CALLING.
GIVE ME A MOMENT!
SURE.

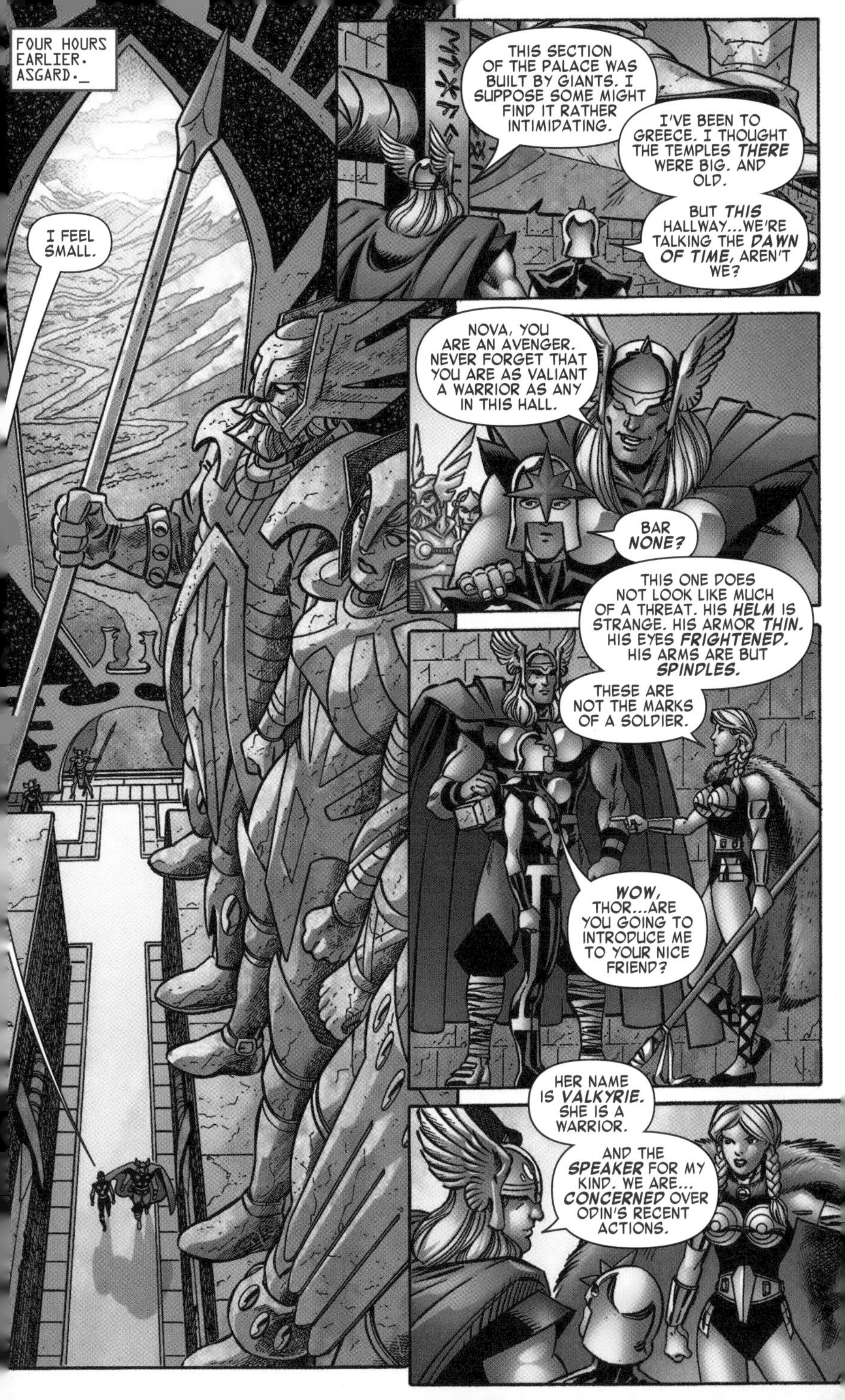

FOUR HOURS EARLIER. ASGARD._
I FEEL SMALL.
THIS SECTION OF THE PALACE WAS BUILT BY GIANTS. I SUPPOSE SOME MIGHT FIND IT RATHER INTIMIDATING.
I'VE BEEN TO GREECE. I THOUGHT THE TEMPLES THERE WERE BIG. AND OLD.
BUT THIS HALLWAY...WE'RE TALKING THE DAWN OF TIME, AREN'T WE?
NOVA, YOU ARE AN AVENGER. NEVER FORGET THAT YOU ARE AS VALIANT A WARRIOR AS ANY IN THIS HALL.
BAR NONE?
THIS ONE DOES NOT LOOK LIKE MUCH OF A THREAT. HIS HELM IS STRANGE. HIS ARMOR THIN. HIS EYES FRIGHTENED. HIS ARMS ARE BUT SPINDLES.
THESE ARE NOT THE MARKS OF A SOLDIER.
WOW, THOR...ARE YOU GOING TO INTRODUCE ME TO YOUR NICE FRIEND?
HER NAME IS VALKYRIE. SHE IS A WARRIOR.
AND THE SPEAKER FOR MY KIND. WE ARE... CONCERNED OVER ODIN'S RECENT ACTIONS.

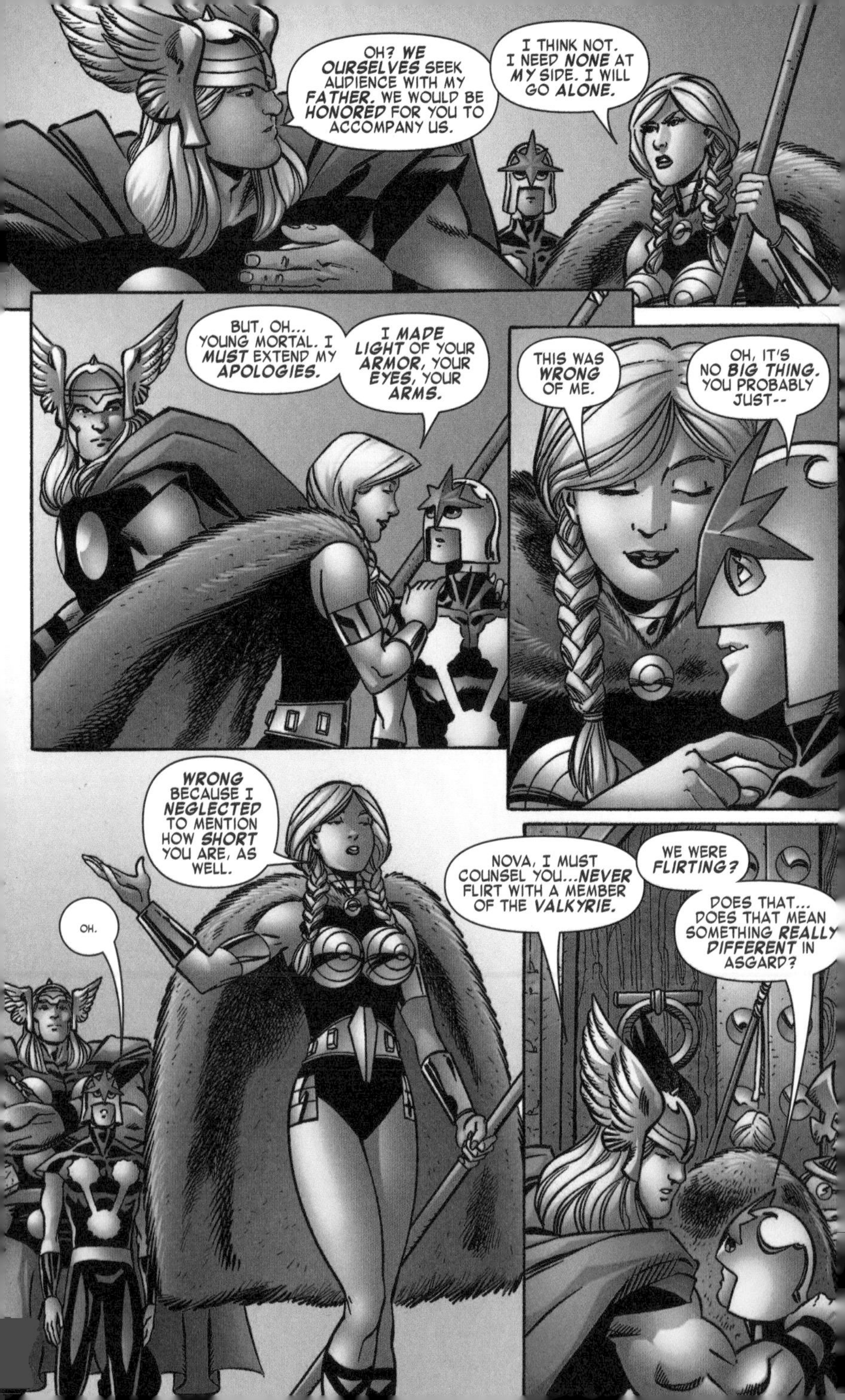
OH? WE OURSELVES SEEK AUDIENCE WITH MY FATHER. WE WOULD BE HONORED FOR YOU TO ACCOMPANY US.
I THINK NOT. I NEED NONE AT MY SIDE. I WILL GO ALONE.
BUT, OH... YOUNG MORTAL. I MUST EXTEND MY APOLOGIES.
I MADE LIGHT OF YOUR ARMOR, YOUR EYES, YOUR ARMS.
THIS WAS WRONG OF ME.
OH, IT'S NO BIG THING. YOU PROBABLY JUST--
WRONG BECAUSE I NEGLECTED TO MENTION HOW SHORT YOU ARE, AS WELL.
OH.
NOVA, I MUST COUNSEL YOU...NEVER FLIRT WITH A MEMBER OF THE VALKYRIE.
WE WERE FLIRTING?
DOES THAT... DOES THAT MEAN SOMETHING REALLY DIFFERENT IN ASGARD?

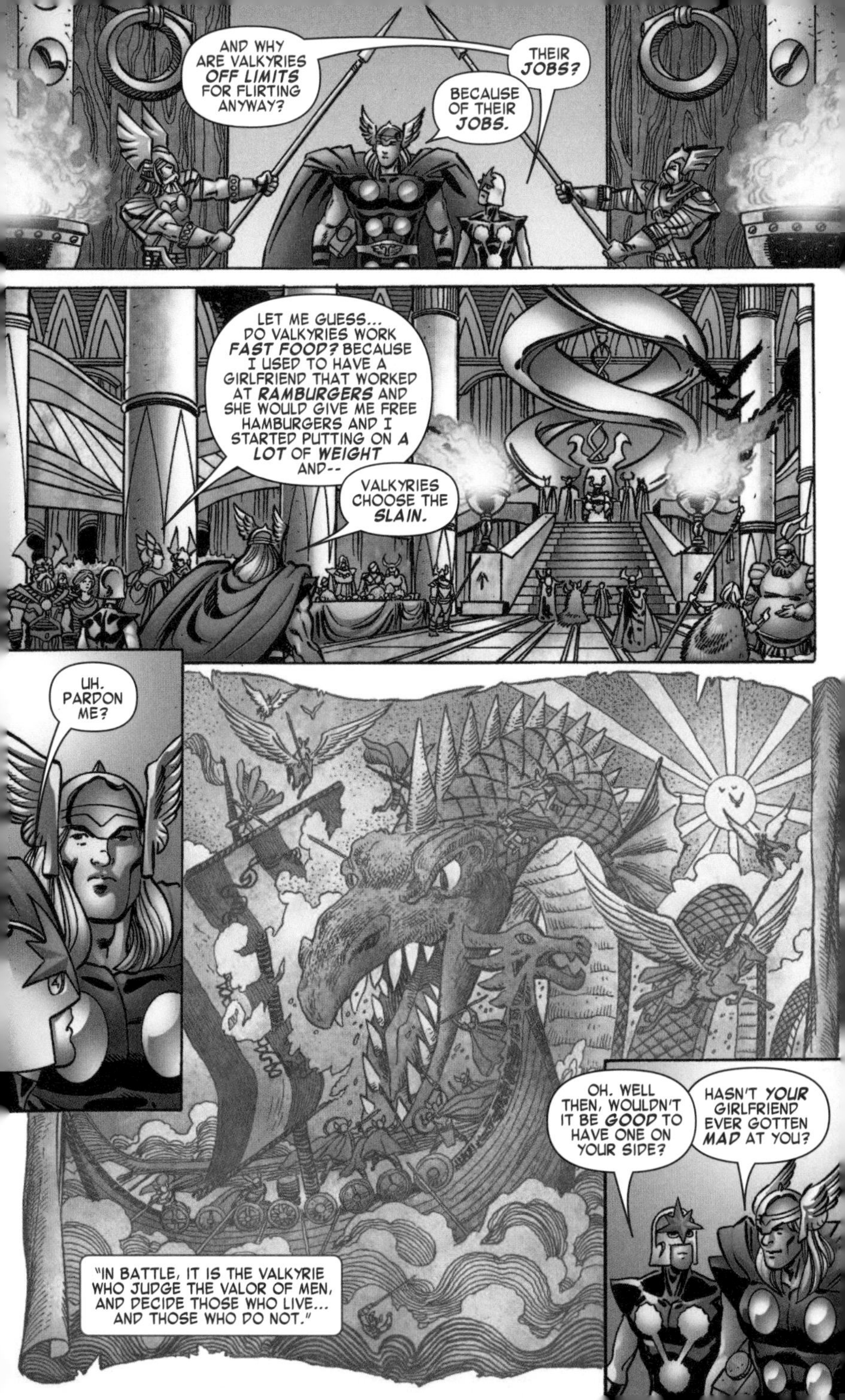
AND WHY ARE VALKYRIES OFF LIMITS FOR FLIRTING ANYWAY?
THEIR JOBS?
BECAUSE OF THEIR JOBS.
LET ME GUESS... DO VALKYRIES WORK FAST FOOD? BECAUSE I USED TO HAVE A GIRLFRIEND THAT WORKED AT RAMBURGERS AND SHE WOULD GIVE ME FREE HAMBURGERS AND I STARTED PUTTING ON A LOT OF WEIGHT AND--
VALKYRIES CHOOSE THE SLAIN.
UH. PARDON ME?
"IN BATTLE, IT IS THE VALKYRIE WHO JUDGE THE VALOR OF MEN, AND DECIDE THOSE WHO LIVE... AND THOSE WHO DO NOT."
OH. WELL THEN, WOULDN'T IT BE GOOD TO HAVE ONE ON YOUR SIDE?
HASN'T YOUR GIRLFRIEND EVER GOTTEN MAD AT YOU?

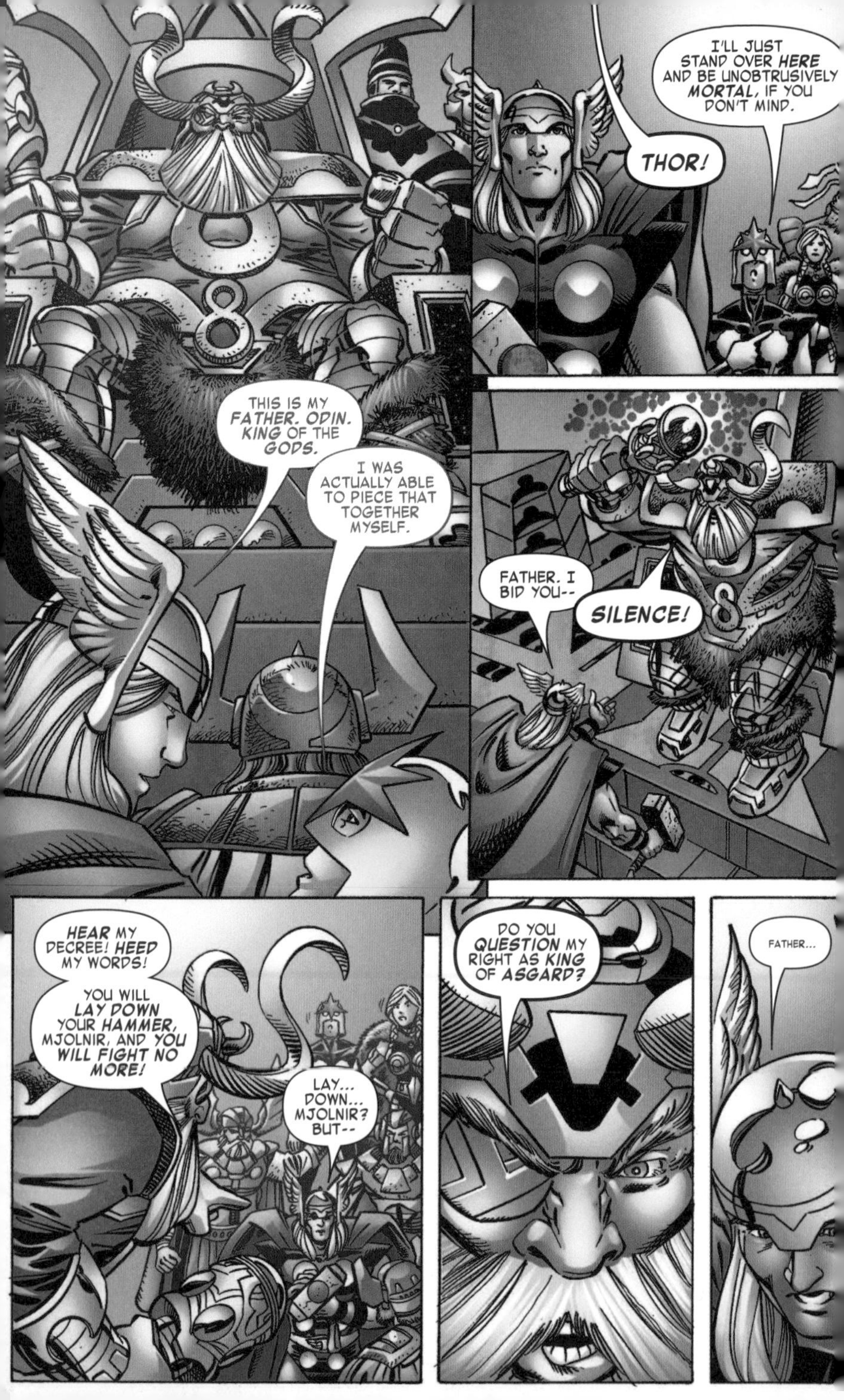
THOR!
I'LL JUST STAND OVER HERE AND BE UNOBTRUSIVELY MORTAL, IF YOU DON'T MIND.
THIS IS MY FATHER. ODIN. KING OF THE GODS.
I WAS ACTUALLY ABLE TO PIECE THAT TOGETHER MYSELF.
FATHER. I BID YOU--
SILENCE!
HEAR MY DECREE! HEED MY WORDS!
YOU WILL LAY DOWN YOUR HAMMER, MJOLNIR, AND YOU WILL FIGHT NO MORE!
LAY... DOWN... MJOLNIR? BUT--
DO YOU QUESTION MY RIGHT AS KING OF ASGARD?
FATHER...

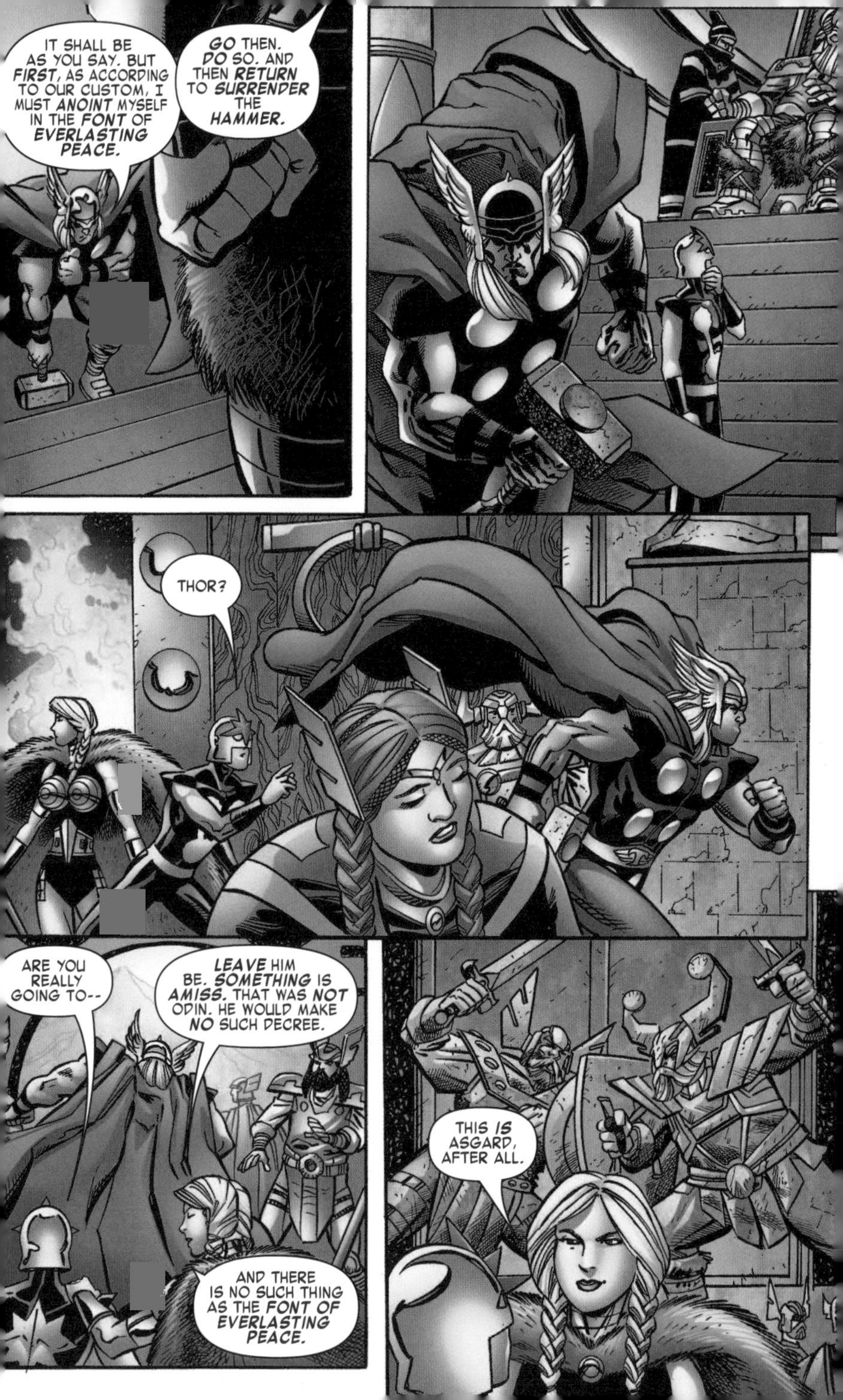
IT SHALL BE AS YOU SAY. BUT FIRST, AS ACCORDING TO OUR CUSTOM, I MUST ANOINT MYSELF IN THE FONT OF EVERLASTING PEACE.
GO THEN. DO SO. AND THEN RETURN TO SURRENDER THE HAMMER.
THOR?
ARE YOU REALLY GOING TO--
LEAVE HIM BE. SOMETHING IS AMISS. THAT WAS NOT ODIN. HE WOULD MAKE NO SUCH DECREE.
AND THERE IS NO SUCH THING AS THE FONT OF EVERLASTING PEACE.
THIS IS ASGARD, AFTER ALL.

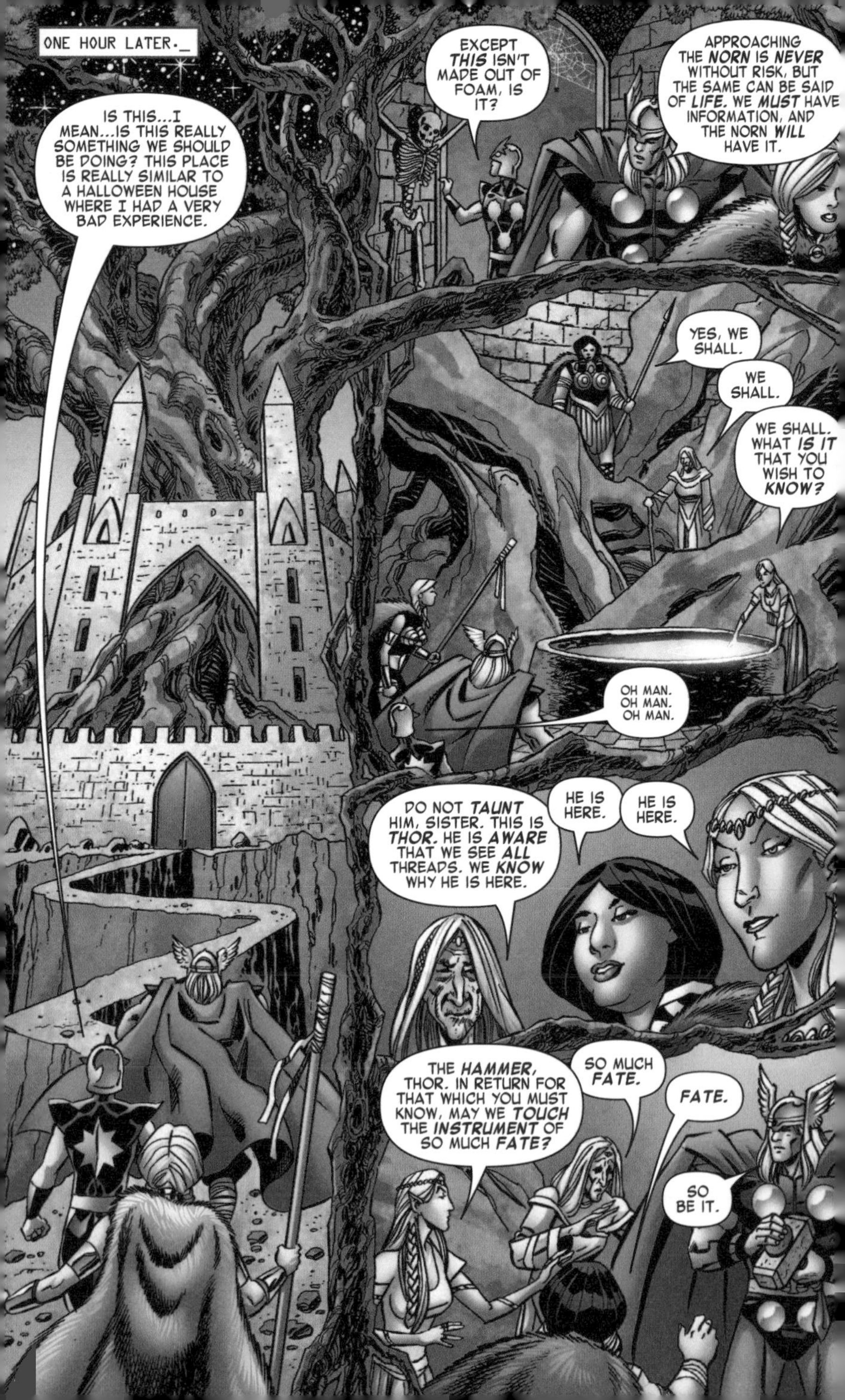
ONE HOUR LATER._
IS THIS...I MEAN...IS THIS REALLY SOMETHING WE SHOULD BE DOING? THIS PLACE IS REALLY SIMILAR TO A HALLOWEEN HOUSE WHERE I HAD A VERY BAD EXPERIENCE.
EXCEPT THIS ISN'T MADE OUT OF FOAM, IS IT?
APPROACHING THE NORN IS NEVER WITHOUT RISK, BUT THE SAME CAN BE SAID OF LIFE. WE MUST HAVE INFORMATION, AND THE NORN WILL HAVE IT.
YES, WE SHALL.
WE SHALL.
WE SHALL. WHAT IS IT THAT YOU WISH TO KNOW?
OH MAN. OH MAN. OH MAN.
DO NOT TAUNT HIM, SISTER. THIS IS THOR. HE IS AWARE THAT WE SEE ALL THREADS. WE KNOW WHY HE IS HERE.
HE IS HERE.
HE IS HERE.
THE HAMMER, THOR. IN RETURN FOR THAT WHICH YOU MUST KNOW, MAY WE TOUCH THE INSTRUMENT OF SO MUCH FATE?
SO MUCH FATE.
FATE.
SO BE IT.

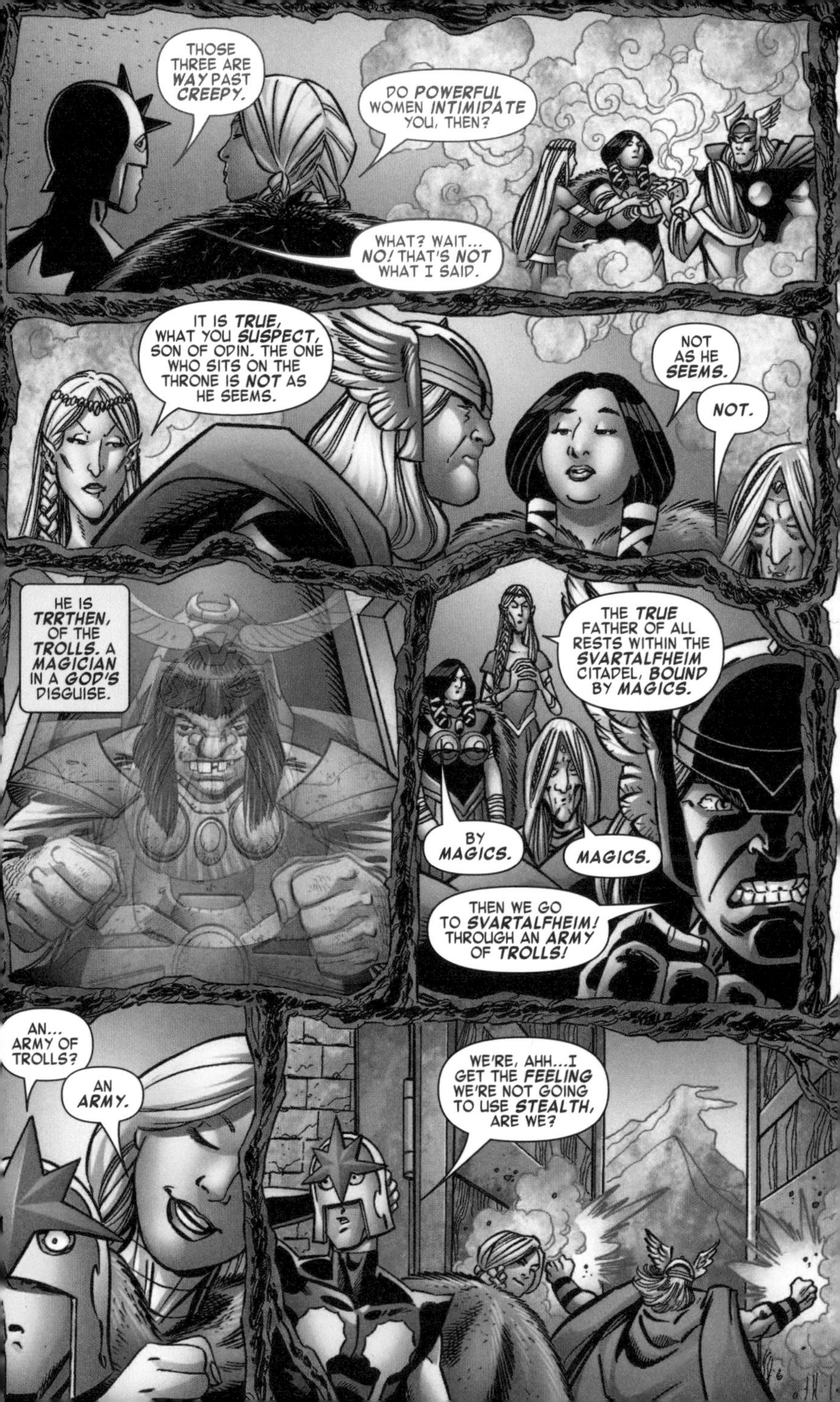

THOSE THREE ARE WAY PAST CREEPY.
DO POWERFUL WOMEN INTIMIDATE YOU, THEN?
WHAT? WAIT... NO! THAT'S NOT WHAT I SAID.
IT IS TRUE, WHAT YOU SUSPECT, SON OF ODIN. THE ONE WHO SITS ON THE THRONE IS NOT AS HE SEEMS.
NOT AS HE SEEMS.
NOT.
HE IS TRRTHEN, OF THE TROLLS. A MAGICIAN IN A GOD'S DISGUISE.
THE TRUE FATHER OF ALL RESTS WITHIN THE SVARTALFHEIM CITADEL, BOUND BY MAGICS.
BY MAGICS.
MAGICS.
THEN WE GO TO SVARTALFHEIM! THROUGH AN ARMY OF TROLLS!
AN... ARMY OF TROLLS?
AN ARMY.
WE'RE, AHH...I GET THE FEELING WE'RE NOT GOING TO USE STEALTH, ARE WE?

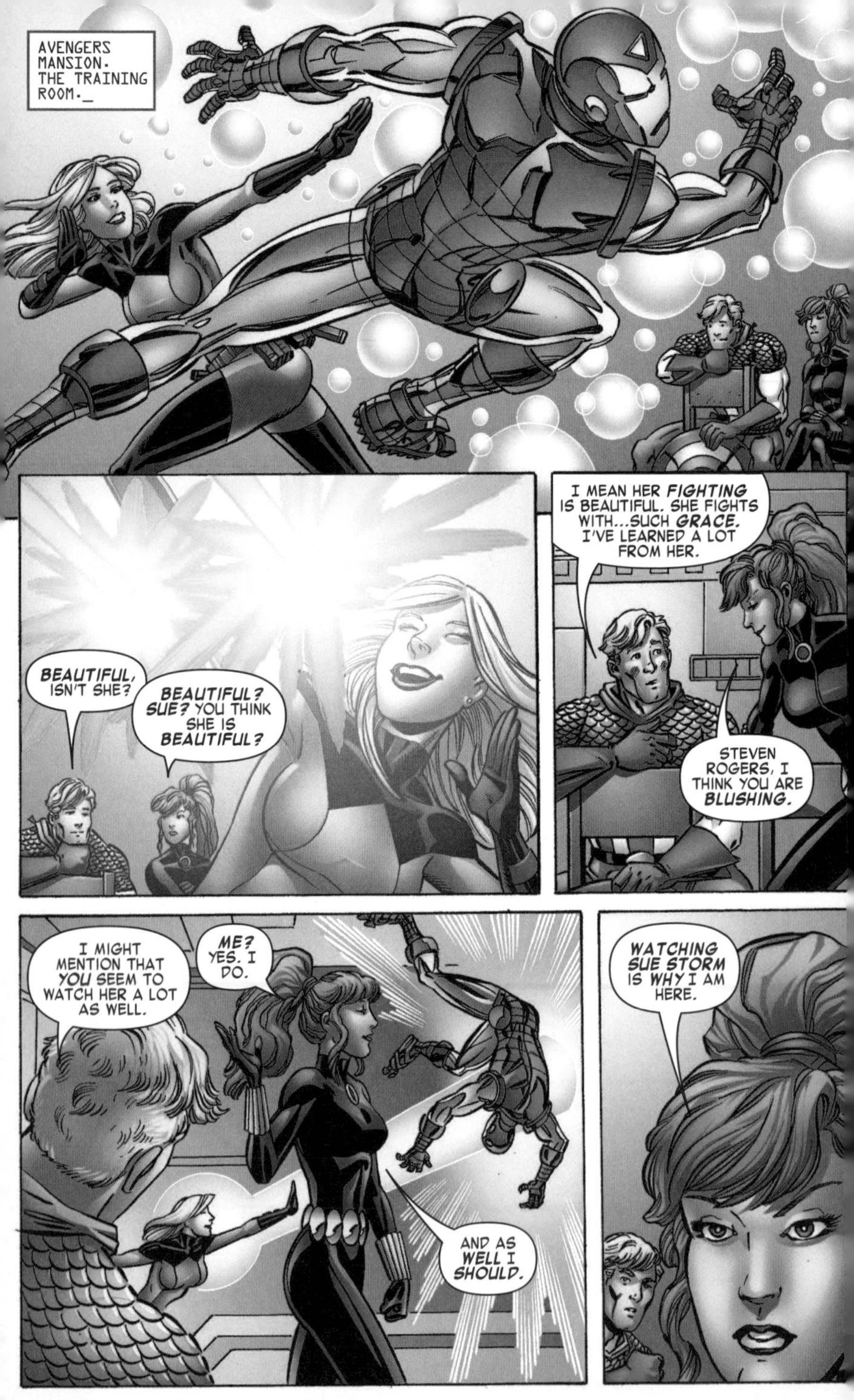
AVENGERS MANSION. THE TRAINING ROOM._
BEAUTIFUL, ISN'T SHE?
BEAUTIFUL? SUE? YOU THINK SHE IS BEAUTIFUL?
I MEAN HER FIGHTING IS BEAUTIFUL. SHE FIGHTS WITH...SUCH GRACE. I'VE LEARNED A LOT FROM HER.
STEVEN ROGERS, I THINK YOU ARE BLUSHING.
I MIGHT MENTION THAT YOU SEEM TO WATCH HER A LOT AS WELL.
ME? YES. I DO.
AND AS WELL I SHOULD.
WATCHING SUE STORM IS WHY I AM HERE.

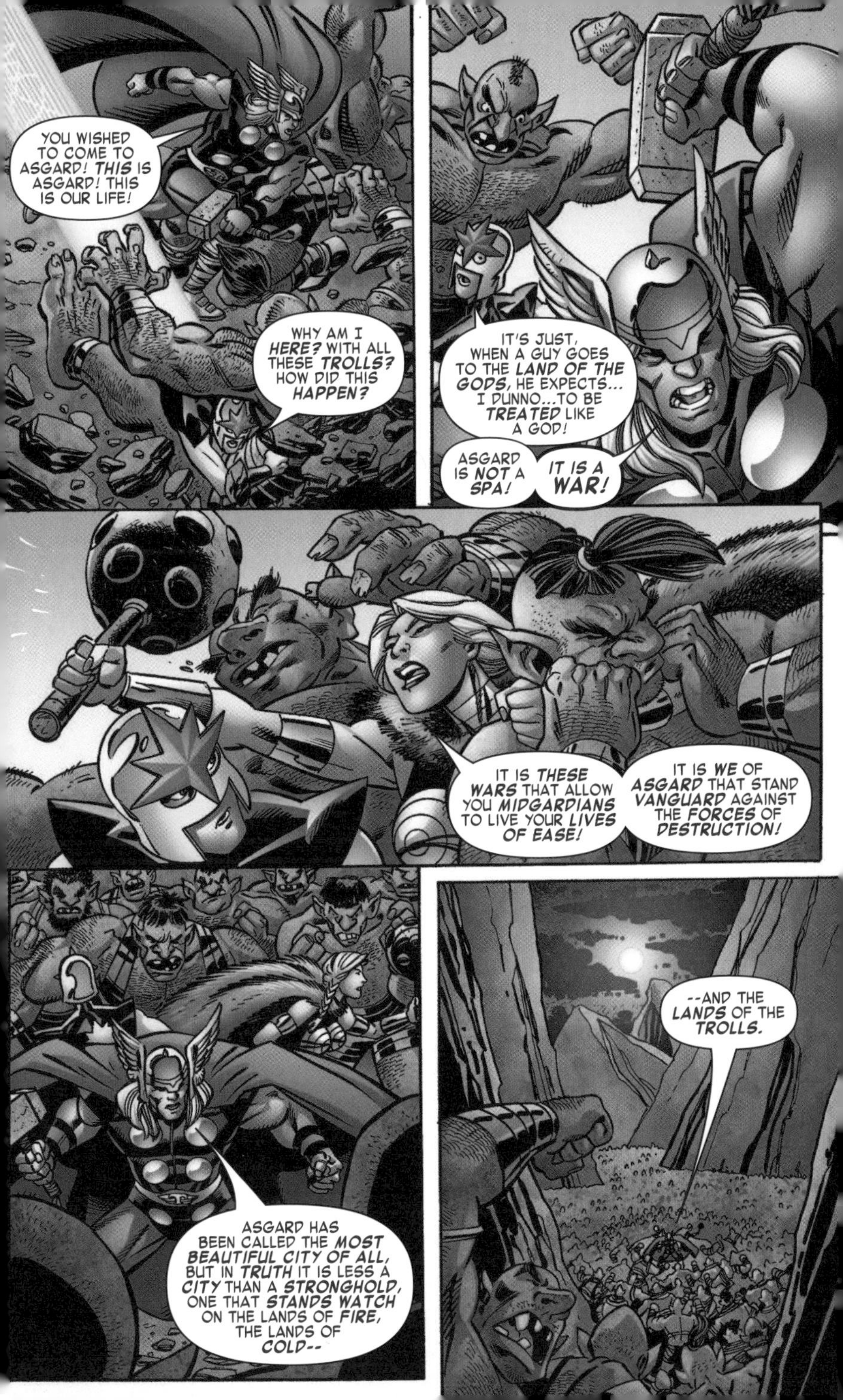
YOU WISHED TO COME TO ASGARD! THIS IS ASGARD! THIS IS OUR LIFE!
WHY AM I HERE? WITH ALL THESE TROLLS? HOW DID THIS HAPPEN?
IT'S JUST, WHEN A GUY GOES TO THE LAND OF THE GODS, HE EXPECTS... I DUNNO...TO BE TREATED LIKE A GOD!
ASGARD IS NOT A SPA!
IT IS A WAR!
IT IS THESE WARS THAT ALLOW YOU MIDGARDIANS TO LIVE YOUR LIVES OF EASE!
IT IS WE OF ASGARD THAT STAND VANGUARD AGAINST THE FORCES OF DESTRUCTION!
ASGARD HAS BEEN CALLED THE MOST BEAUTIFUL CITY OF ALL, BUT IN TRUTH IT IS LESS A CITY THAN A STRONGHOLD, ONE THAT STANDS WATCH ON THE LANDS OF FIRE, THE LANDS OF COLD--
--AND THE LANDS OF THE TROLLS.

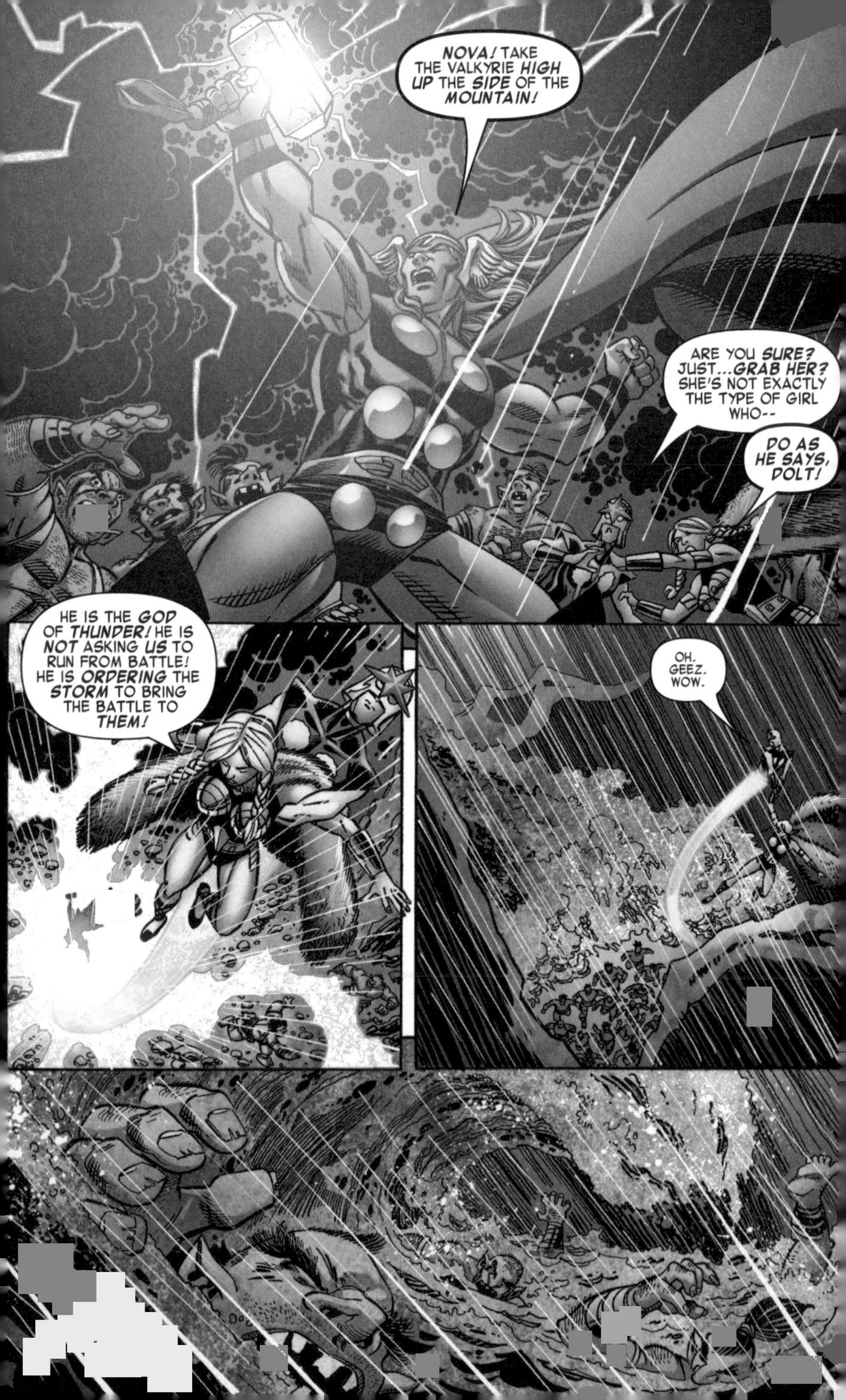
NOVA! TAKE THE VALKYRIE HIGH UP THE SIDE OF THE MOUNTAIN!
ARE YOU SURE? JUST...GRAB HER? SHE'S NOT EXACTLY THE TYPE OF GIRL WHO--
DO AS HE SAYS, DOLT!
HE IS THE GOD OF THUNDER! HE IS NOT ASKING US TO RUN FROM BATTLE! HE IS ORDERING THE STORM TO BRING THE BATTLE TO THEM!
OH. GEEZ. WOW.

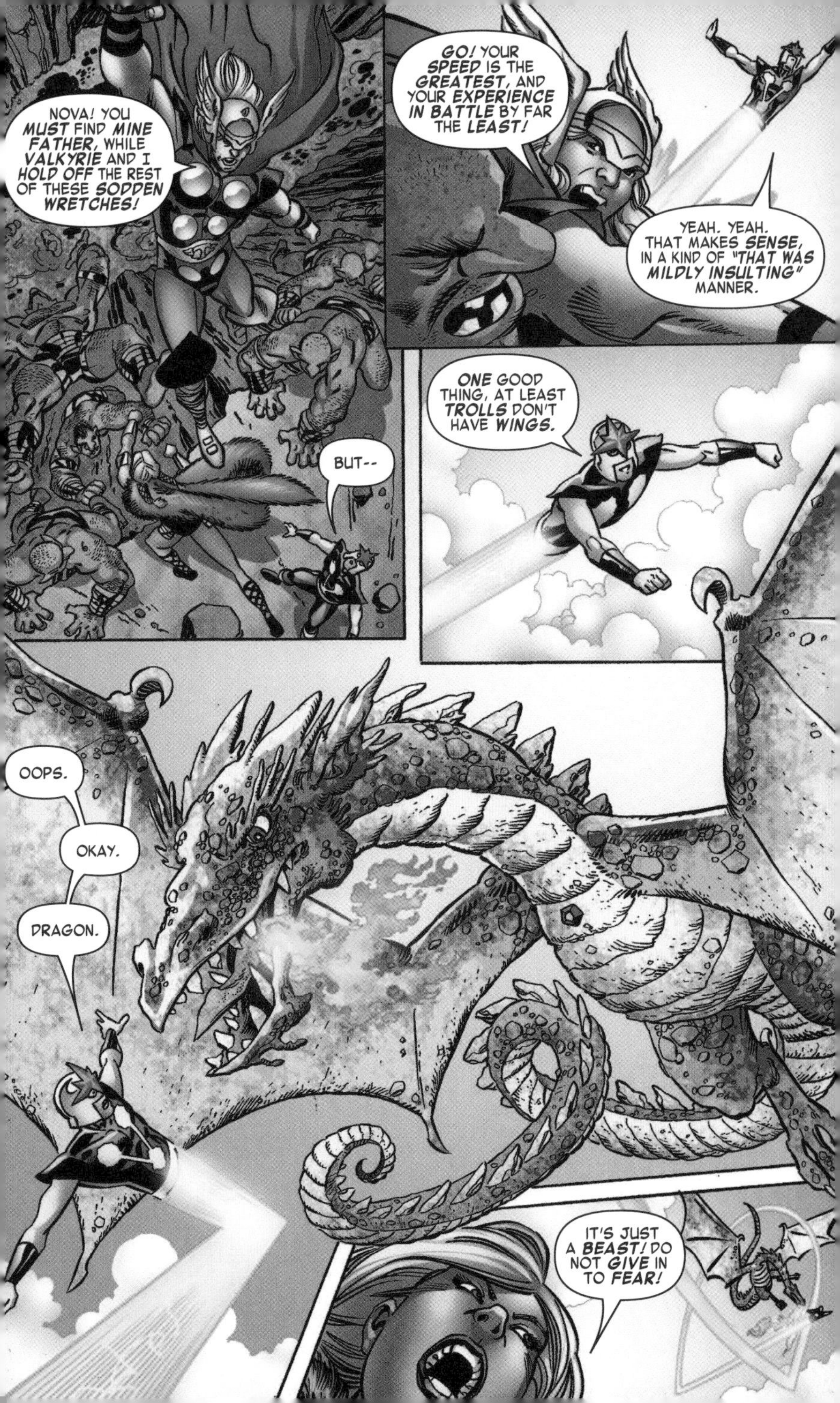
NOVA! YOU MUST FIND MINE FATHER, WHILE VALKYRIE AND I HOLD OFF THE REST OF THESE SODDEN WRETCHES!
BUT--
GO! YOUR SPEED IS THE GREATEST, AND YOUR EXPERIENCE IN BATTLE BY FAR THE LEAST!
YEAH. YEAH. THAT MAKES SENSE, IN A KIND OF "THAT WAS MILDLY INSULTING" MANNER.
ONE GOOD THING, AT LEAST TROLLS DON'T HAVE WINGS.
OOPS.
OKAY.
DRAGON.
IT'S JUST A BEAST! DO NOT GIVE IN TO FEAR!

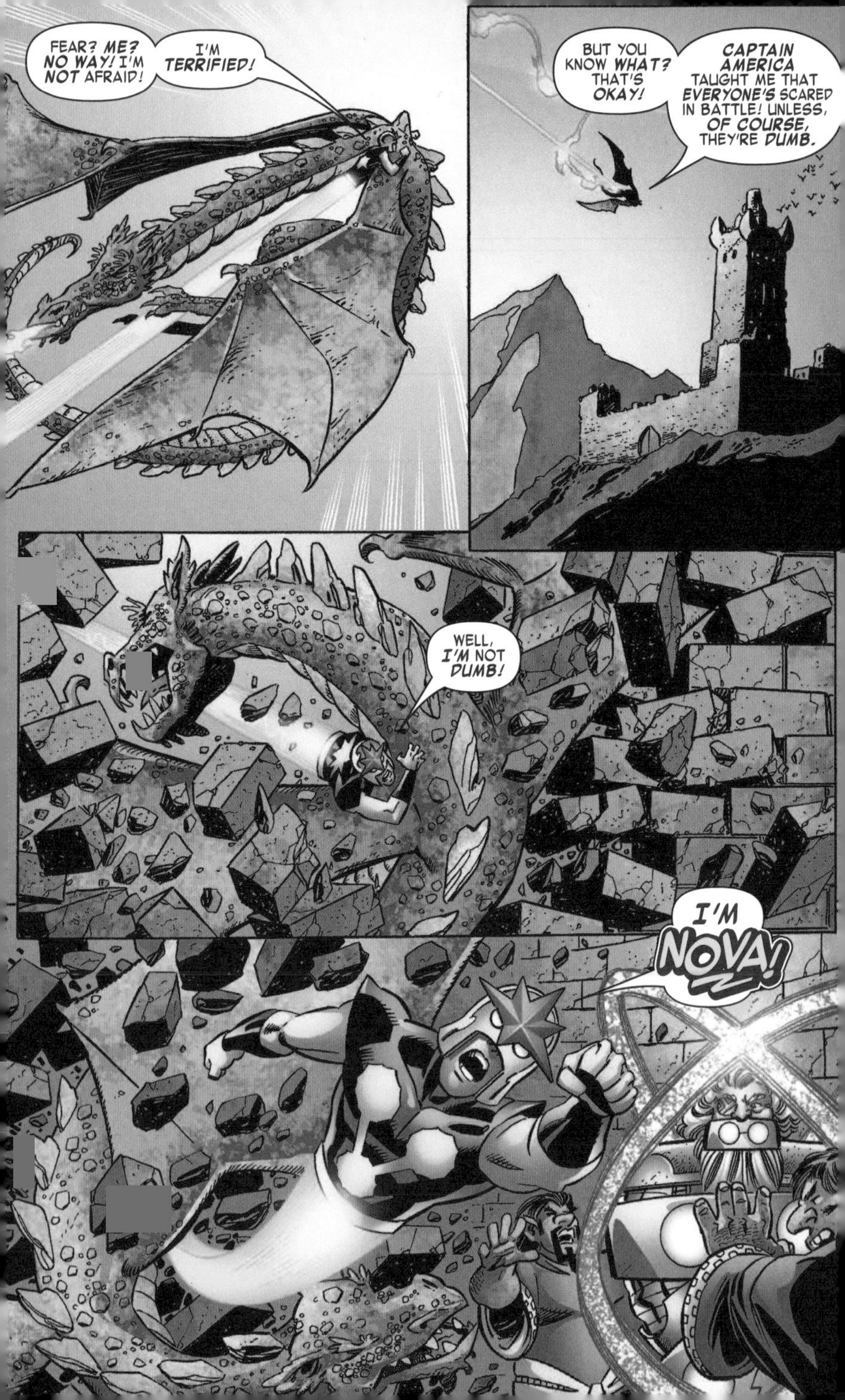
FEAR? ME? NO WAY! I'M NOT AFRAID!
I'M TERRIFIED!
BUT YOU KNOW WHAT? THAT'S OKAY!
CAPTAIN AMERICA TAUGHT ME THAT EVERYONE'S SCARED IN BATTLE! UNLESS, OF COURSE, THEY'RE DUMB.
WELL, I'M NOT DUMB!
I'M NOVA!

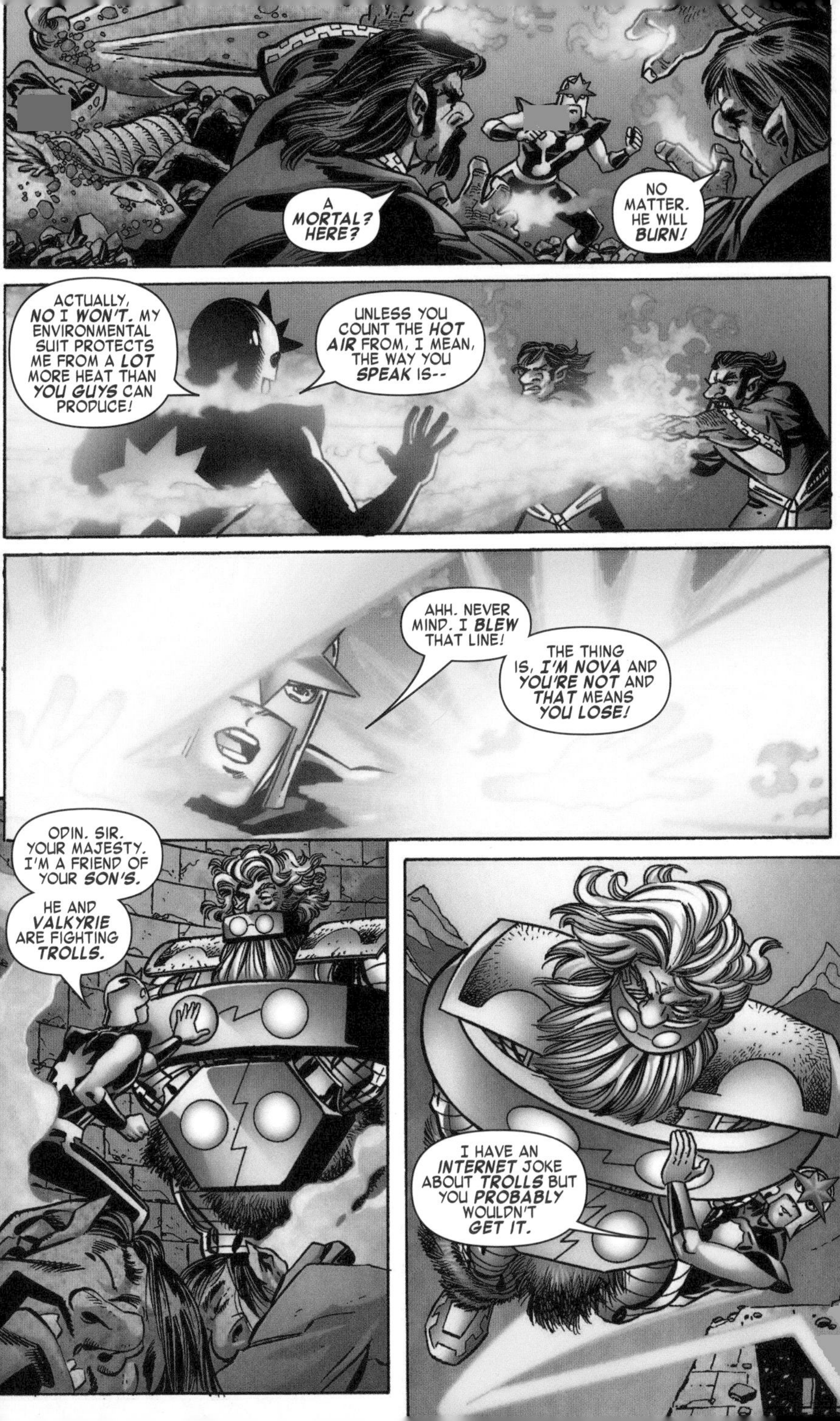
A MORTAL? HERE?
NO MATTER. HE WILL BURN!
ACTUALLY, NO I WON'T. MY ENVIRONMENTAL SUIT PROTECTS ME FROM A LOT MORE HEAT THAN YOU GUYS CAN PRODUCE!
UNLESS YOU COUNT THE HOT AIR FROM, I MEAN, THE WAY YOU SPEAK IS--
AHH. NEVER MIND. I BLEW THAT LINE!
THE THING IS, I'M NOVA AND YOU'RE NOT AND THAT MEANS YOU LOSE!
ODIN. SIR. YOUR MAJESTY. I'M A FRIEND OF YOUR SON'S.
HE AND VALKYRIE ARE FIGHTING TROLLS.
I HAVE AN INTERNET JOKE ABOUT TROLLS BUT YOU PROBABLY WOULDN'T GET IT.

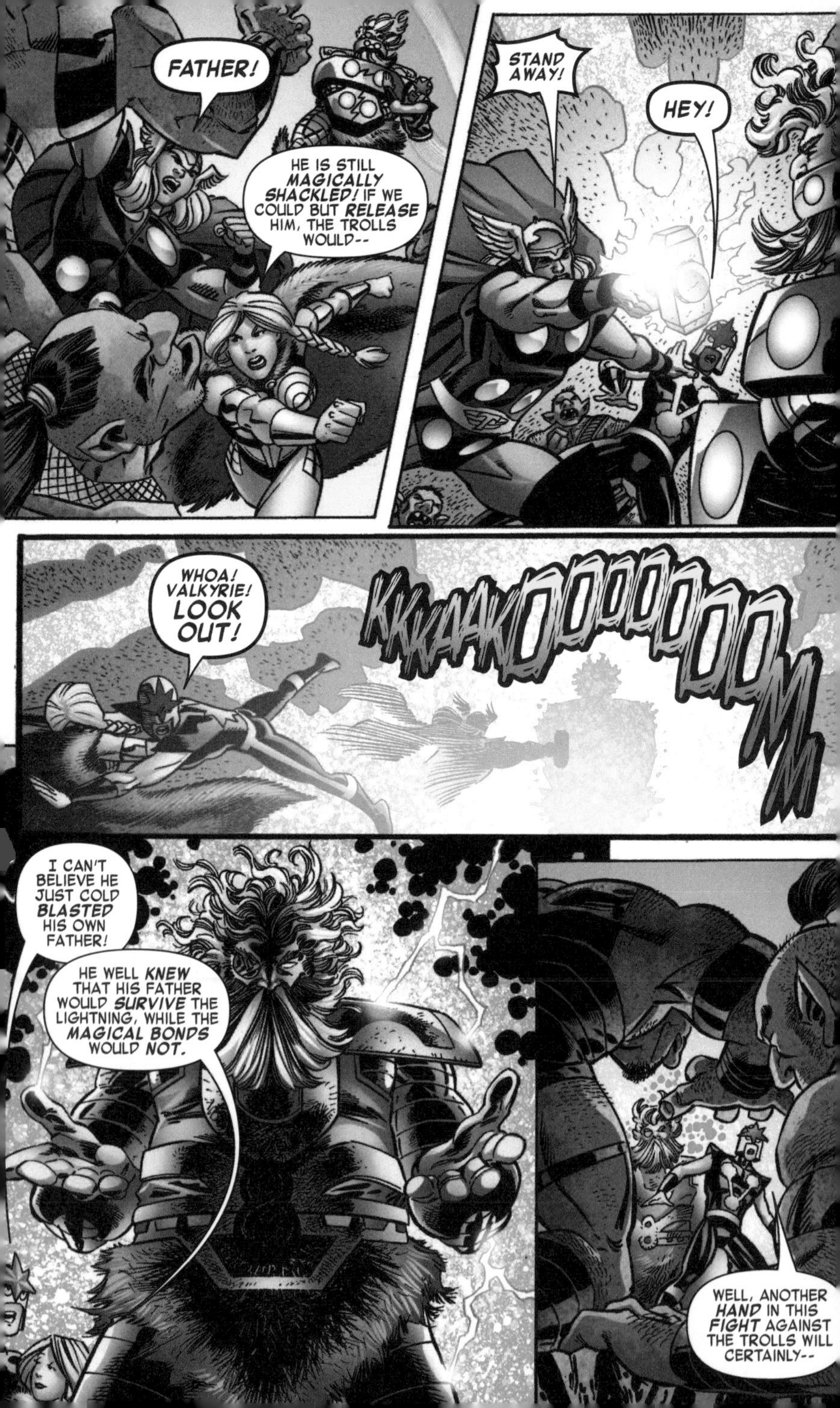
FATHER!
HE IS STILL MAGICALLY SHACKLED! IF WE COULD BUT RELEASE HIM, THE TROLLS WOULD--
STAND AWAY!
HEY!
WHOA! VALKYRIE! LOOK OUT!
KKKAAKOOOOOOOM
I CAN'T BELIEVE HE JUST COLD BLASTED HIS OWN FATHER!
HE WELL KNEW THAT HIS FATHER WOULD SURVIVE THE LIGHTNING, WHILE THE MAGICAL BONDS WOULD NOT.
WELL, ANOTHER HAND IN THIS FIGHT AGAINST THE TROLLS WILL CERTAINLY--

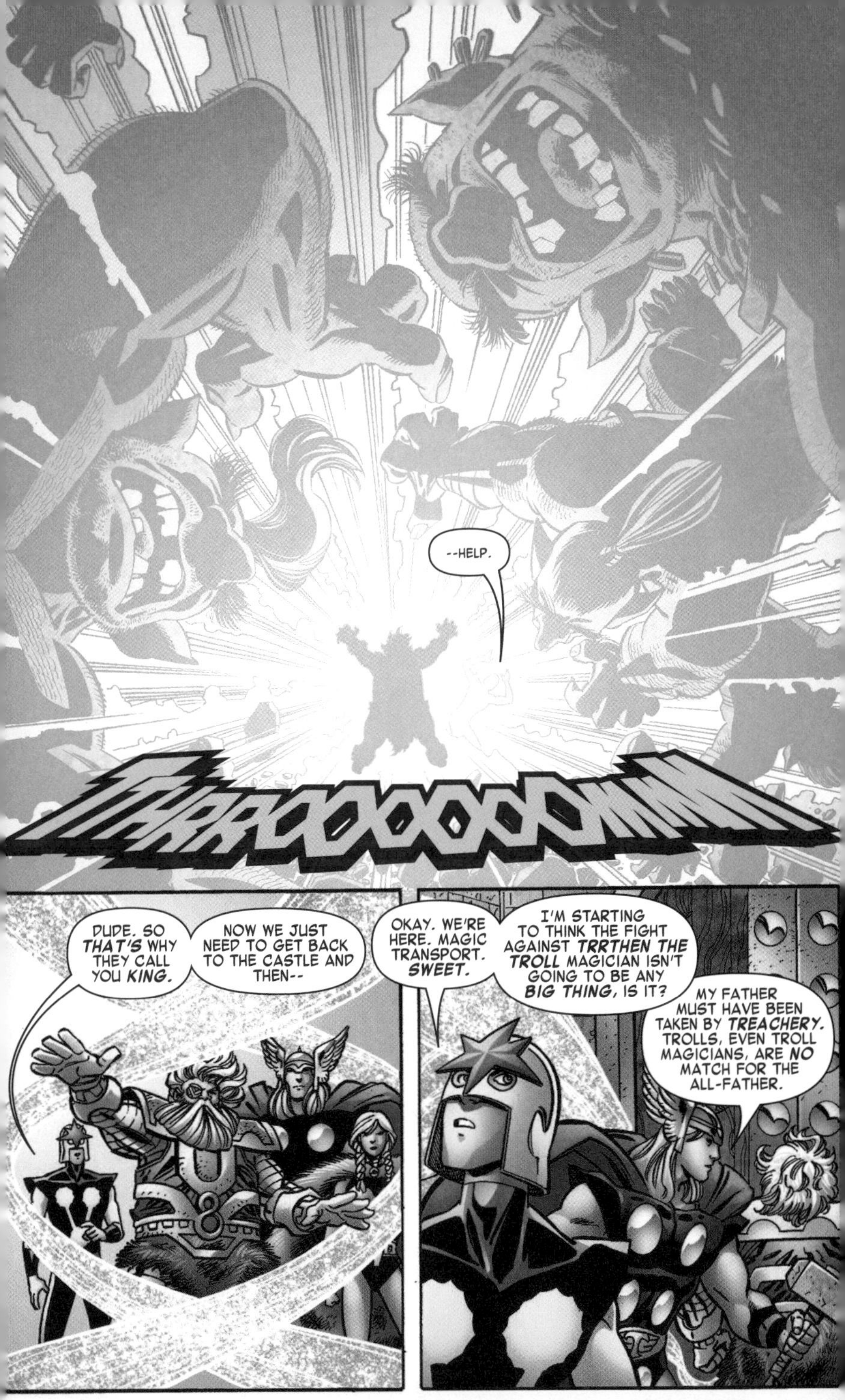
--HELP.
THRROOOOOOMMM
DUDE. SO THAT'S WHY THEY CALL YOU KING.
NOW WE JUST NEED TO GET BACK TO THE CASTLE AND THEN--
OKAY. WE'RE HERE. MAGIC TRANSPORT. SWEET.
I'M STARTING TO THINK THE FIGHT AGAINST TRRTHEN THE TROLL MAGICIAN ISN'T GOING TO BE ANY BIG THING, IS IT?
MY FATHER MUST HAVE BEEN TAKEN BY TREACHERY. TROLLS, EVEN TROLL MAGICIANS, ARE NO MATCH FOR THE ALL-FATHER.

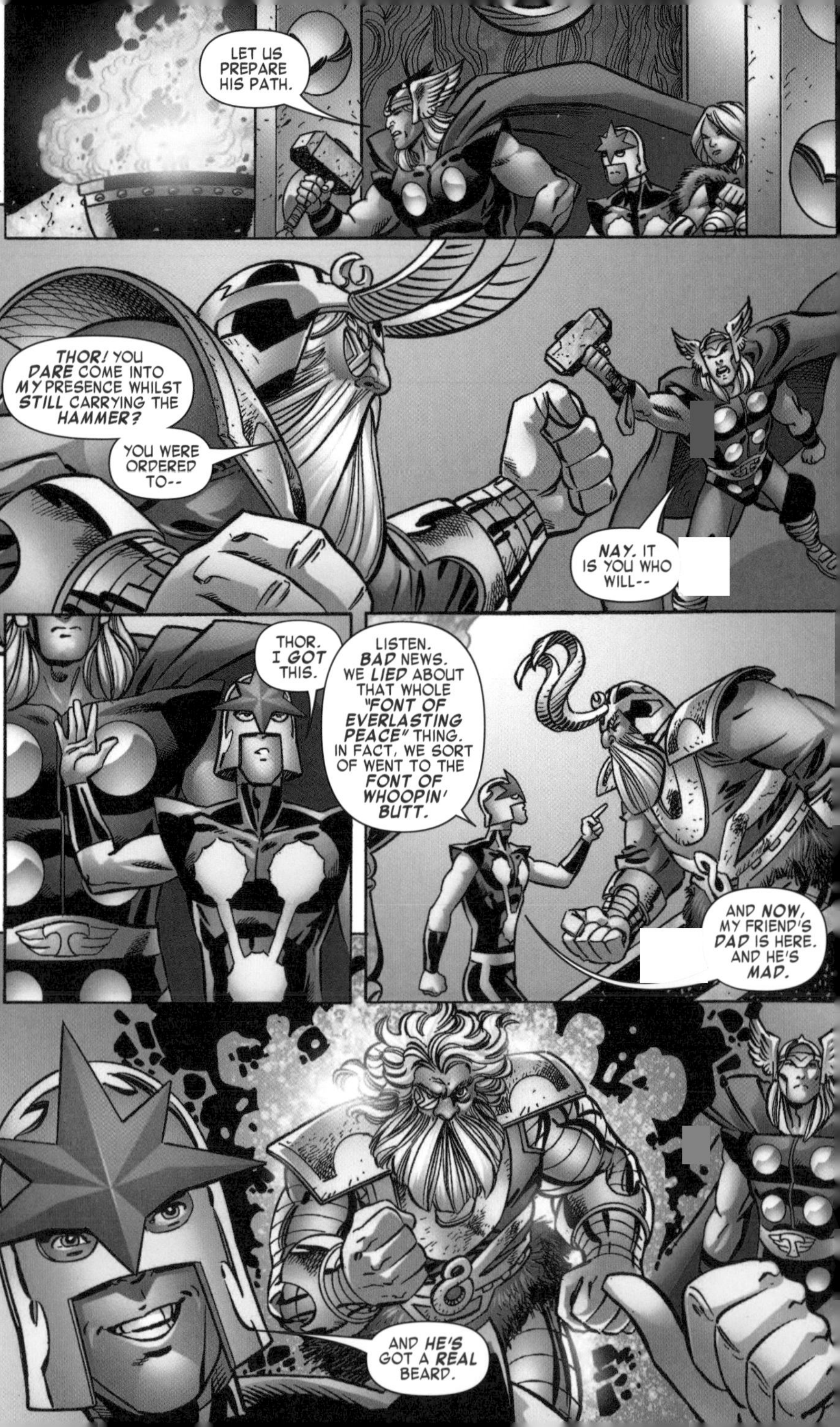
LET US PREPARE HIS PATH.
THOR! YOU DARE COME INTO MY PRESENCE WHILST STILL CARRYING THE HAMMER?
YOU WERE ORDERED TO--
NAY. IT IS YOU WHO WILL--
THOR. I GOT THIS.
LISTEN. BAD NEWS. WE LIED ABOUT THAT WHOLE "FONT OF EVERLASTING PEACE" THING. IN FACT, WE SORT OF WENT TO THE FONT OF WHOOPIN' BUTT.
AND NOW, MY FRIEND'S DAD IS HERE. AND HE'S MAD.
AND HE'S GOT A REAL BEARD.

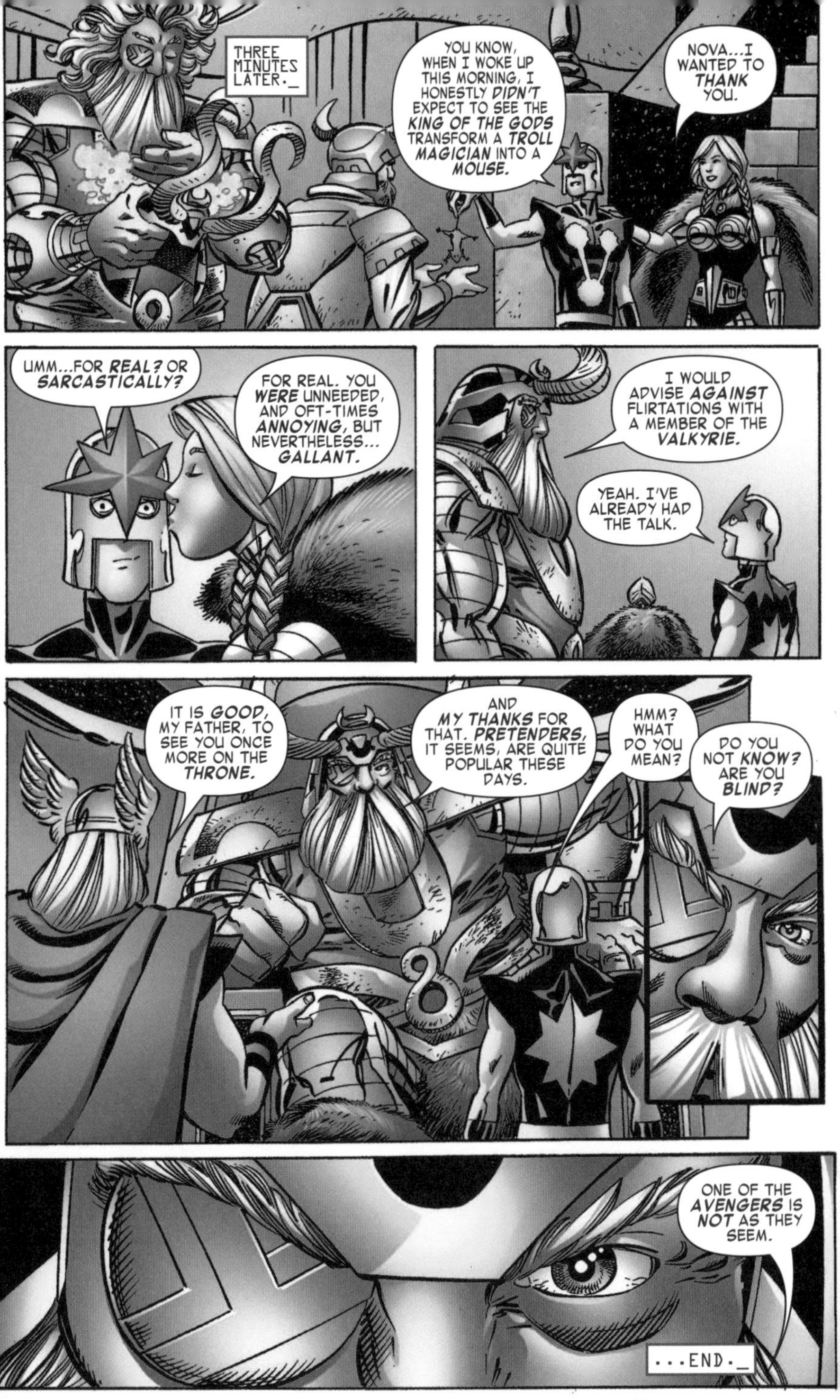
THREE MINUTES LATER._
YOU KNOW, WHEN I WOKE UP THIS MORNING, I HONESTLY DIDN'T EXPECT TO SEE THE KING OF THE GODS TRANSFORM A TROLL MAGICIAN INTO A MOUSE.
NOVA...I WANTED TO THANK YOU.
UMM...FOR REAL? OR SARCASTICALLY?
FOR REAL. YOU WERE UNNEEDED, AND OFT-TIMES ANNOYING, BUT NEVERTHELESS... GALLANT.
I WOULD ADVISE AGAINST FLIRTATIONS WITH A MEMBER OF THE VALKYRIE.
YEAH. I'VE ALREADY HAD THE TALK.
IT IS GOOD, MY FATHER, TO SEE YOU ONCE MORE ON THE THRONE.
AND MY THANKS FOR THAT. PRETENDERS, IT SEEMS, ARE QUITE POPULAR THESE DAYS.
HMM? WHAT DO YOU MEAN?
DO YOU NOT KNOW? ARE YOU BLIND?
ONE OF THE AVENGERS IS NOT AS THEY SEEM.
...END._

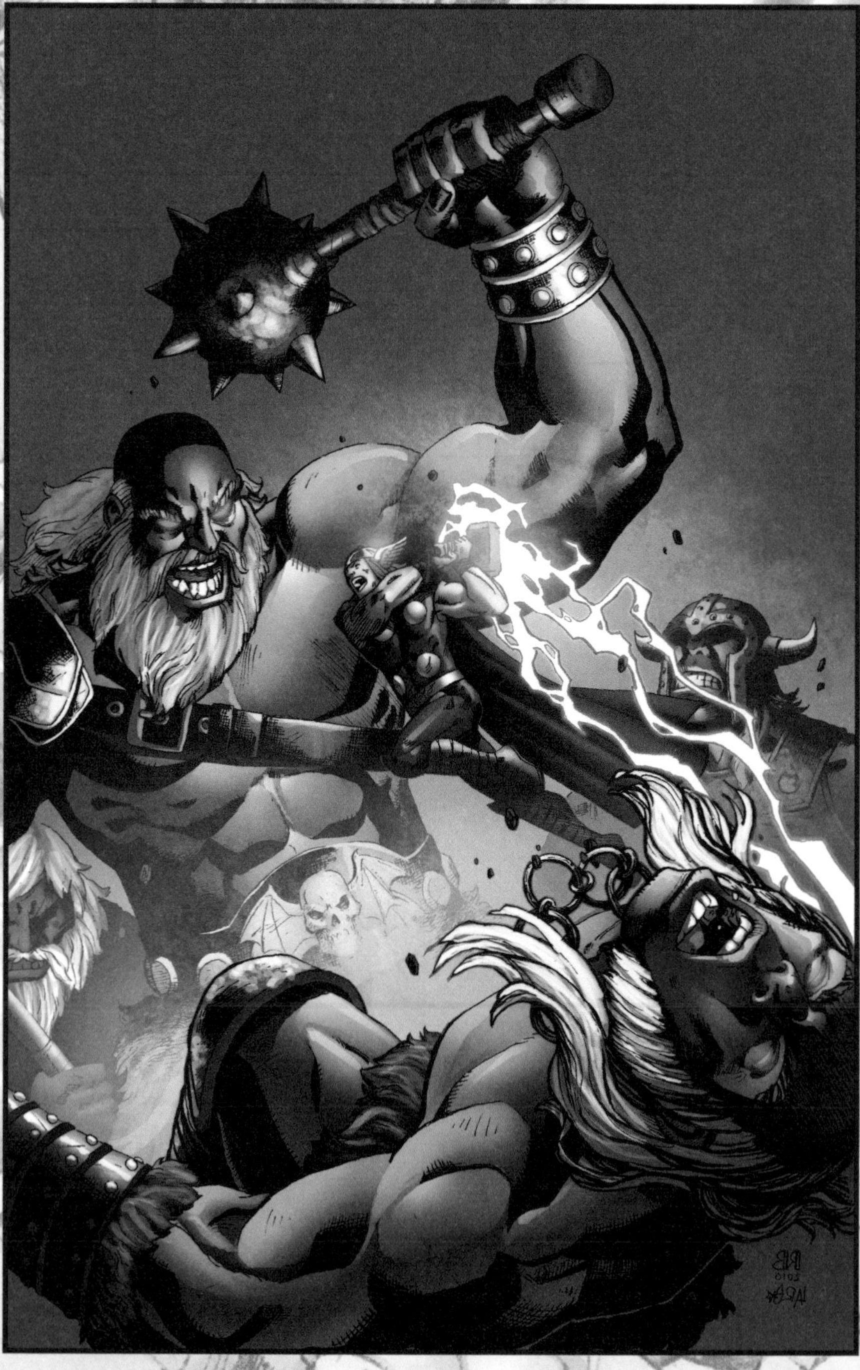

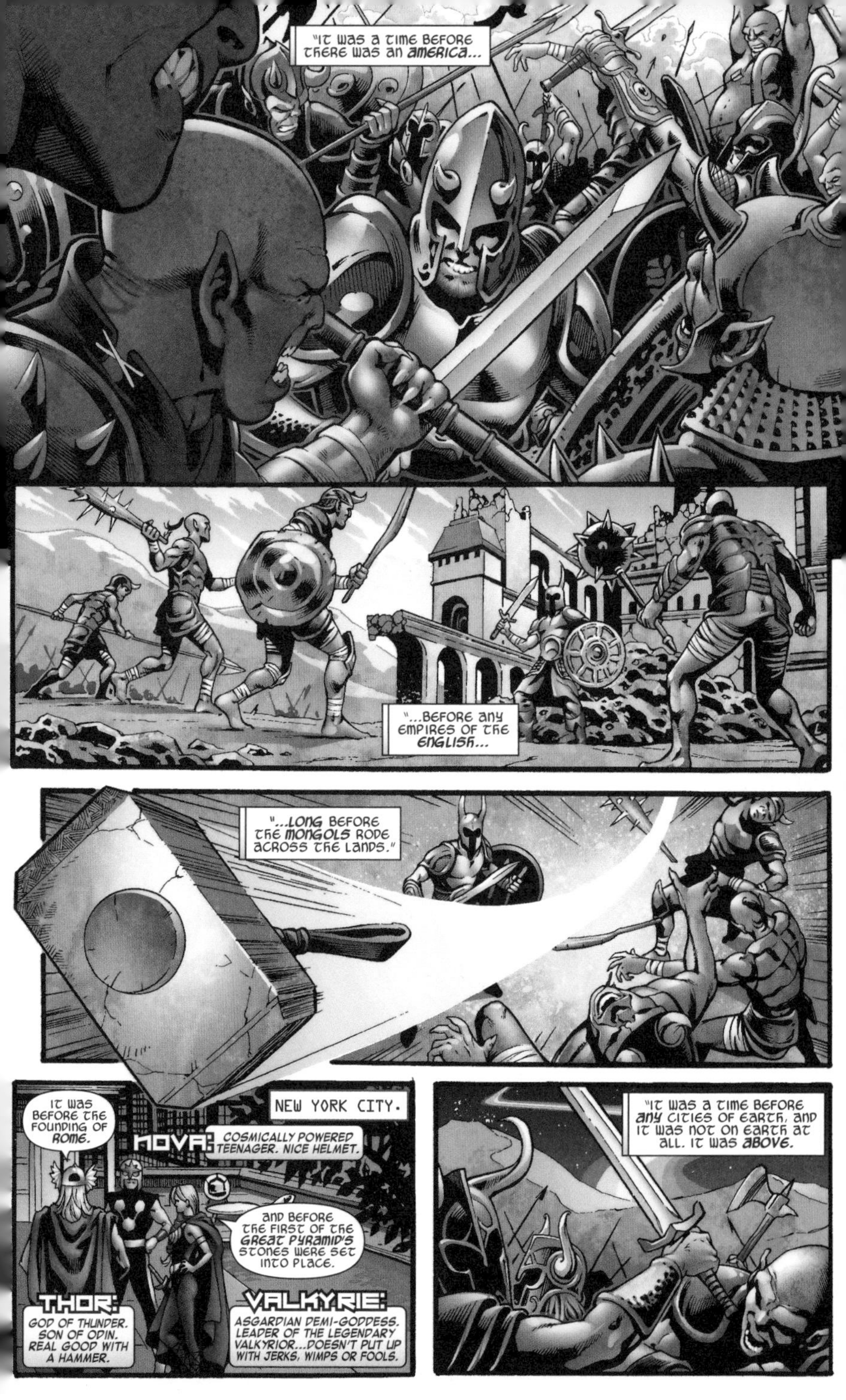
"IT WAS A TIME BEFORE THERE WAS AN AMERICA...
"...BEFORE ANY EMPIRES OF THE ENGLISH...
"...LONG BEFORE THE MONGOLS RODE ACROSS THE LANDS."
NEW YORK CITY.
IT WAS BEFORE THE FOUNDING OF ROME.
NOVA: COSMICALLY POWERED TEENAGER. NICE HELMET.
AND BEFORE THE FIRST OF THE GREAT PYRAMID'S STONES WERE SET INTO PLACE.
THOR: GOD OF THUNDER. SON OF ODIN. REAL GOOD WITH A HAMMER.
VALKYRIE: ASGARDIAN DEMI-GODDESS. LEADER OF THE LEGENDARY VALKYRIOR...DOESN'T PUT UP WITH JERKS, WIMPS OR FOOLS.
"IT WAS A TIME BEFORE ANY CITIES OF EARTH, AND IT WAS NOT ON EARTH AT ALL. IT WAS ABOVE.

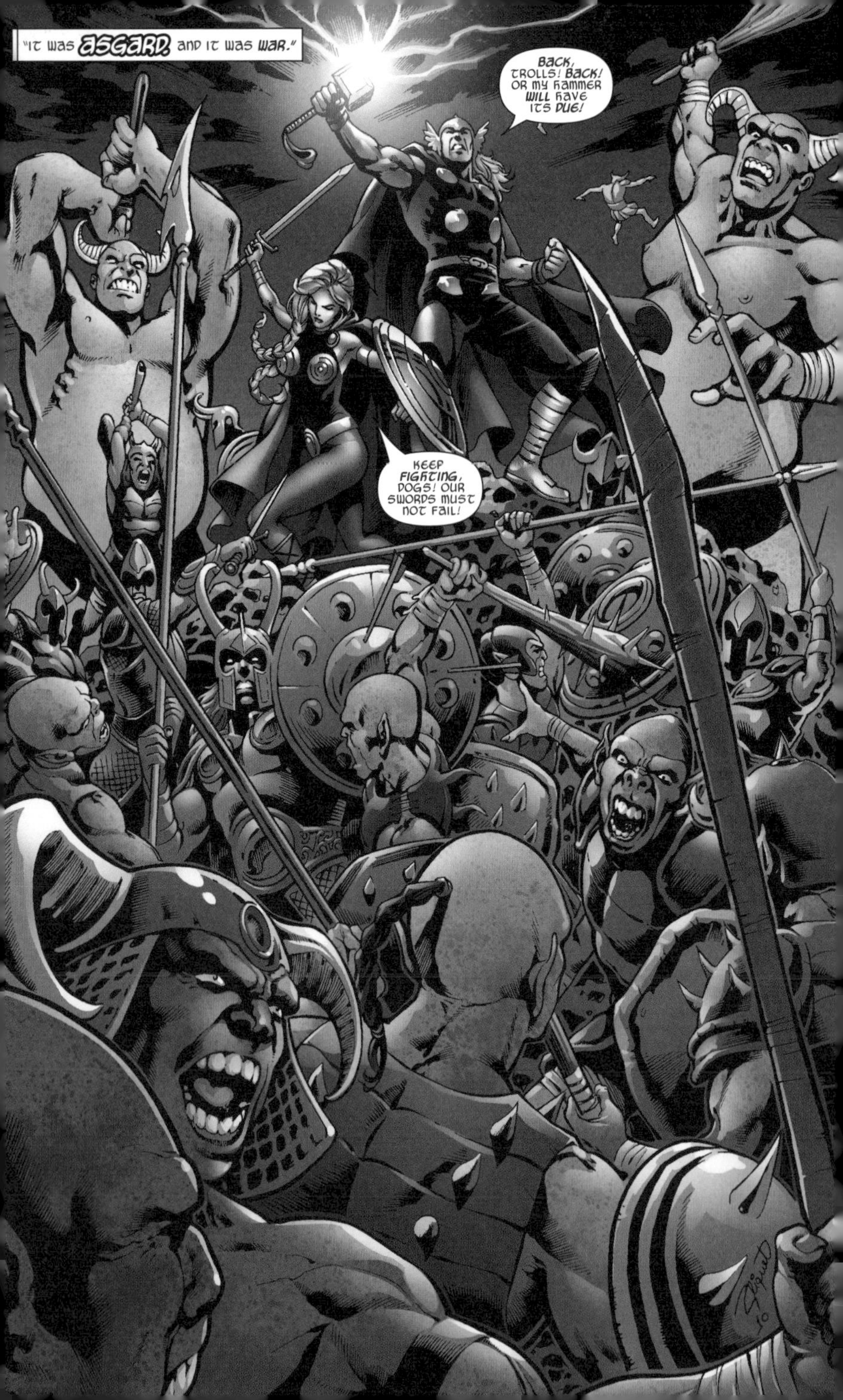
"IT WAS ASGARD, AND IT WAS WAR."
BACK, TROLLS! BACK! OR MY HAMMER WILL HAVE ITS DUE!
KEEP FIGHTING, DOGS! OUR SWORDS MUST NOT FAIL!

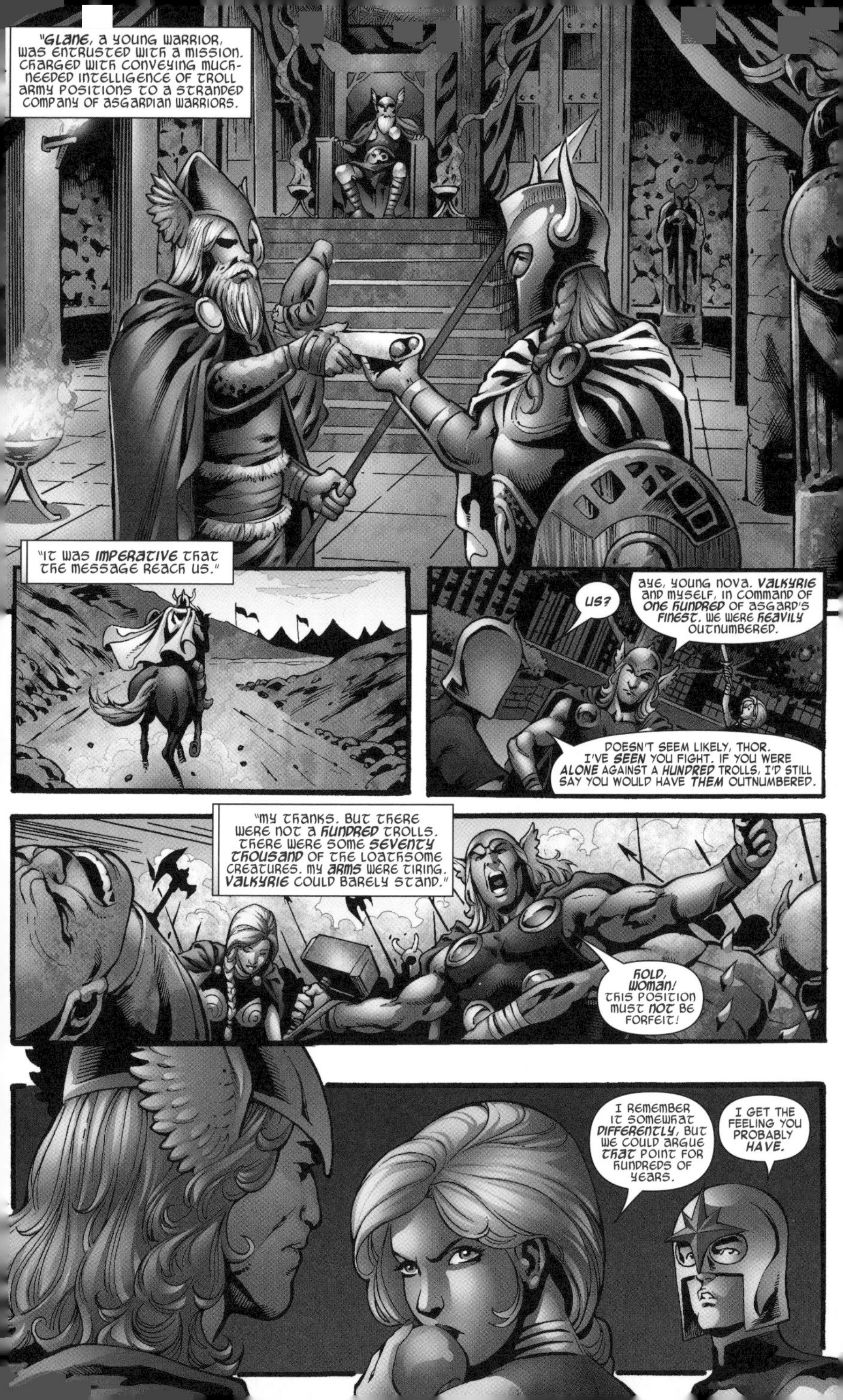
"GLANE, A YOUNG WARRIOR, WAS ENTRUSTED WITH A MISSION. CHARGED WITH CONVEYING MUCH-NEEDED INTELLIGENCE OF TROLL ARMY POSITIONS TO A STRANDED COMPANY OF ASGARDIAN WARRIORS.
"IT WAS IMPERATIVE THAT THE MESSAGE REACH US."
US?
AYE, YOUNG NOVA. VALKYRIE AND MYSELF, IN COMMAND OF ONE HUNDRED OF ASGARD'S FINEST. WE WERE HEAVILY OUTNUMBERED.
DOESN'T SEEM LIKELY, THOR. I'VE SEEN YOU FIGHT. IF YOU WERE ALONE AGAINST A HUNDRED TROLLS, I'D STILL SAY YOU WOULD HAVE THEM OUTNUMBERED.
"MY THANKS. BUT THERE WERE NOT A HUNDRED TROLLS. THERE WERE SOME SEVENTY THOUSAND OF THE LOATHSOME CREATURES. MY ARMS WERE TIRING. VALKYRIE COULD BARELY STAND."
HOLD, WOMAN! THIS POSITION MUST NOT BE FORFEIT!
I REMEMBER IT SOMEWHAT DIFFERENTLY, BUT WE COULD ARGUE THAT POINT FOR HUNDREDS OF YEARS.
I GET THE FEELING YOU PROBABLY HAVE.

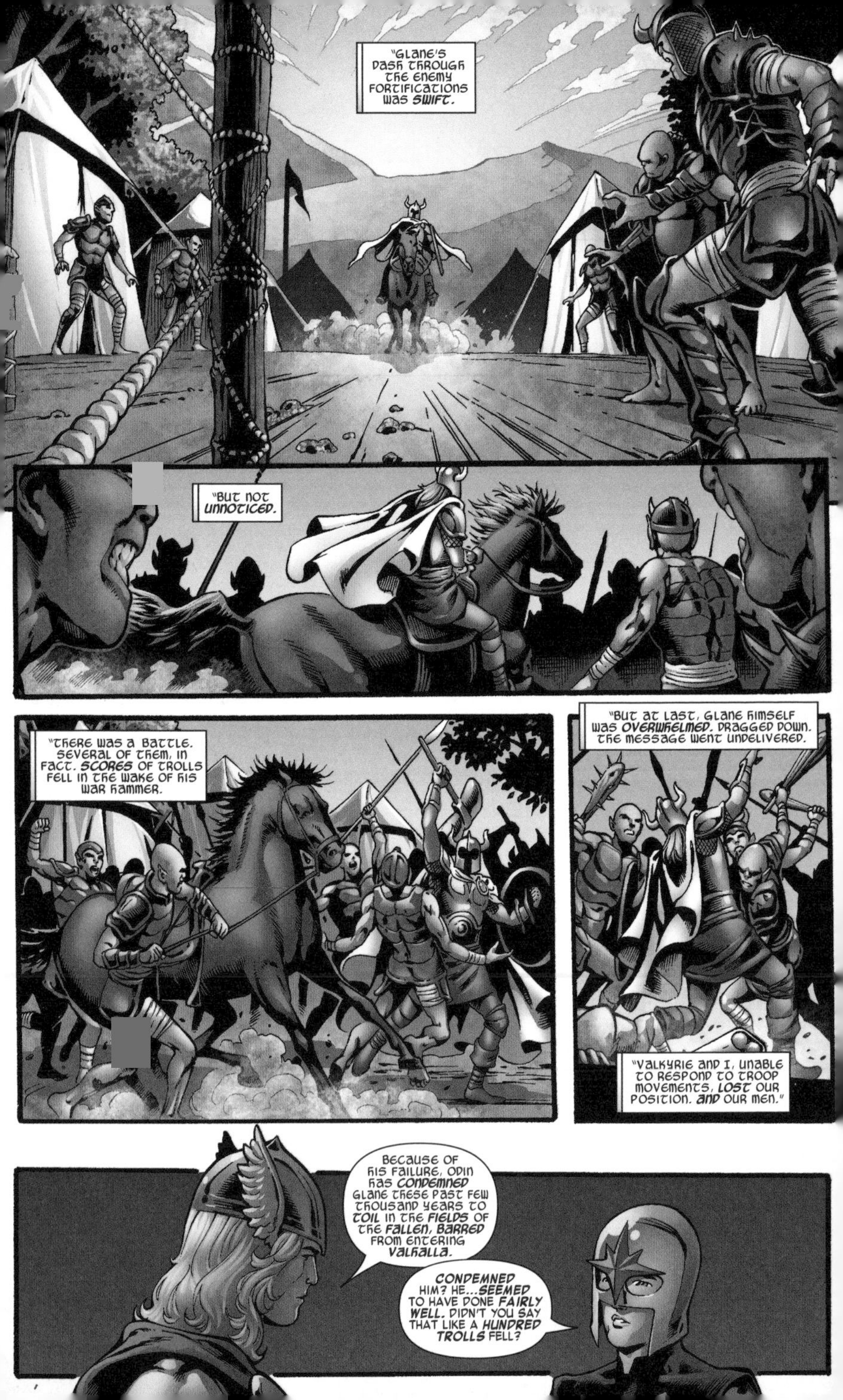
"GLANE'S DASH THROUGH THE ENEMY FORTIFICATIONS WAS SWIFT.
"BUT NOT UNNOTICED.
"THERE WAS A BATTLE. SEVERAL OF THEM, IN FACT. SCORES OF TROLLS FELL IN THE WAKE OF HIS WAR HAMMER.
"BUT AT LAST, GLANE HIMSELF WAS OVERWHELMED. DRAGGED DOWN. THE MESSAGE WENT UNDELIVERED.
"VALKYRIE AND I, UNABLE TO RESPOND TO TROOP MOVEMENTS, LOST OUR POSITION. AND OUR MEN."
BECAUSE OF HIS FAILURE, ODIN HAS CONDEMNED GLANE THESE PAST FEW THOUSAND YEARS TO TOIL IN THE FIELDS OF THE FALLEN, BARRED FROM ENTERING VALHALLA.
CONDEMNED HIM? HE...SEEMED TO HAVE DONE FAIRLY WELL. DIDN'T YOU SAY THAT LIKE A HUNDRED TROLLS FELL?

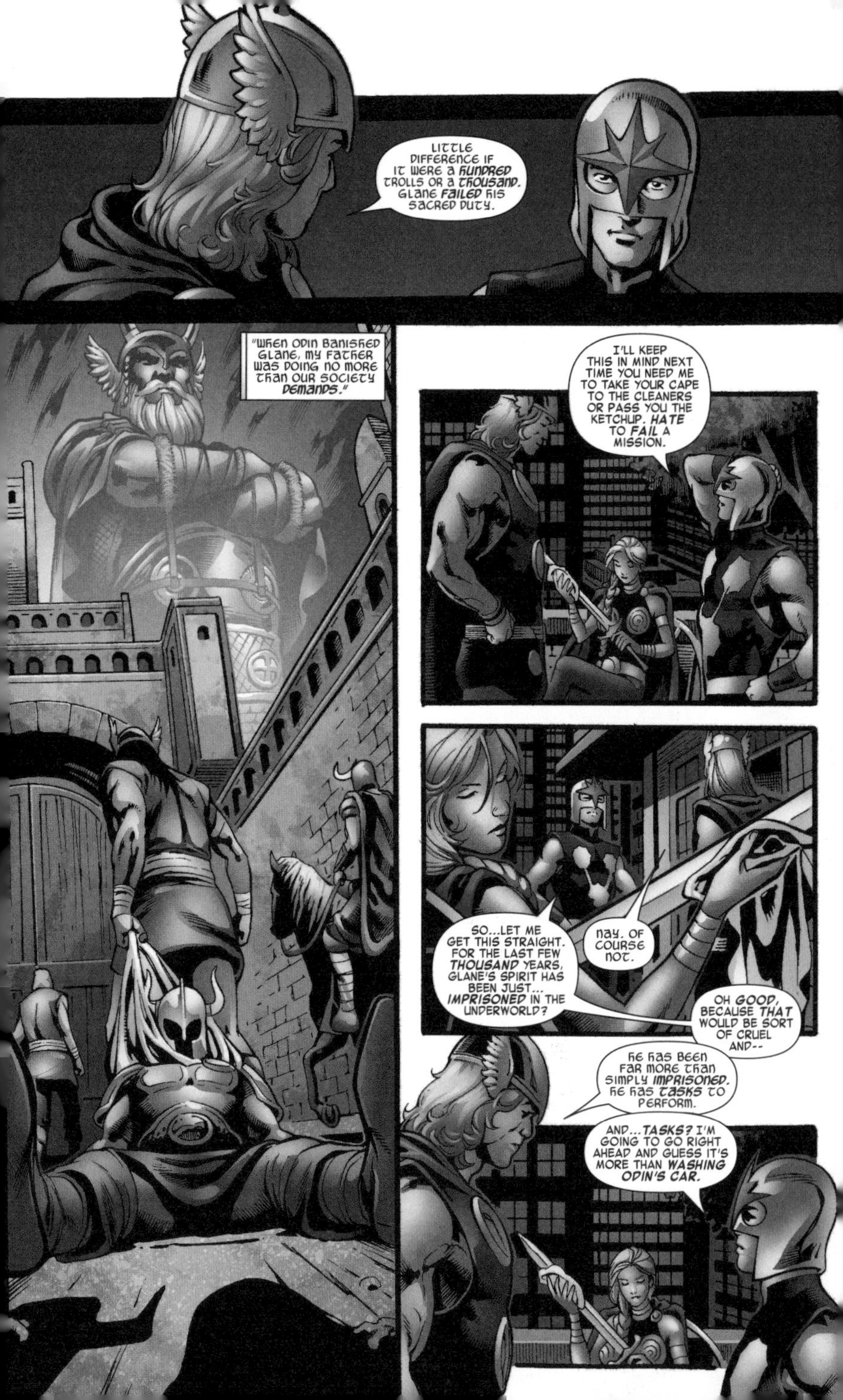

LITTLE DIFFERENCE IF IT WERE A HUNDRED TROLLS OR A THOUSAND. GLANE FAILED HIS SACRED DUTY.
"WHEN ODIN BANISHED GLANE, MY FATHER WAS DOING NO MORE THAN OUR SOCIETY DEMANDS."
I'LL KEEP THIS IN MIND NEXT TIME YOU NEED ME TO TAKE YOUR CAPE TO THE CLEANERS OR PASS YOU THE KETCHUP. HATE TO FAIL A MISSION.
SO...LET ME GET THIS STRAIGHT. FOR THE LAST FEW THOUSAND YEARS, GLANE'S SPIRIT HAS BEEN JUST... IMPRISONED IN THE UNDERWORLD?
NAY. OF COURSE NOT.
OH GOOD, BECAUSE THAT WOULD BE SORT OF CRUEL AND--
HE HAS BEEN FAR MORE THAN SIMPLY IMPRISONED. HE HAS TASKS TO PERFORM.
AND...TASKS? I'M GOING TO GO RIGHT AHEAD AND GUESS IT'S MORE THAN WASHING ODIN'S CAR.

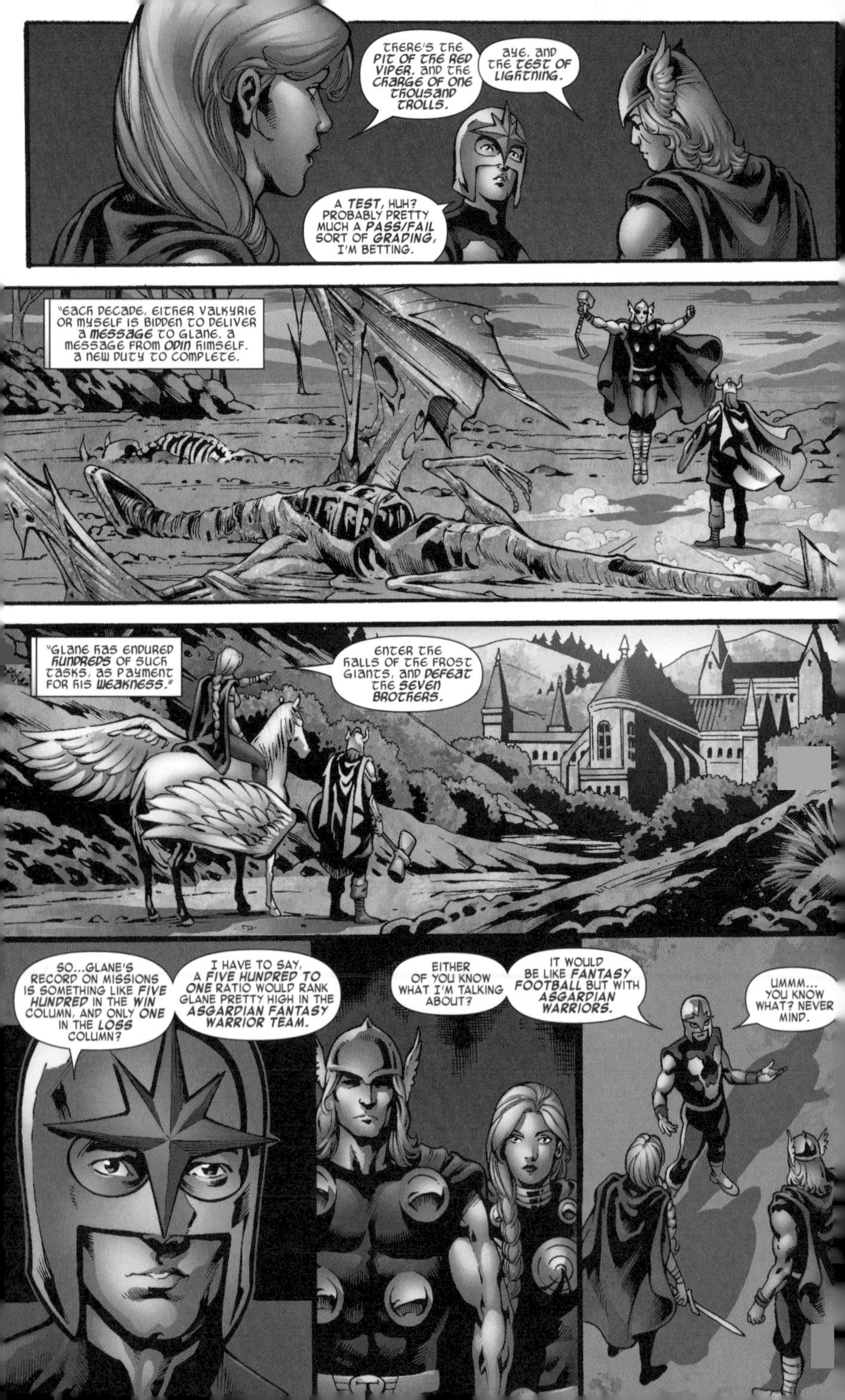
THERE'S THE PIT OF THE RED VIPER. AND THE CHARGE OF ONE THOUSAND TROLLS.
AYE. AND THE TEST OF LIGHTNING.
A TEST, HUH? PROBABLY PRETTY MUCH A PASS/FAIL SORT OF GRADING, I'M BETTING.
"EACH DECADE, EITHER VALKYRIE OR MYSELF IS BIDDEN TO DELIVER A MESSAGE TO GLANE. A MESSAGE FROM ODIN HIMSELF. A NEW DUTY TO COMPLETE.
"GLANE HAS ENDURED HUNDREDS OF SUCH TASKS, AS PAYMENT FOR HIS WEAKNESS."
ENTER THE HALLS OF THE FROST GIANTS, AND DEFEAT THE SEVEN BROTHERS.
SO...GLANE'S RECORD ON MISSIONS IS SOMETHING LIKE FIVE HUNDRED IN THE WIN COLUMN, AND ONLY ONE IN THE LOSS COLUMN?
I HAVE TO SAY, A FIVE HUNDRED TO ONE RATIO WOULD RANK GLANE PRETTY HIGH IN THE ASGARDIAN FANTASY WARRIOR TEAM.
EITHER OF YOU KNOW WHAT I'M TALKING ABOUT?
IT WOULD BE LIKE FANTASY FOOTBALL BUT WITH ASGARDIAN WARRIORS.
UMMM... YOU KNOW WHAT? NEVER MIND.

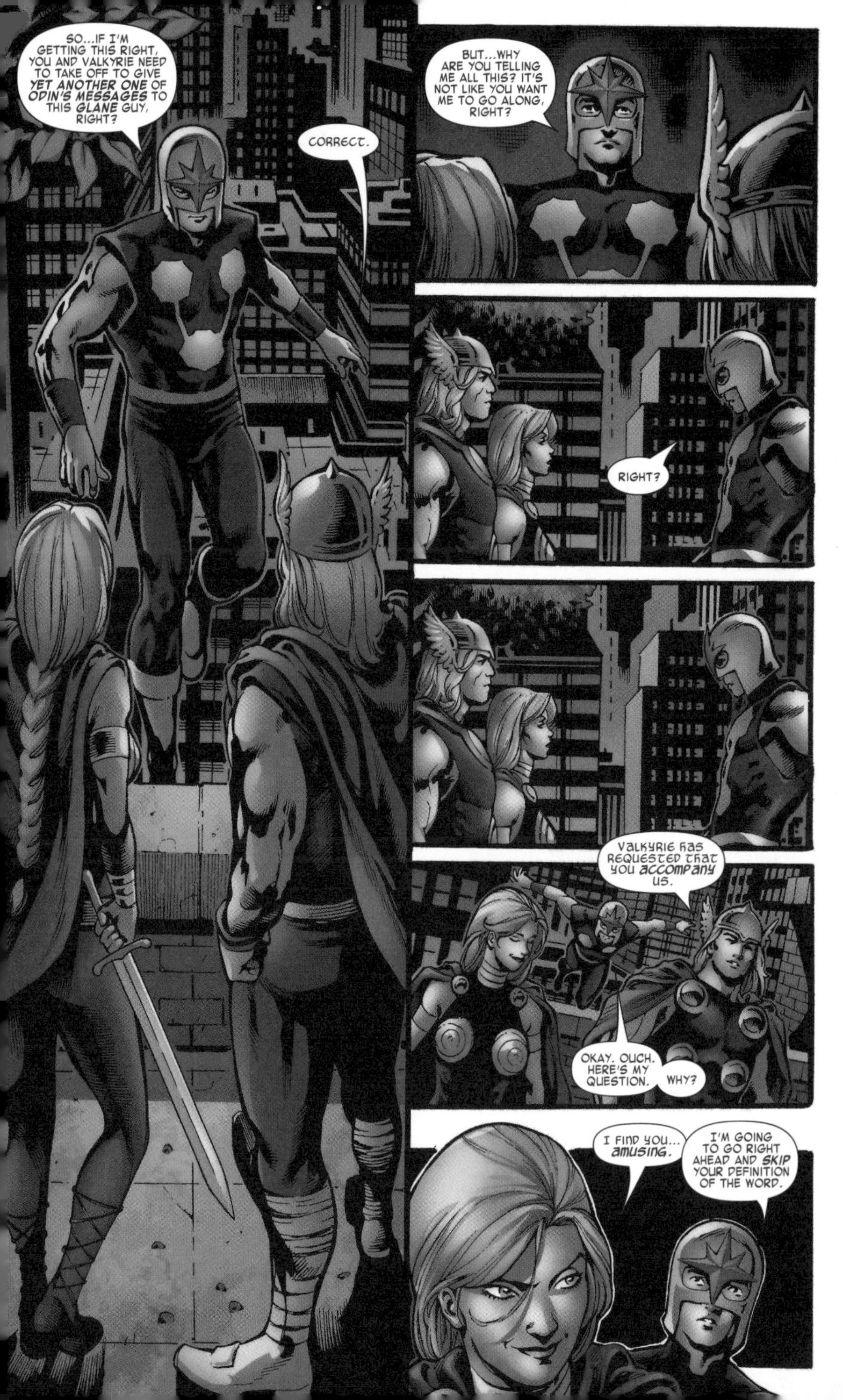
SO...IF I'M GETTING THIS RIGHT, YOU AND VALKYRIE NEED TO TAKE OFF TO GIVE YET ANOTHER ONE OF ODIN'S MESSAGES TO THIS GLANE GUY, RIGHT?
CORRECT.
BUT...WHY ARE YOU TELLING ME ALL THIS? IT'S NOT LIKE YOU WANT ME TO GO ALONG, RIGHT?
RIGHT?
VALKYRIE HAS REQUESTED THAT YOU ACCOMPANY US.
OKAY. OUCH. HERE'S MY QUESTION.
WHY?
I FIND YOU... AMUSING.
I'M GOING TO GO RIGHT AHEAD AND SKIP YOUR DEFINITION OF THE WORD.

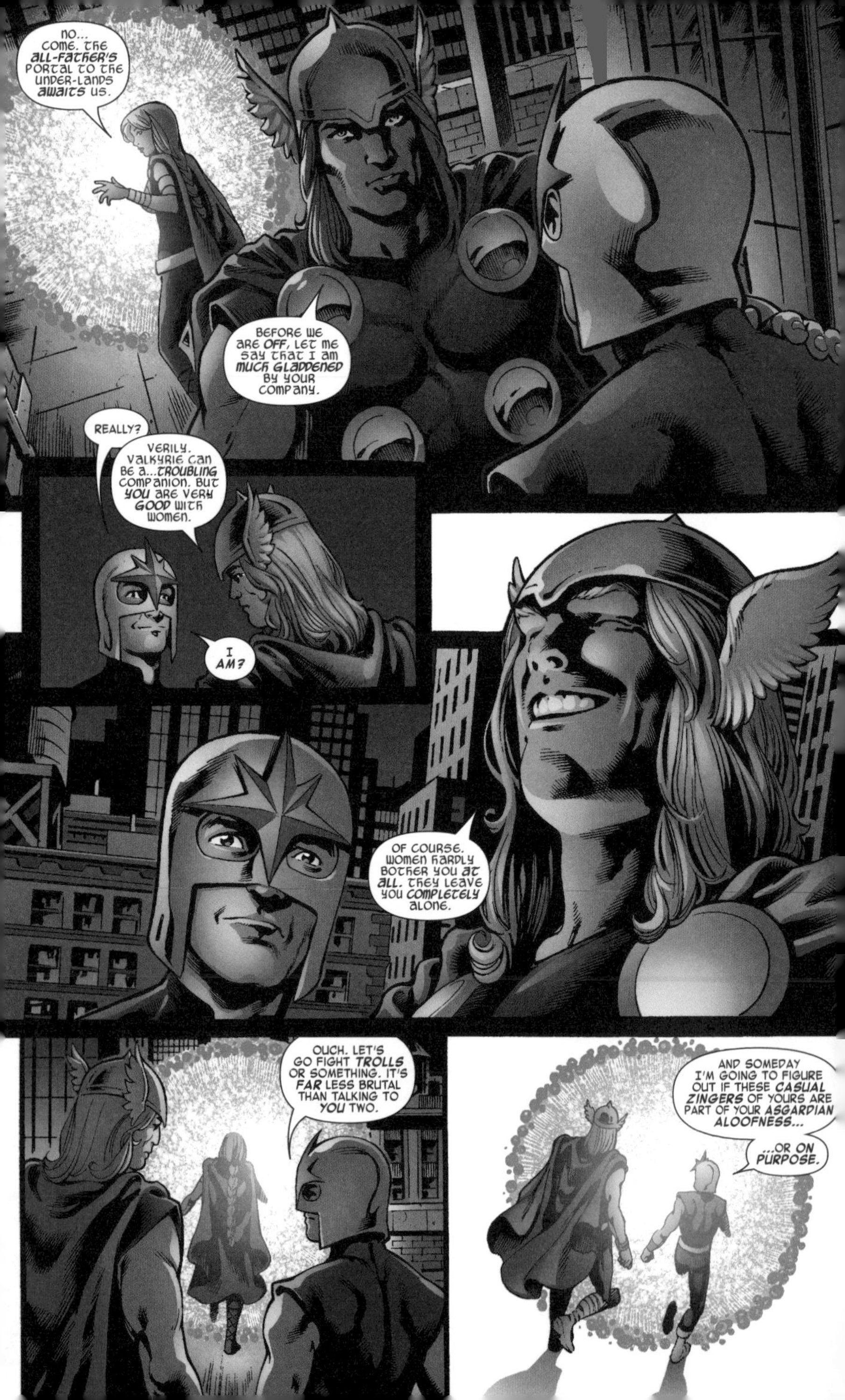
NO... COME. THE ALL-FATHER'S PORTAL TO THE UNDER-LANDS AWAITS US.
BEFORE WE ARE OFF, LET ME SAY THAT I AM MUCH GLADDENED BY YOUR COMPANY.
REALLY?
VERILY. VALKYRIE CAN BE A...TROUBLING COMPANION. BUT YOU ARE VERY GOOD WITH WOMEN.
I AM?
OF COURSE. WOMEN HARDLY BOTHER YOU AT ALL. THEY LEAVE YOU COMPLETELY ALONE.
OUCH. LET'S GO FIGHT TROLLS OR SOMETHING. IT'S FAR LESS BRUTAL THAN TALKING TO YOU TWO.
AND SOMEDAY I'M GOING TO FIGURE OUT IF THESE CASUAL ZINGERS OF YOURS ARE PART OF YOUR ASGARDIAN ALOOFNESS...
...OR ON PURPOSE.

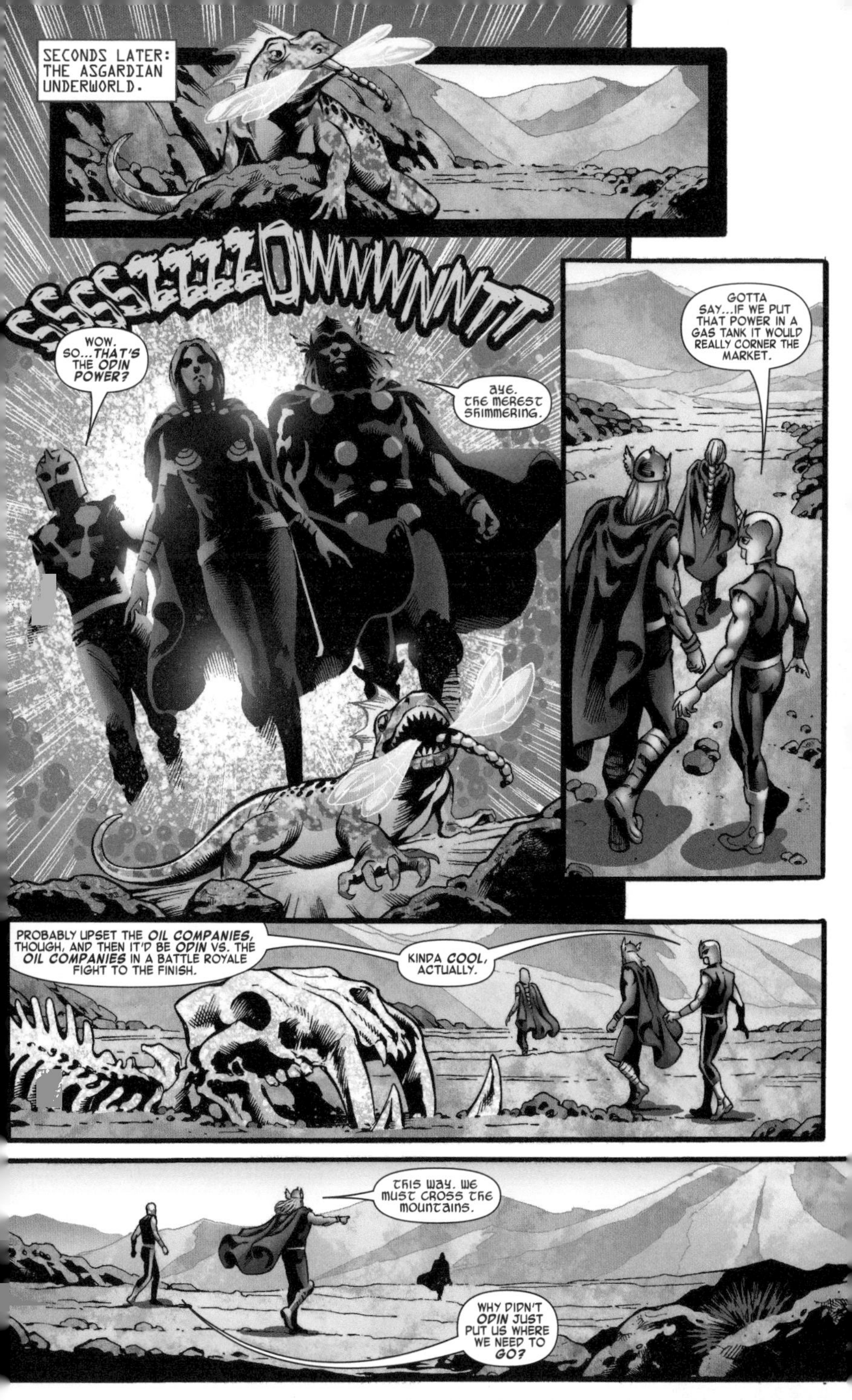
SECONDS LATER: THE ASGARDIAN UNDERWORLD.
SSSSZZZZOWWWNNTT
WOW. SO...THAT'S THE ODIN POWER?
AYE. THE MEREST SHIMMERING.
GOTTA SAY...IF WE PUT THAT POWER IN A GAS TANK IT WOULD REALLY CORNER THE MARKET.
PROBABLY UPSET THE OIL COMPANIES, THOUGH, AND THEN IT'D BE ODIN VS. THE OIL COMPANIES IN A BATTLE ROYALE FIGHT TO THE FINISH.
KINDA COOL, ACTUALLY.
THIS WAY. WE MUST CROSS THE MOUNTAINS.
WHY DIDN'T ODIN JUST PUT US WHERE WE NEED TO GO?

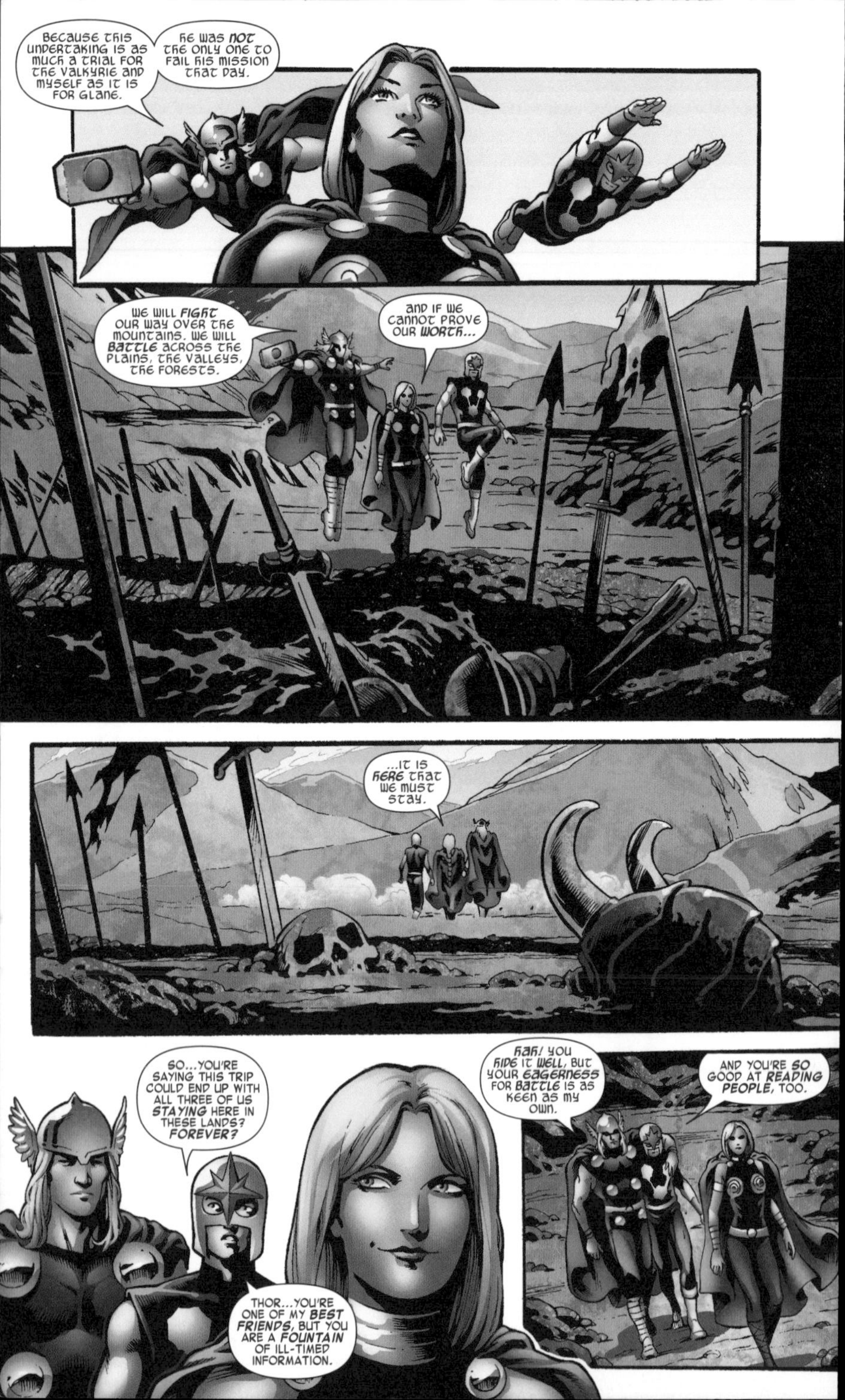
BECAUSE THIS UNDERTAKING IS AS MUCH A TRIAL FOR THE VALKYRIE AND MYSELF AS IT IS FOR GLANE.
HE WAS NOT THE ONLY ONE TO FAIL HIS MISSION THAT DAY.
WE WILL FIGHT OUR WAY OVER THE MOUNTAINS. WE WILL BATTLE ACROSS THE PLAINS, THE VALLEYS, THE FORESTS.
AND IF WE CANNOT PROVE OUR WORTH...
...IT IS HERE THAT WE MUST STAY.
SO...YOU'RE SAYING THIS TRIP COULD END UP WITH ALL THREE OF US STAYING HERE IN THESE LANDS? FOREVER?
THOR...YOU'RE ONE OF MY BEST FRIENDS, BUT YOU ARE A FOUNTAIN OF ILL-TIMED INFORMATION.
HAH! YOU HIDE IT WELL, BUT YOUR EAGERNESS FOR BATTLE IS AS KEEN AS MY OWN.
AND YOU'RE SO GOOD AT READING PEOPLE, TOO.

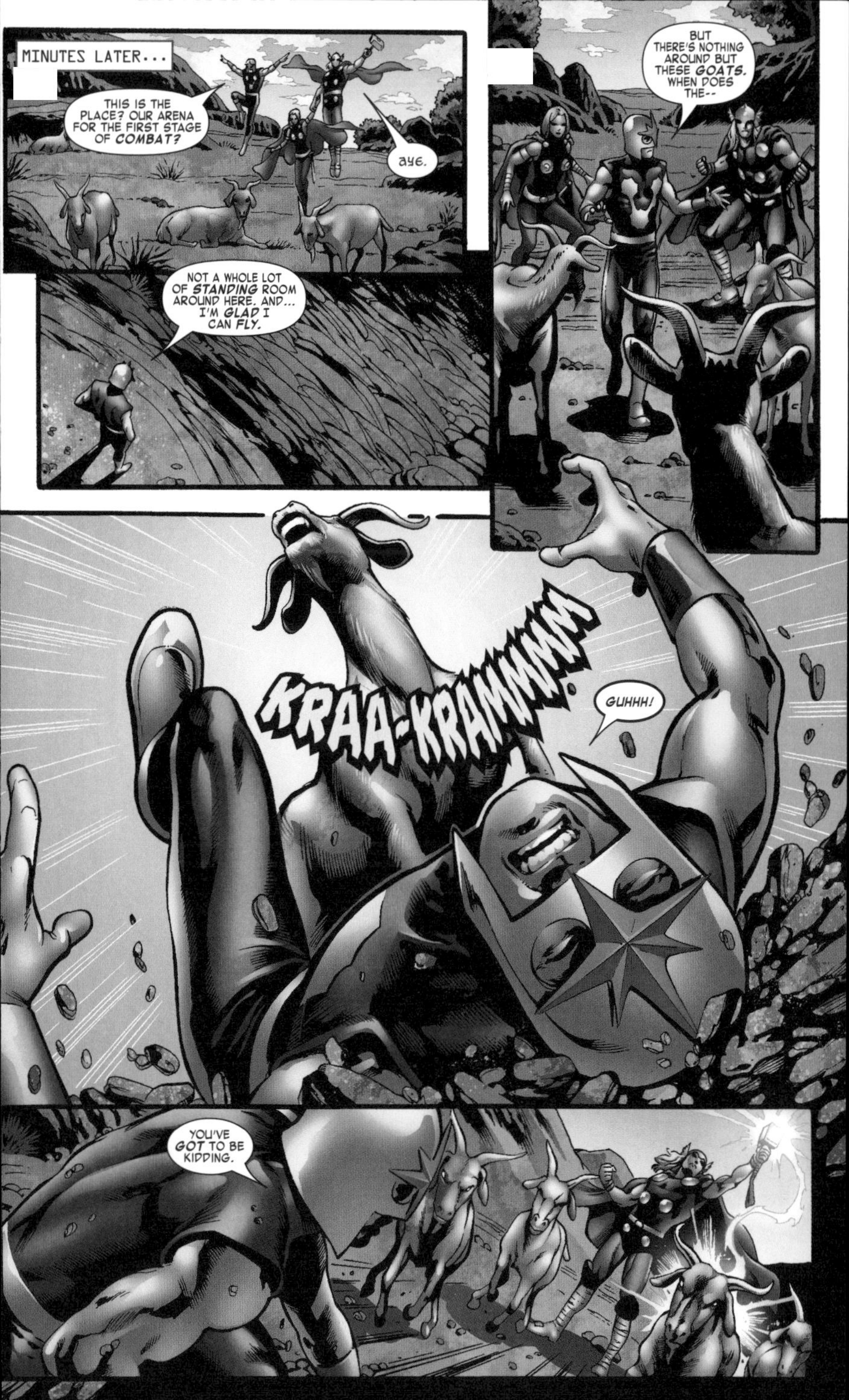
MINUTES LATER...
THIS IS THE PLACE? OUR ARENA FOR THE FIRST STAGE OF COMBAT?
AYE.
BUT THERE'S NOTHING AROUND BUT THESE GOATS. WHEN DOES THE--
NOT A WHOLE LOT OF STANDING ROOM AROUND HERE. AND... I'M GLAD I CAN FLY.
KRAA-KRAMMMM
GUHHH!
YOU'VE GOT TO BE KIDDING.

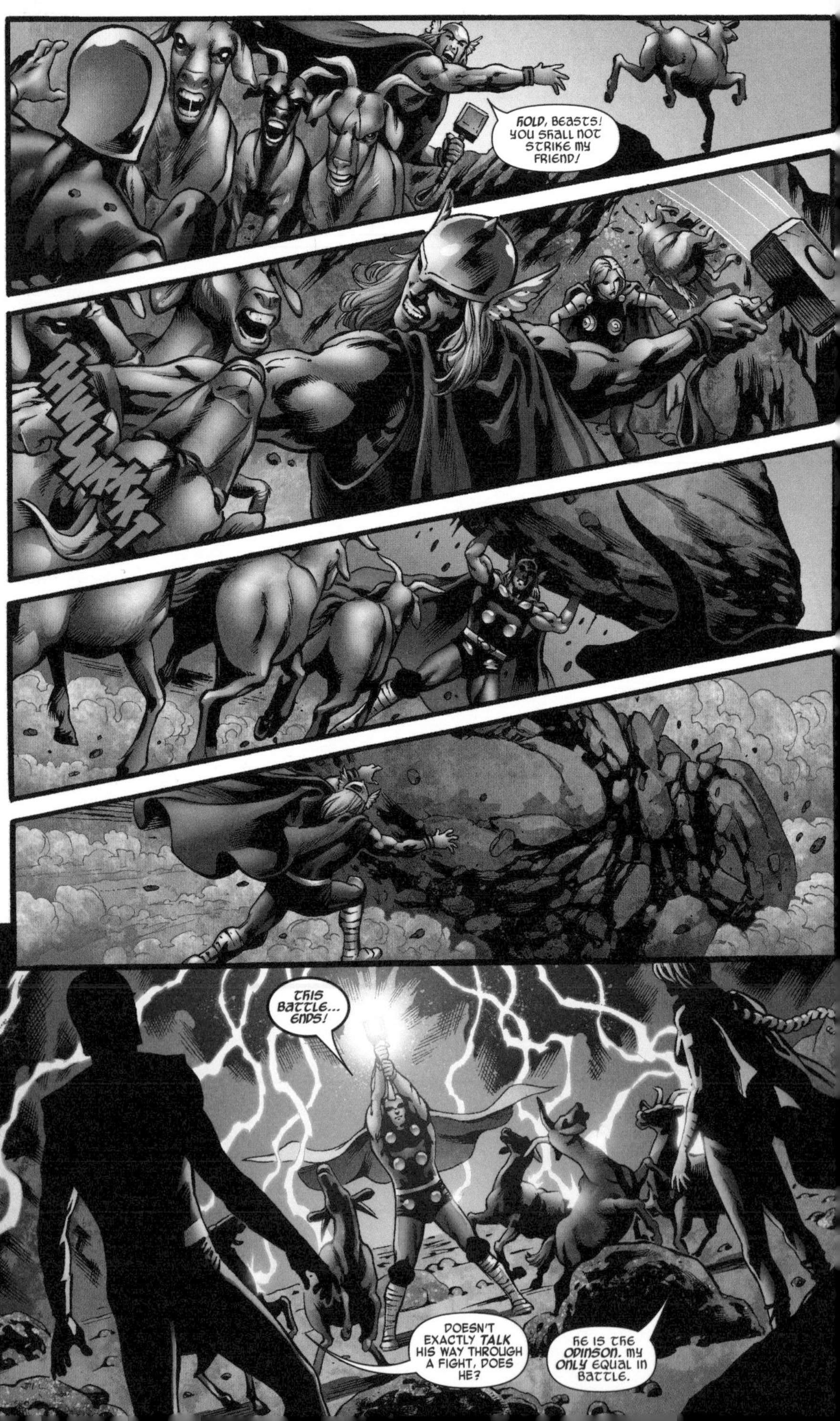
HOLD, BEASTS! YOU SHALL NOT STRIKE MY FRIEND!
THWAKKT!
THIS BATTLE... ENDS!
DOESN'T EXACTLY TALK HIS WAY THROUGH A FIGHT, DOES HE?
HE IS THE ODINSON. MY ONLY EQUAL IN BATTLE.

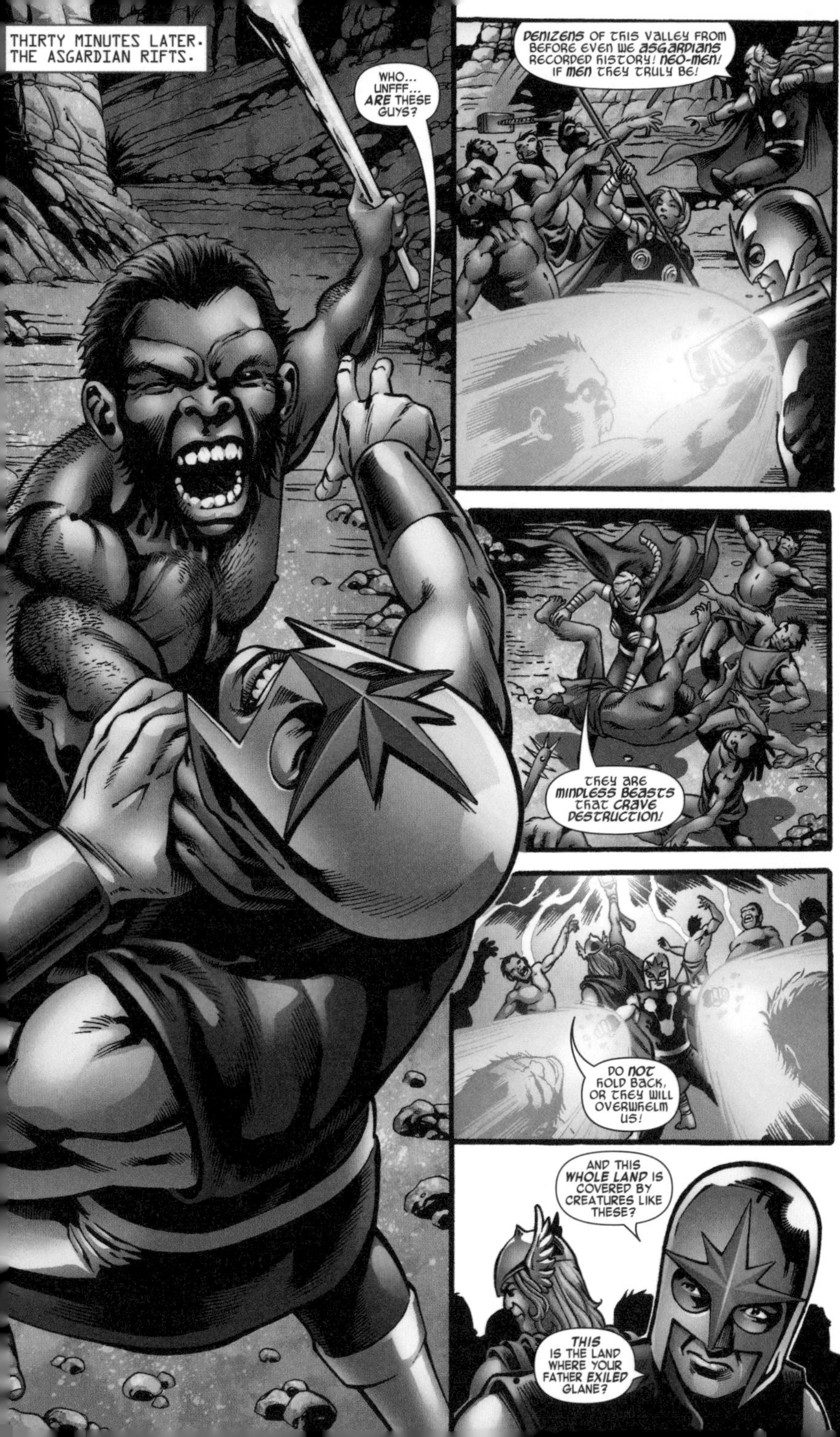
THIRTY MINUTES LATER. THE ASGARDIAN RIFTS.
WHO... UNFFF... ARE THESE GUYS?
DENIZENS OF THIS VALLEY FROM BEFORE EVEN WE ASGARDIANS RECORDED HISTORY! NEO-MEN! IF MEN THEY TRULY BE!
THEY ARE MINDLESS BEASTS THAT CRAVE DESTRUCTION!
DO NOT HOLD BACK, OR THEY WILL OVERWHELM US!
AND THIS WHOLE LAND IS COVERED BY CREATURES LIKE THESE?
THIS IS THE LAND WHERE YOUR FATHER EXILED GLANE?

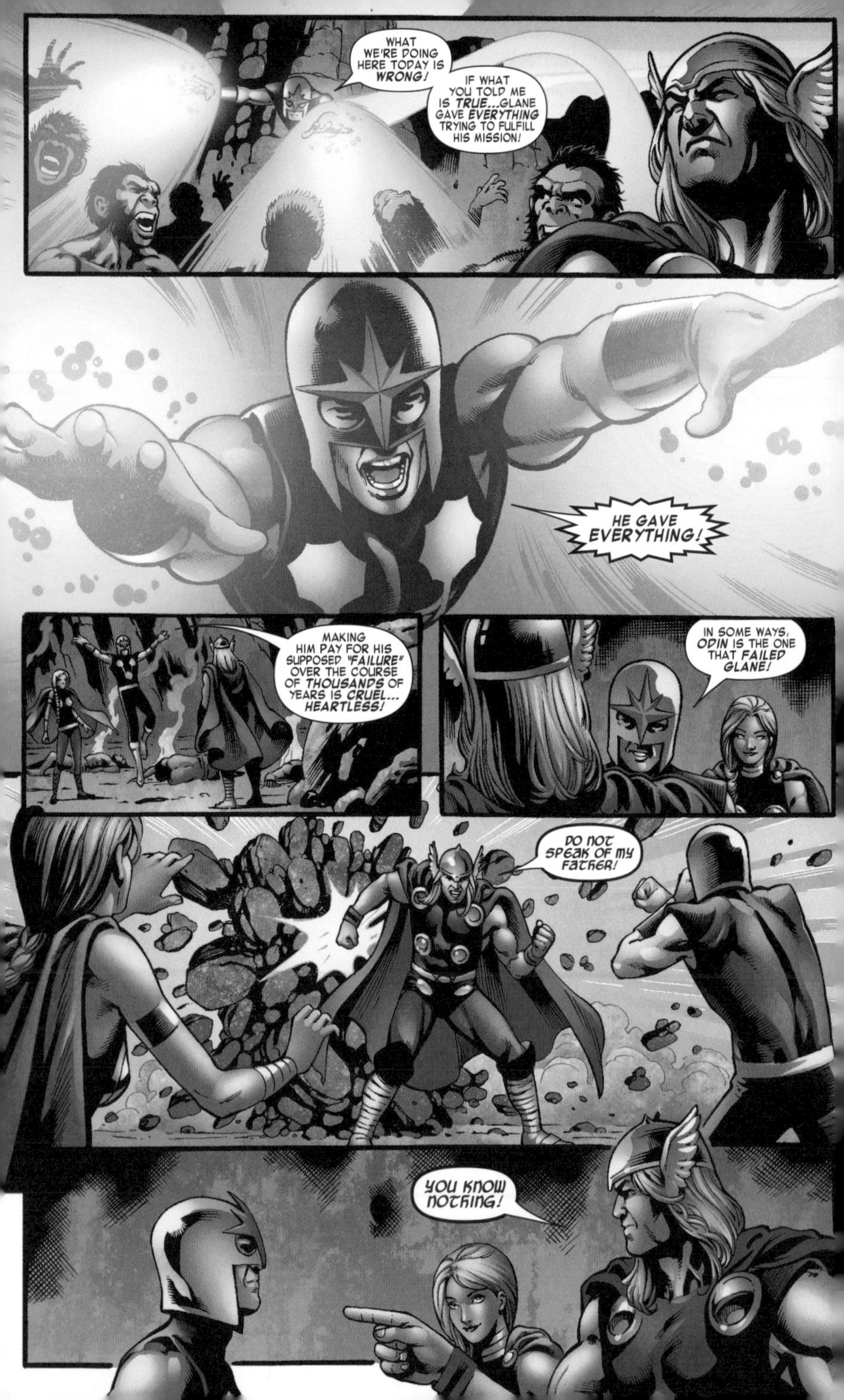
WHAT WE'RE DOING HERE TODAY IS WRONG!
IF WHAT YOU TOLD ME IS TRUE...GLANE GAVE EVERYTHING TRYING TO FULFILL HIS MISSION!
HE GAVE EVERYTHING!
MAKING HIM PAY FOR HIS SUPPOSED "FAILURE" OVER THE COURSE OF THOUSANDS OF YEARS IS CRUEL... HEARTLESS!
IN SOME WAYS, ODIN IS THE ONE THAT FAILED GLANE!
DO NOT SPEAK OF MY FATHER!
YOU KNOW NOTHING!

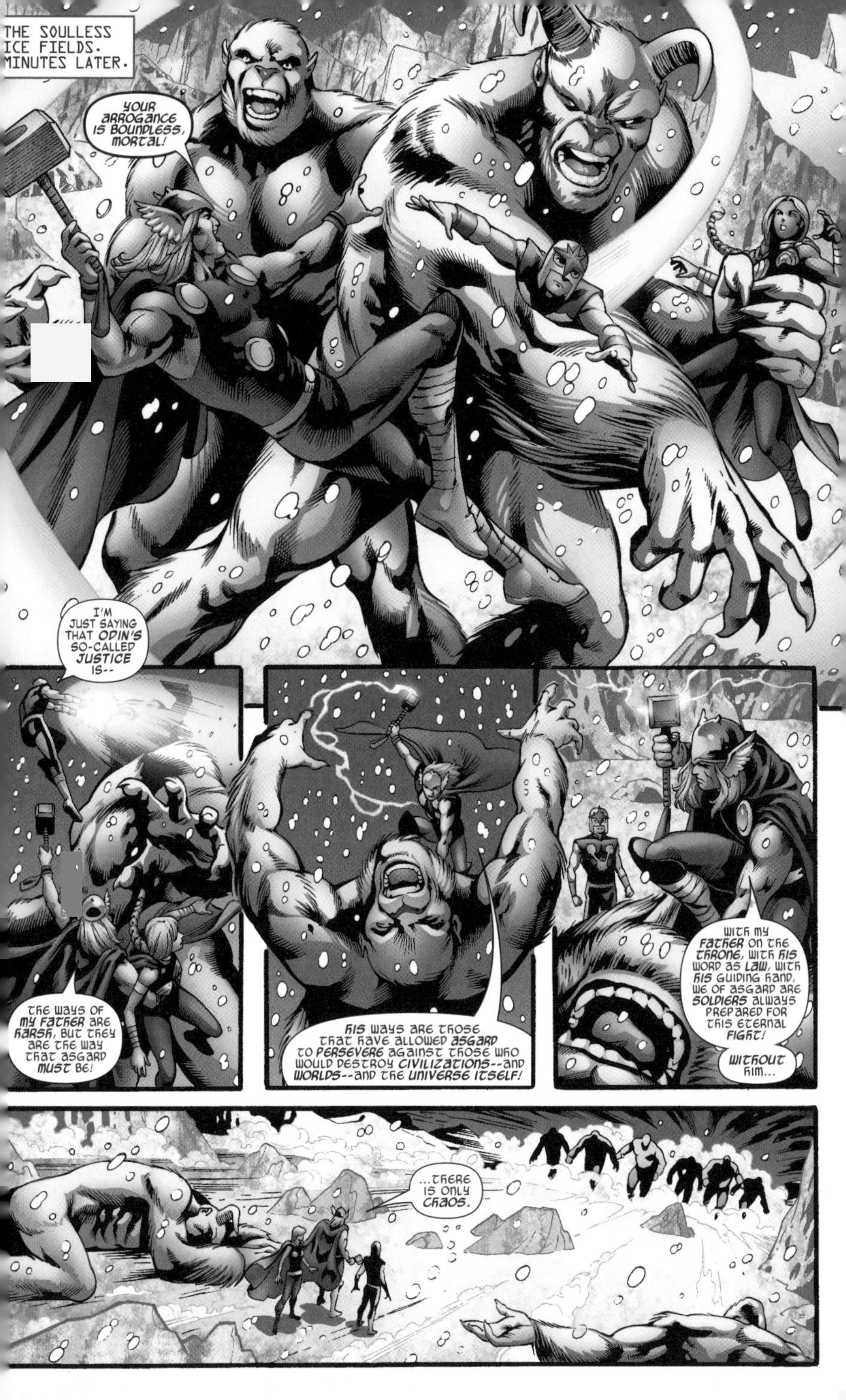
THE SOULLESS ICE FIELDS. MINUTES LATER.
YOUR ARROGANCE IS BOUNDLESS, MORTAL!
I'M JUST SAYING THAT ODIN'S SO-CALLED JUSTICE IS--
THE WAYS OF MY FATHER ARE HARSH, BUT THEY ARE THE WAY THAT ASGARD MUST BE!
HIS WAYS ARE THOSE THAT HAVE ALLOWED ASGARD TO PERSEVERE AGAINST THOSE WHO WOULD DESTROY CIVILIZATIONS--AND WORLDS--AND THE UNIVERSE ITSELF!
WITH MY FATHER ON THE THRONE, WITH HIS WORD AS LAW, WITH HIS GUIDING HAND, WE OF ASGARD ARE SOLDIERS ALWAYS PREPARED FOR THIS ETERNAL FIGHT!
WITHOUT HIM...
...THERE IS ONLY CHAOS.

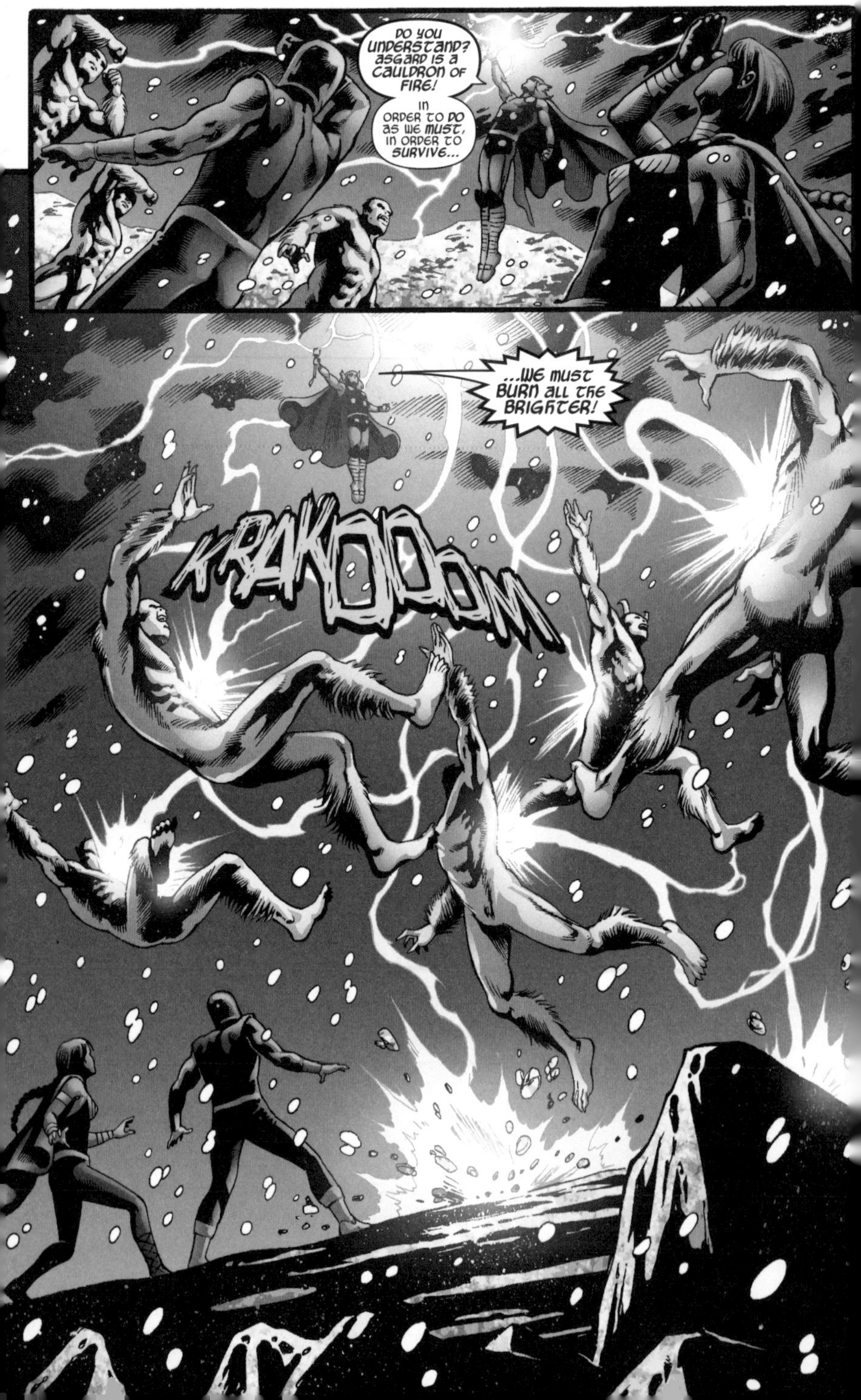
DO YOU UNDERSTAND? ASGARD IS A CAULDRON OF FIRE!
IN ORDER TO DO AS WE MUST, IN ORDER TO SURVIVE...
...WE MUST BURN ALL THE BRIGHTER!
KRAKOOOOM

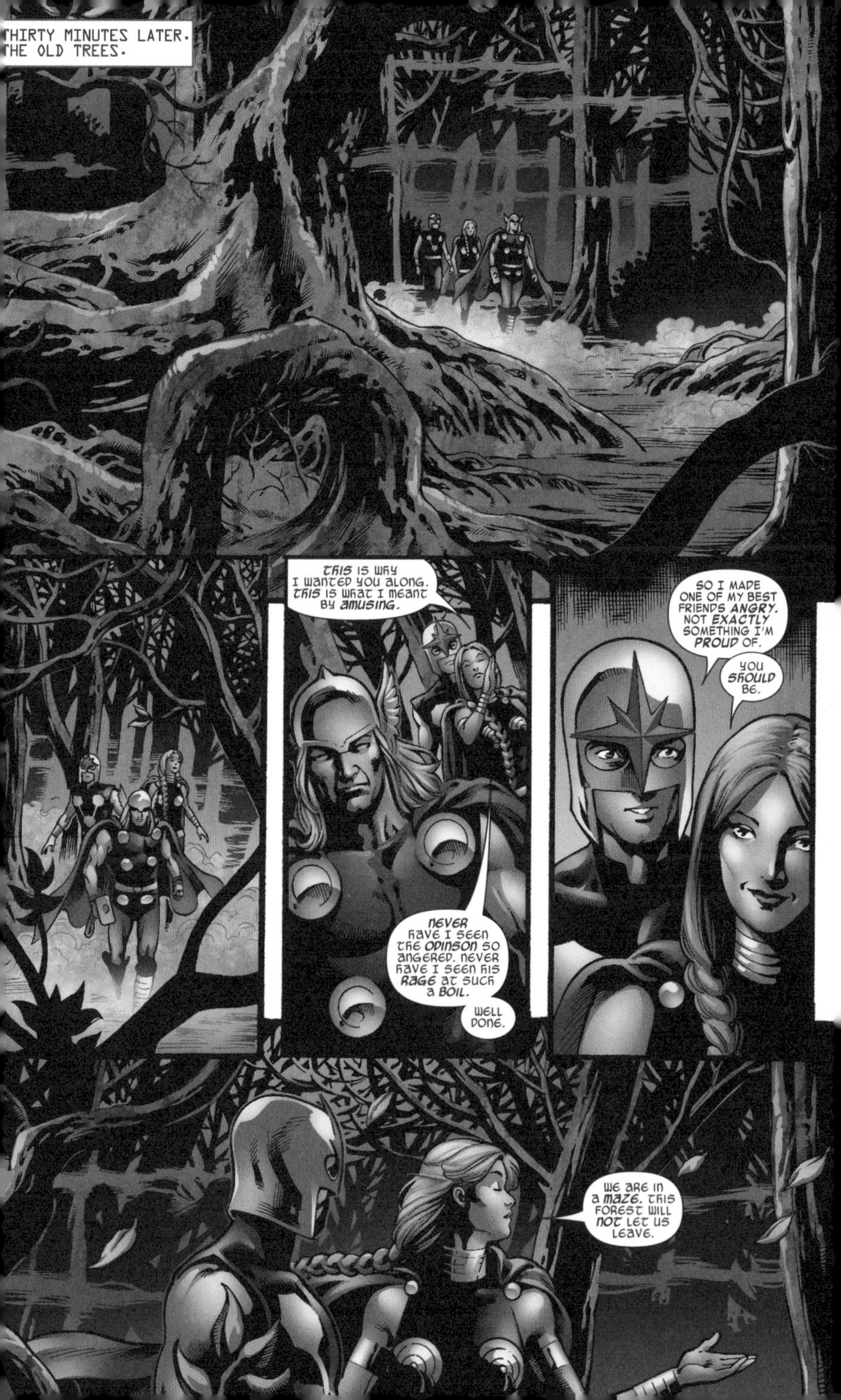
THIRTY MINUTES LATER. THE OLD TREES.
THIS IS WHY I WANTED YOU ALONG. THIS IS WHAT I MEANT BY AMUSING.
NEVER HAVE I SEEN THE ODINSON SO ANGERED. NEVER HAVE I SEEN HIS RAGE AT SUCH A BOIL.
WELL DONE.
SO I MADE ONE OF MY BEST FRIENDS ANGRY. NOT EXACTLY SOMETHING I'M PROUD OF.
YOU SHOULD BE.
WE ARE IN A MAZE. THIS FOREST WILL NOT LET US LEAVE.

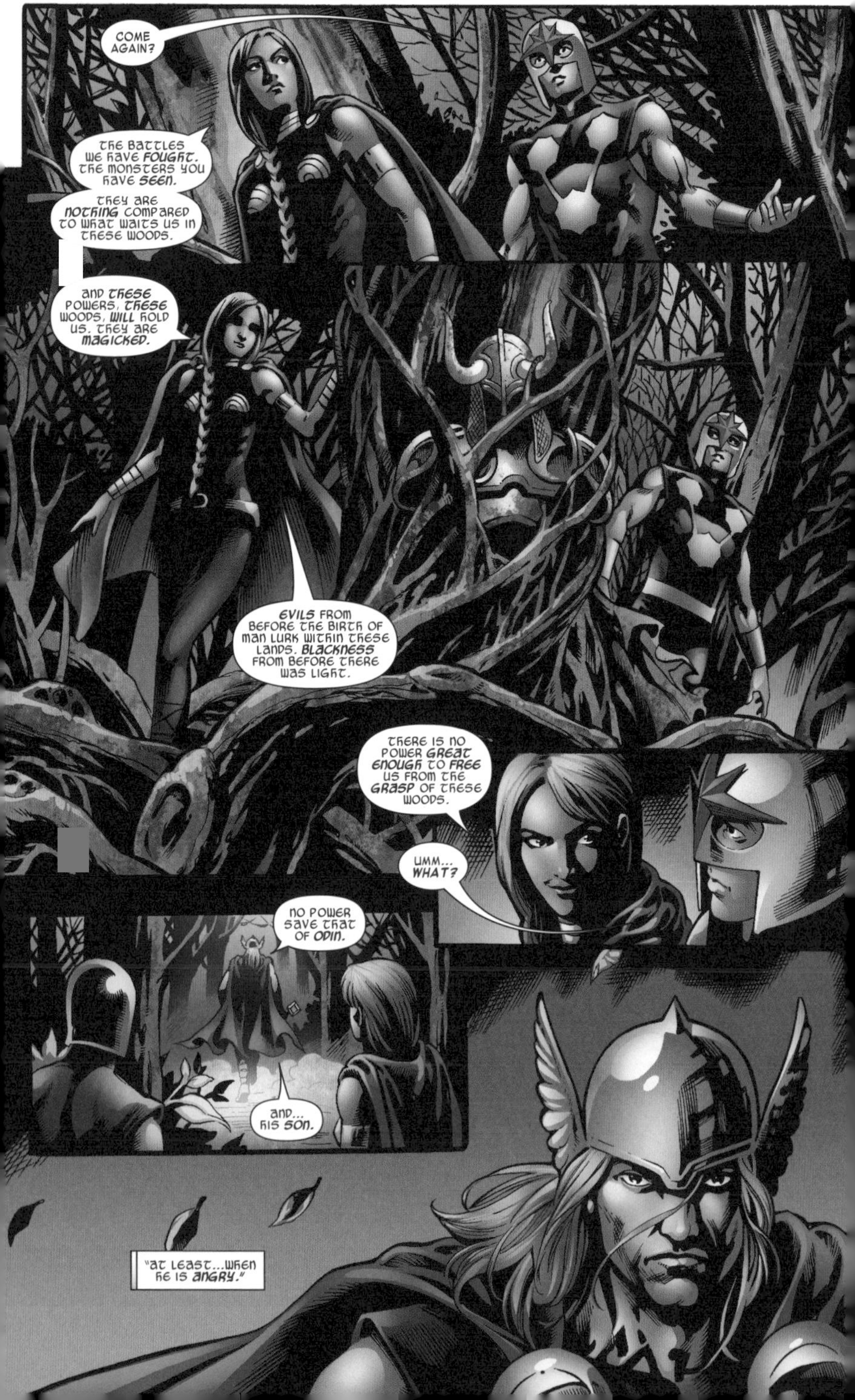
COME AGAIN?
THE BATTLES WE HAVE FOUGHT. THE MONSTERS YOU HAVE SEEN.
THEY ARE NOTHING COMPARED TO WHAT WAITS US IN THESE WOODS.
AND THESE POWERS, THESE WOODS, WILL HOLD US. THEY ARE MAGICKED.
EVILS FROM BEFORE THE BIRTH OF MAN LURK WITHIN THESE LANDS. BLACKNESS FROM BEFORE THERE WAS LIGHT.
THERE IS NO POWER GREAT ENOUGH TO FREE US FROM THE GRASP OF THESE WOODS.
UMM... WHAT?
NO POWER SAVE THAT OF ODIN.
AND... HIS SON.
"AT LEAST...WHEN HE IS ANGRY."

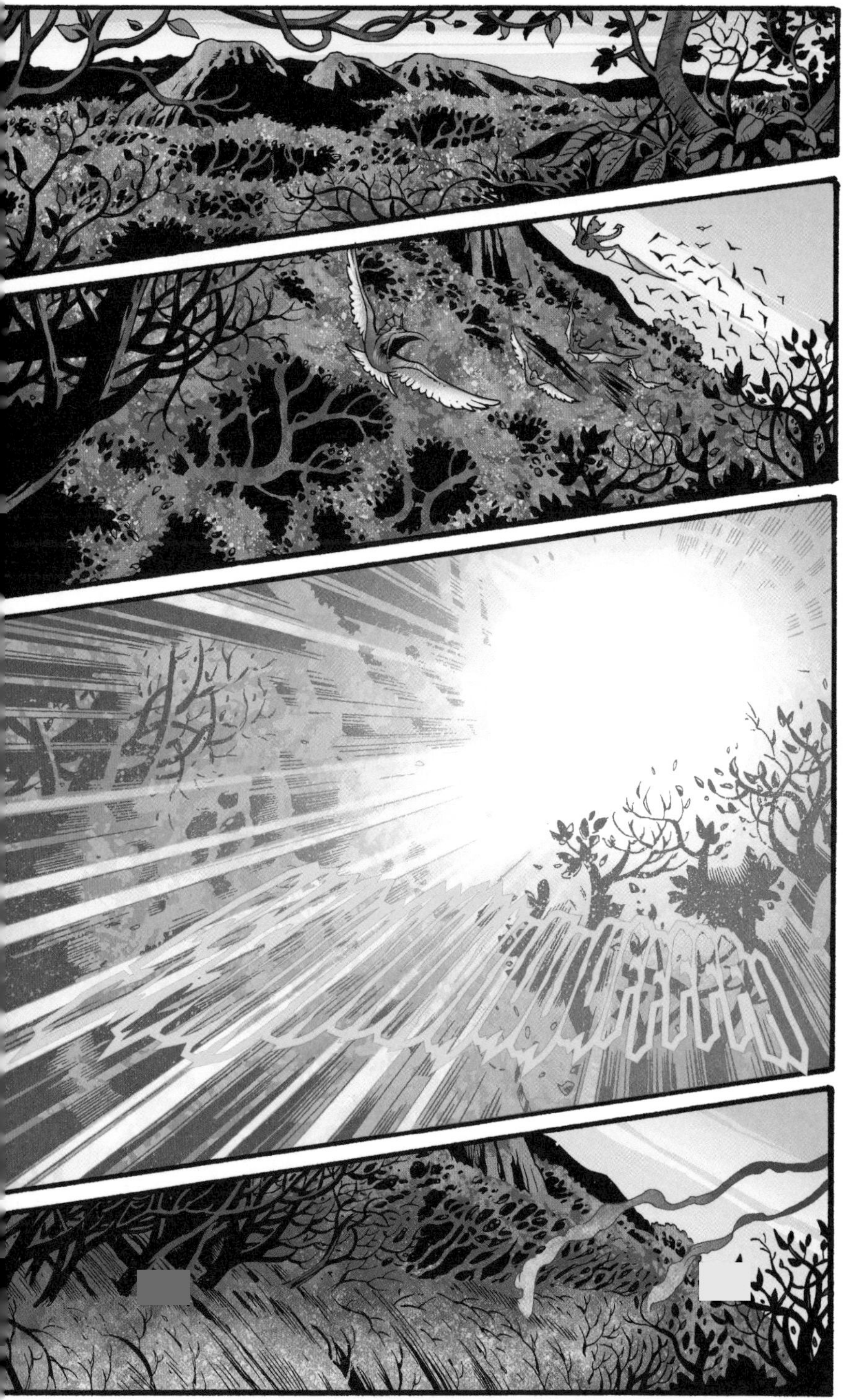

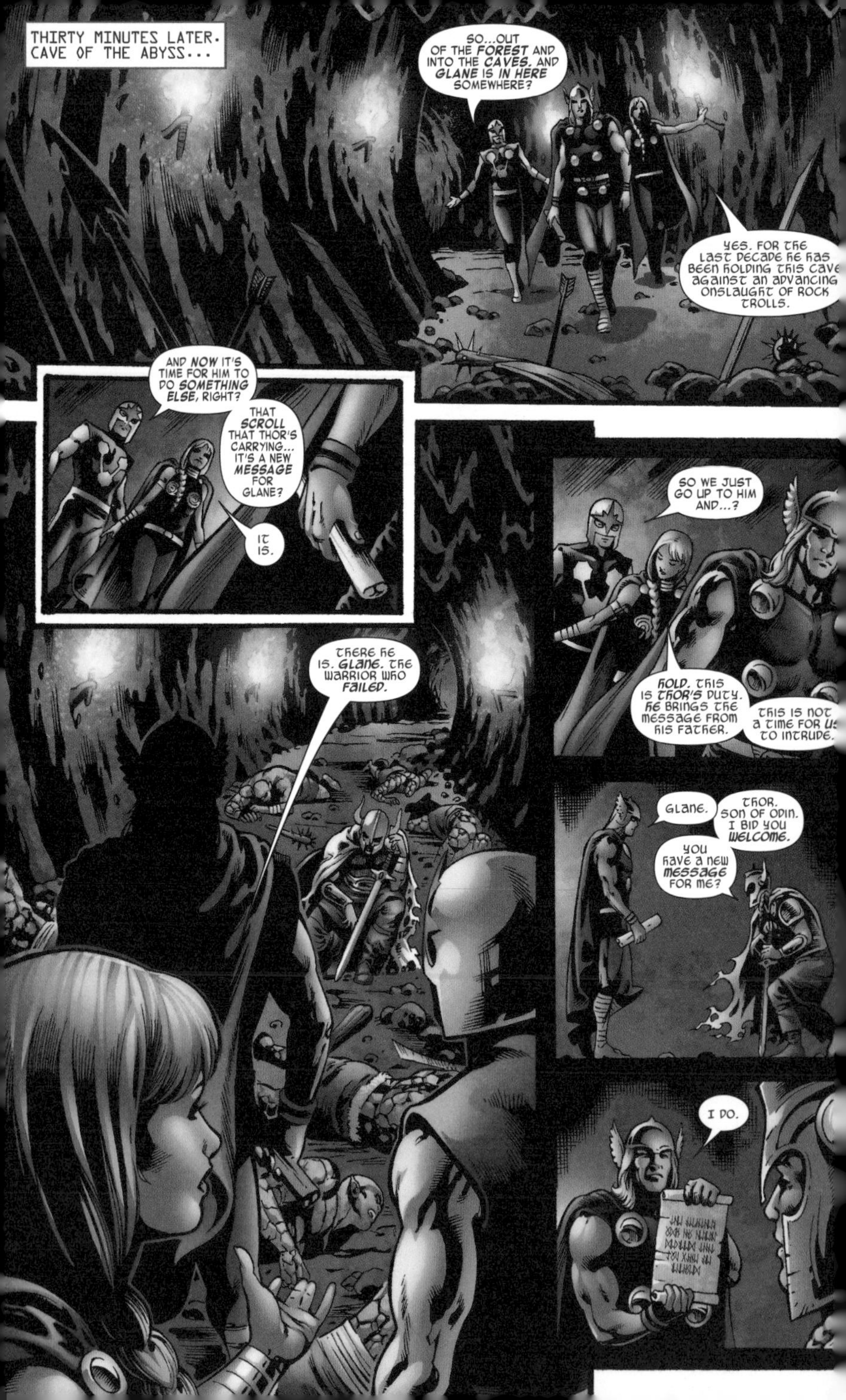

THIRTY MINUTES LATER. CAVE OF THE ABYSS...
SO...OUT OF THE FOREST AND INTO THE CAVES. AND GLANE IS IN HERE SOMEWHERE?
YES. FOR THE LAST DECADE HE HAS BEEN HOLDING THIS CAVE AGAINST AN ADVANCING ONSLAUGHT OF ROCK TROLLS.
AND NOW IT'S TIME FOR HIM TO DO SOMETHING ELSE, RIGHT?
THAT SCROLL THAT THOR'S CARRYING... IT'S A NEW MESSAGE FOR GLANE?
IT IS.
SO WE JUST GO UP TO HIM AND...?
HOLD. THIS IS THOR'S DUTY. HE BRINGS THE MESSAGE FROM HIS FATHER.
THIS IS NOT A TIME FOR US TO INTRUDE.
THERE HE IS. GLANE. THE WARRIOR WHO FAILED.
GLANE.
THOR. SON OF ODIN. I BID YOU WELCOME.
YOU HAVE A NEW MESSAGE FOR ME?
I DO.

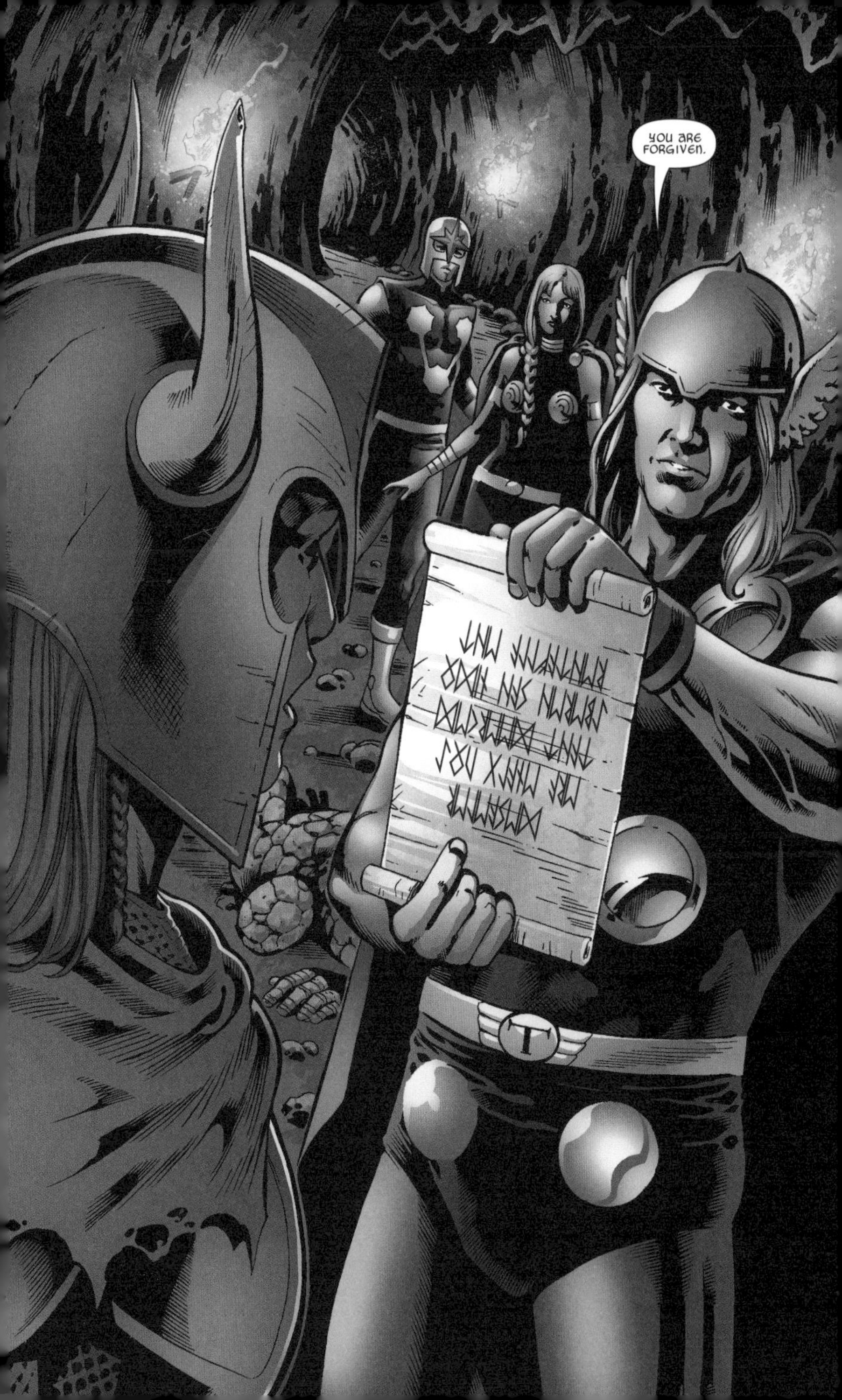
YOU ARE FORGIVEN.

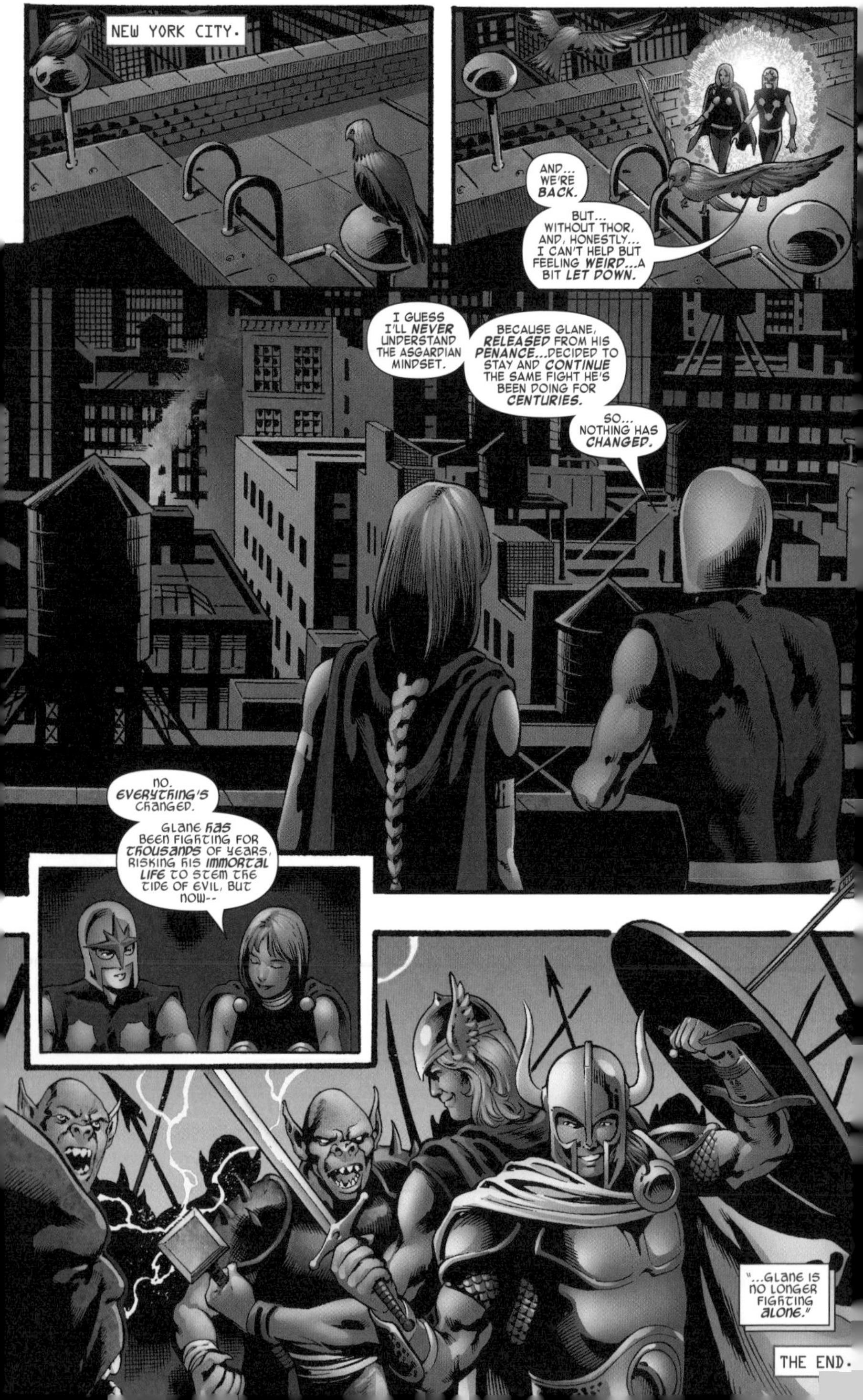
NEW YORK CITY.
AND... WE'RE BACK.
BUT... WITHOUT THOR. AND, HONESTLY... I CAN'T HELP BUT FEELING WEIRD...A BIT LET DOWN.
I GUESS I'LL NEVER UNDERSTAND THE ASGARDIAN MINDSET.
BECAUSE GLANE, RELEASED FROM HIS PENANCE...DECIDED TO STAY AND CONTINUE THE SAME FIGHT HE'S BEEN DOING FOR CENTURIES.
SO... NOTHING HAS CHANGED.
NO. EVERYTHING'S CHANGED.
GLANE HAS BEEN FIGHTING FOR THOUSANDS OF YEARS, RISKING HIS IMMORTAL LIFE TO STEM THE TIDE OF EVIL, BUT NOW--
"...GLANE IS NO LONGER FIGHTING ALONE."
THE END.

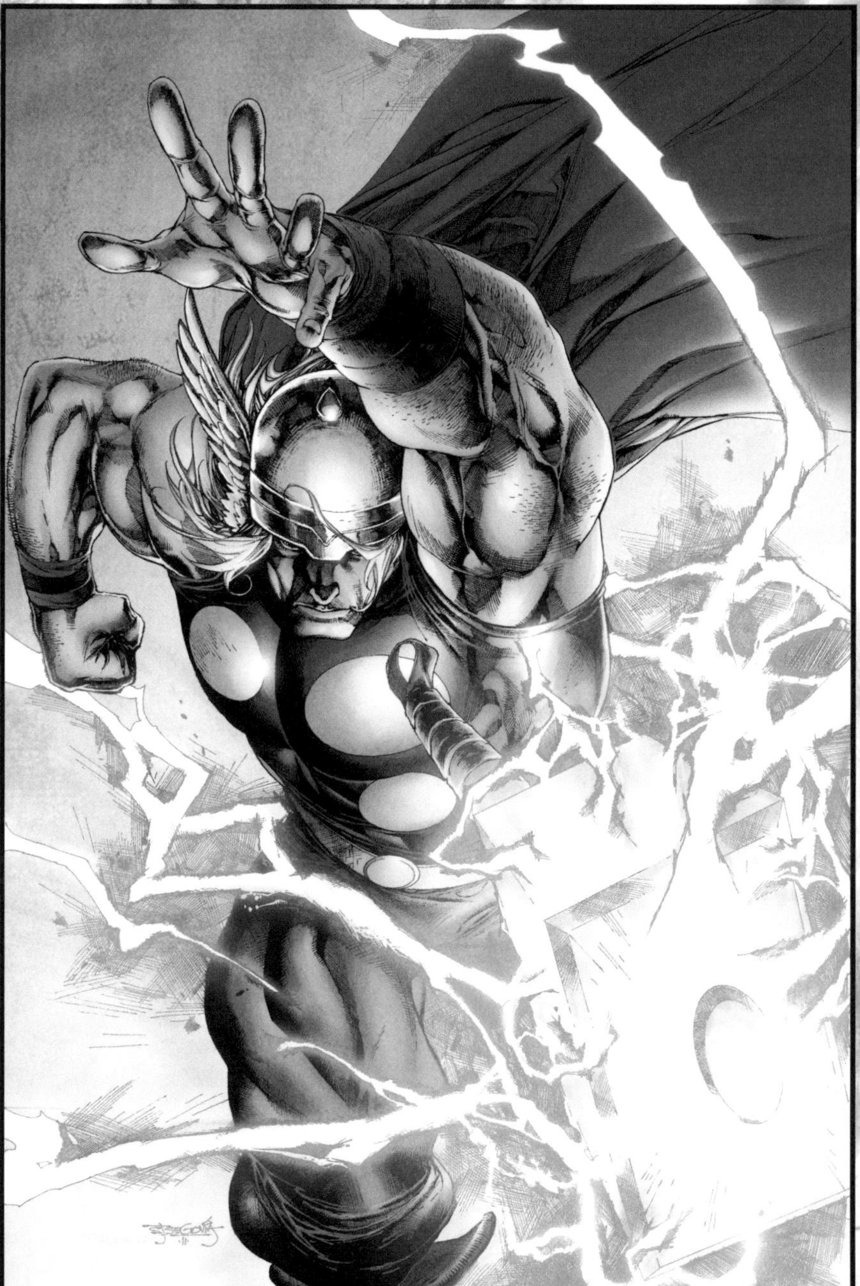

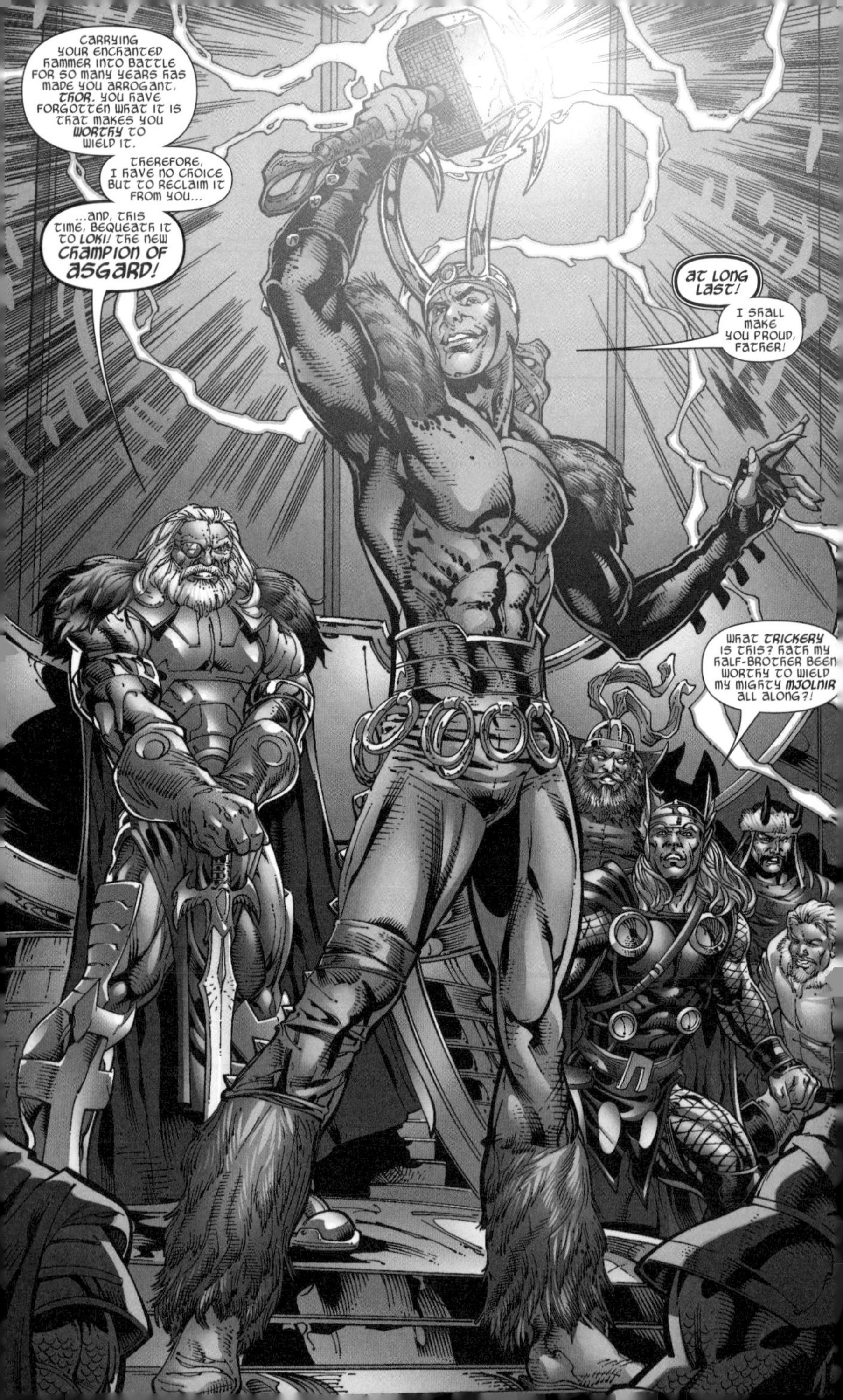
CARRYING YOUR ENCHANTED HAMMER INTO BATTLE FOR SO MANY YEARS HAS MADE YOU ARROGANT, THOR. YOU HAVE FORGOTTEN WHAT IT IS THAT MAKES YOU WORTHY TO WIELD IT.
THEREFORE, I HAVE NO CHOICE BUT TO RECLAIM IT FROM YOU...
...AND, THIS TIME, BEQUEATH IT TO LOKI! THE NEW CHAMPION OF ASGARD!
AT LONG LAST!
I SHALL MAKE YOU PROUD, FATHER!
WHAT TRICKERY IS THIS? HATH MY HALF-BROTHER BEEN WORTHY TO WIELD MY MIGHTY MJOLNIR ALL ALONG?!

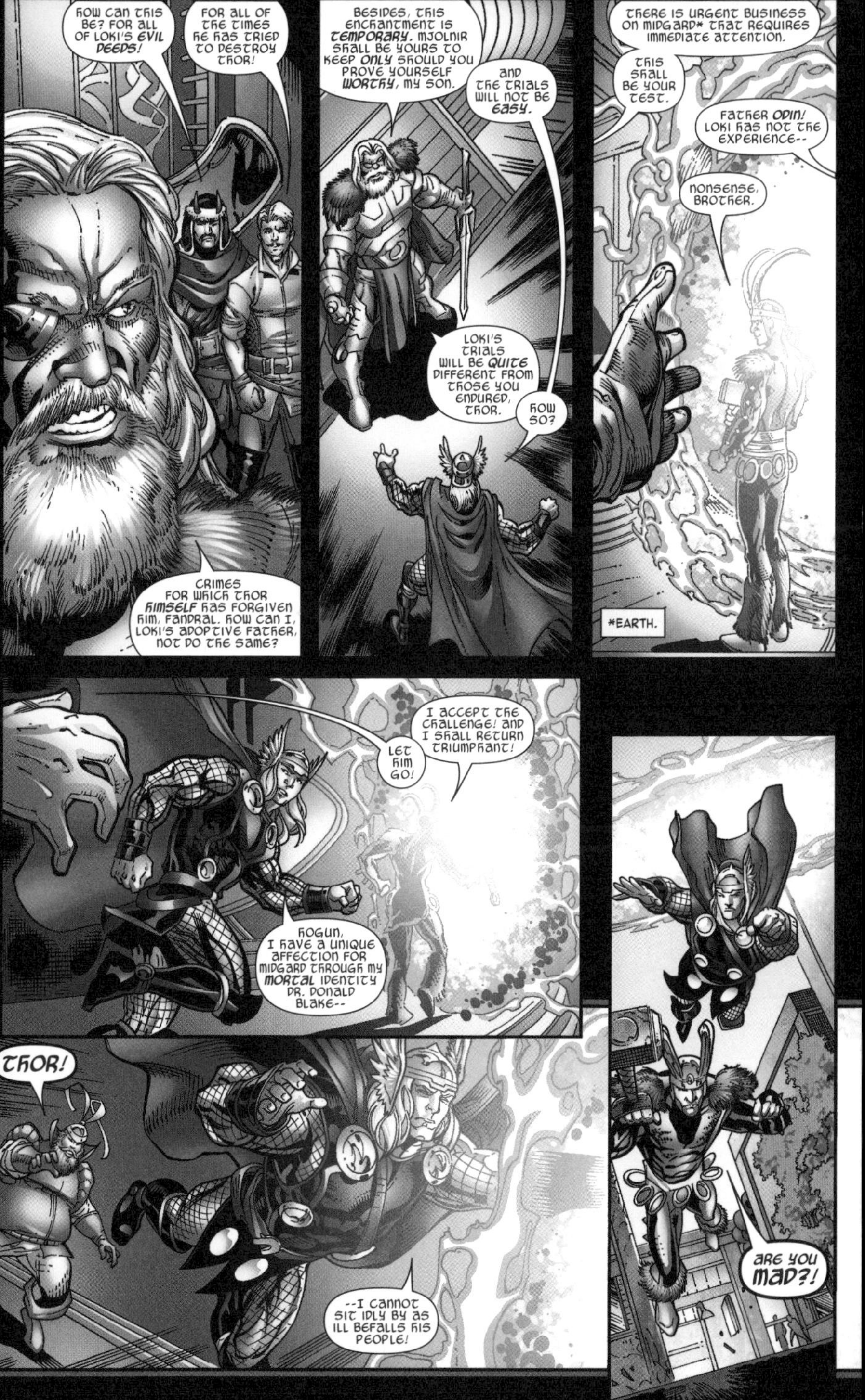
HOW CAN THIS BE? FOR ALL OF LOKI'S EVIL DEEDS!
FOR ALL OF THE TIMES HE HAS TRIED TO DESTROY THOR!
CRIMES FOR WHICH THOR HIMSELF HAS FORGIVEN HIM, FANDRAL. HOW CAN I, LOKI'S ADOPTIVE FATHER, NOT DO THE SAME?
BESIDES, THIS ENCHANTMENT IS TEMPORARY. MJOLNIR SHALL BE YOURS TO KEEP ONLY SHOULD YOU PROVE YOURSELF WORTHY, MY SON.
AND THE TRIALS WILL NOT BE EASY.
LOKI'S TRIALS WILL BE QUITE DIFFERENT FROM THOSE YOU ENDURED, THOR.
HOW SO?
THERE IS URGENT BUSINESS ON MIDGARD* THAT REQUIRES IMMEDIATE ATTENTION.
THIS SHALL BE YOUR TEST.
FATHER ODIN! LOKI HAS NOT THE EXPERIENCE--
NONSENSE, BROTHER.
*EARTH.
LET HIM GO!
I ACCEPT THE CHALLENGE! AND I SHALL RETURN TRIUMPHANT!
HOGUN, I HAVE A UNIQUE AFFECTION FOR MIDGARD THROUGH MY MORTAL IDENTITY DR. DONALD BLAKE--
THOR!
--I CANNOT SIT IDLY BY AS ILL BEFALLS HIS PEOPLE!
ARE YOU MAD?!

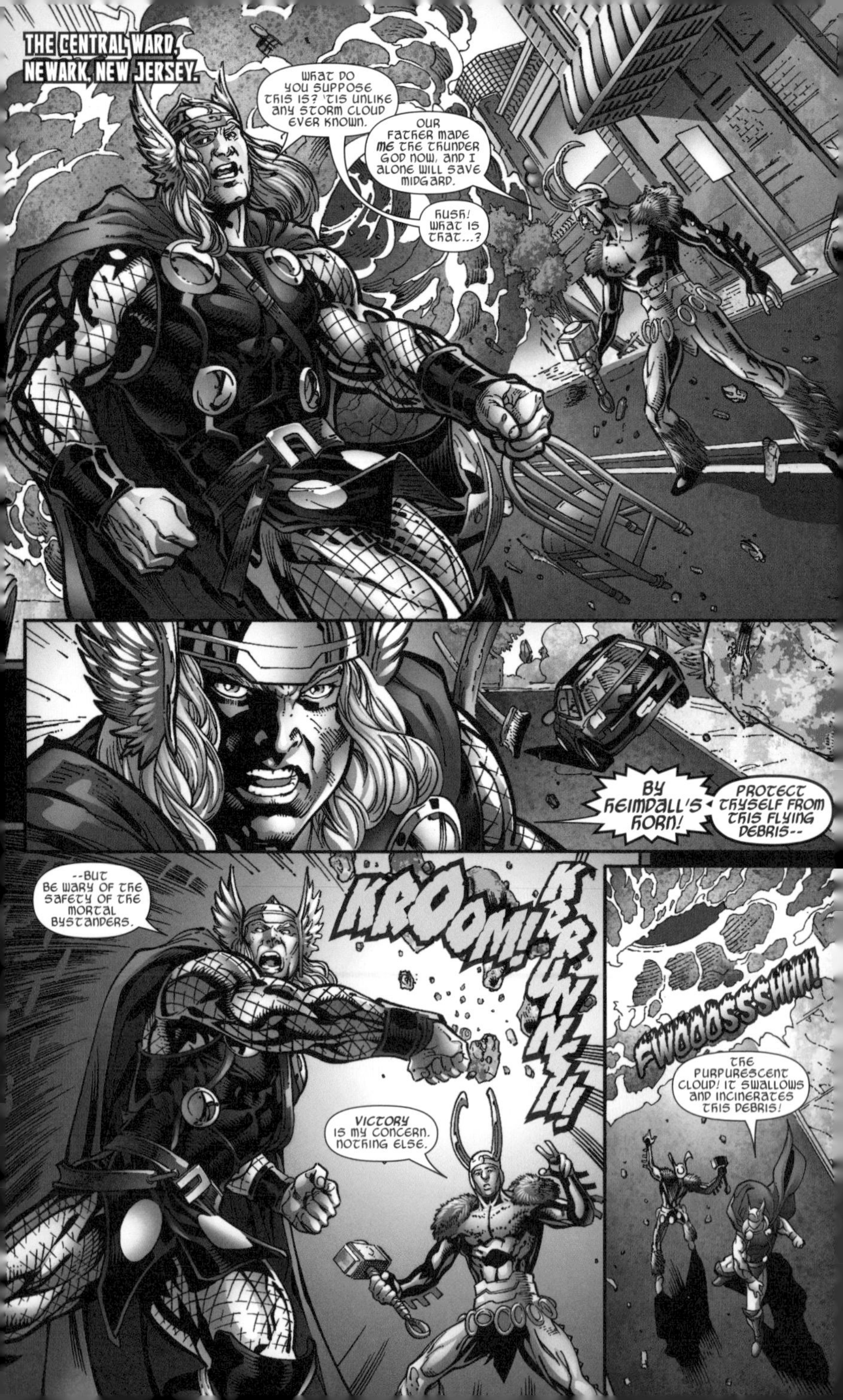
THE CENTRAL WARD, NEWARK, NEW JERSEY.
WHAT DO YOU SUPPOSE THIS IS? 'TIS UNLIKE ANY STORM CLOUD EVER KNOWN.
OUR FATHER MADE ME THE THUNDER GOD NOW, AND I ALONE WILL SAVE MIDGARD.
HUSH! WHAT IS THAT...?
BY HEIMDALL'S HORN!
PROTECT THYSELF FROM THIS FLYING DEBRIS--
--BUT BE WARY OF THE SAFETY OF THE MORTAL BYSTANDERS.
KROOM!
KRUNNCH!
VICTORY IS MY CONCERN. NOTHING ELSE.
FWOOOSSSHHH!
THE PURPURESCENT CLOUD! IT SWALLOWS AND INCINERATES THIS DEBRIS!

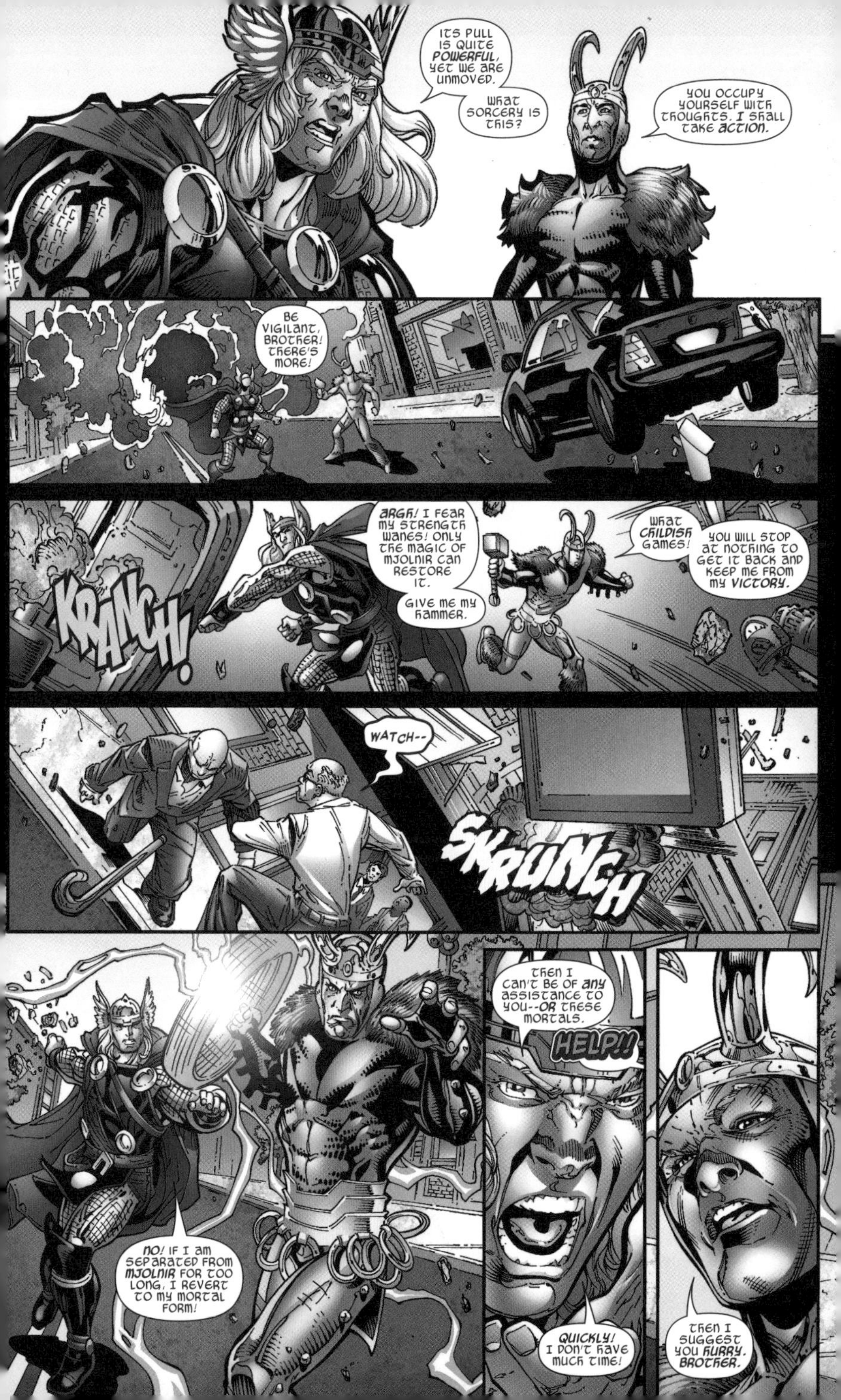
ITS PULL IS QUITE POWERFUL, YET WE ARE UNMOVED.
WHAT SORCERY IS THIS?
YOU OCCUPY YOURSELF WITH THOUGHTS. I SHALL TAKE ACTION.
BE VIGILANT, BROTHER! THERE'S MORE!
KRANCH!
ARGH! I FEAR MY STRENGTH WANES! ONLY THE MAGIC OF MJOLNIR CAN RESTORE IT.
GIVE ME MY HAMMER.
WHAT CHILDISH GAMES!
YOU WILL STOP AT NOTHING TO GET IT BACK AND KEEP ME FROM MY VICTORY.
WATCH--
SKRUNCH
NO! IF I AM SEPARATED FROM MJOLNIR FOR TOO LONG, I REVERT TO MY MORTAL FORM!
THEN I CAN'T BE OF ANY ASSISTANCE TO YOU--OR THESE MORTALS.
HELP!!
QUICKLY! I DON'T HAVE MUCH TIME!
THEN I SUGGEST YOU HURRY, BROTHER.

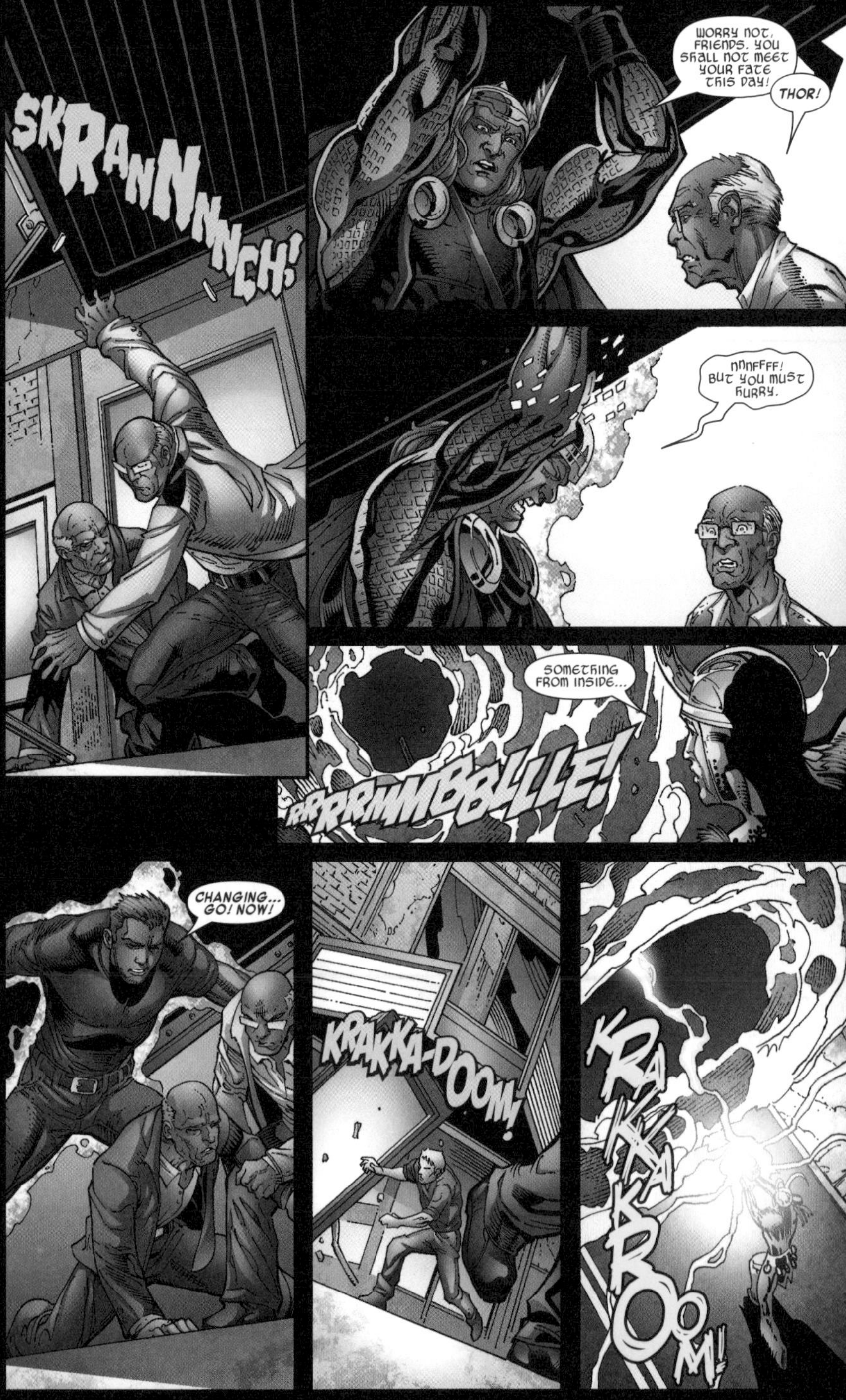
SKRANNNNNCH!
WORRY NOT, FRIENDS. YOU SHALL NOT MEET YOUR FATE THIS DAY!
THOR!
NNNFFFF! BUT YOU MUST HURRY.
SOMETHING FROM INSIDE...
RRRRMMBBLLLE!
CHANGING... GO! NOW!
KRAKKA-DOOM!
KRAKKAKABROOM!

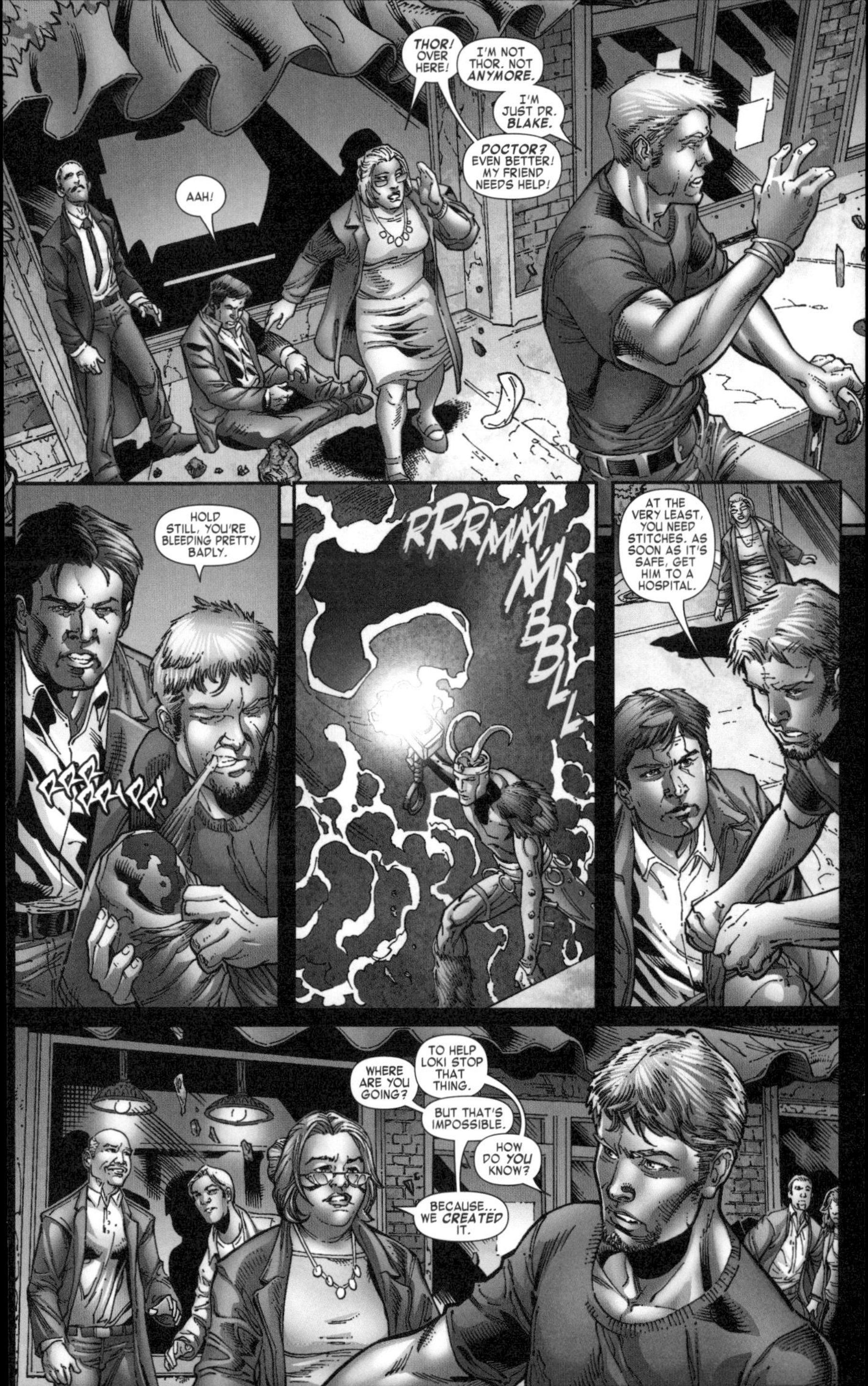
THOR! OVER HERE!
I'M NOT THOR. NOT ANYMORE.
I'M JUST DR. BLAKE.
DOCTOR? EVEN BETTER! MY FRIEND NEEDS HELP!
AAH!
HOLD STILL, YOU'RE BLEEDING PRETTY BADLY.
RRRRIPP!
RRRMMMMBBLLL
AT THE VERY LEAST, YOU NEED STITCHES. AS SOON AS IT'S SAFE, GET HIM TO A HOSPITAL.
WHERE ARE YOU GOING?
TO HELP LOKI STOP THAT THING.
BUT THAT'S IMPOSSIBLE.
HOW DO YOU KNOW?
BECAUSE... WE CREATED IT.

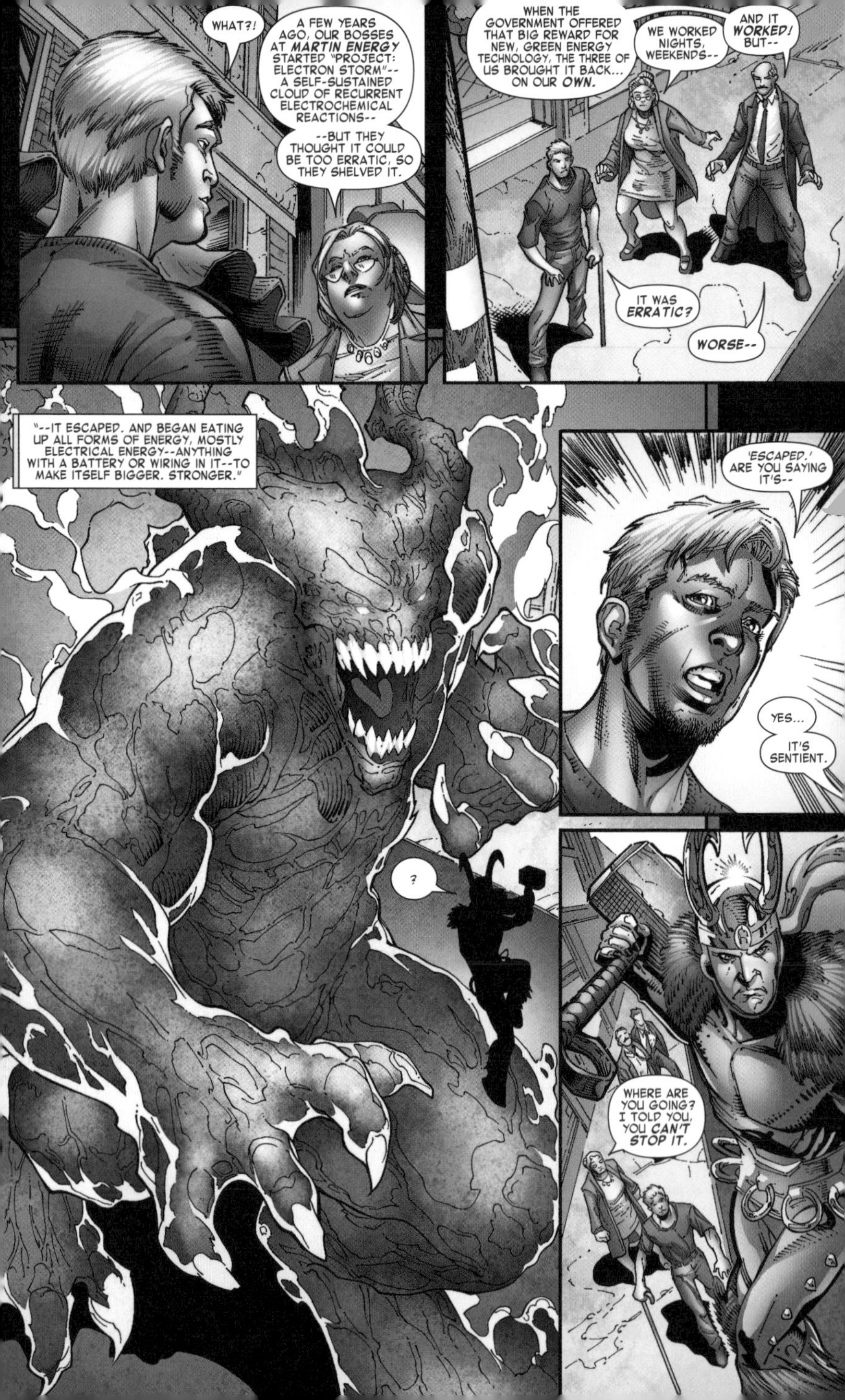
WHAT?!
A FEW YEARS AGO, OUR BOSSES AT MARTIN ENERGY STARTED "PROJECT: ELECTRON STORM"--A SELF-SUSTAINED CLOUD OF RECURRENT ELECTROCHEMICAL REACTIONS--
--BUT THEY THOUGHT IT COULD BE TOO ERRATIC, SO THEY SHELVED IT.
WHEN THE GOVERNMENT OFFERED THAT BIG REWARD FOR NEW, GREEN ENERGY TECHNOLOGY, THE THREE OF US BROUGHT IT BACK... ON OUR OWN.
WE WORKED NIGHTS, WEEKENDS--
AND IT WORKED! BUT--
IT WAS ERRATIC?
WORSE--
"--IT ESCAPED. AND BEGAN EATING UP ALL FORMS OF ENERGY, MOSTLY ELECTRICAL ENERGY--ANYTHING WITH A BATTERY OR WIRING IN IT--TO MAKE ITSELF BIGGER. STRONGER."
'ESCAPED.' ARE YOU SAYING IT'S--
YES...
IT'S SENTIENT.
?
WHERE ARE YOU GOING? I TOLD YOU, YOU CAN'T STOP IT.

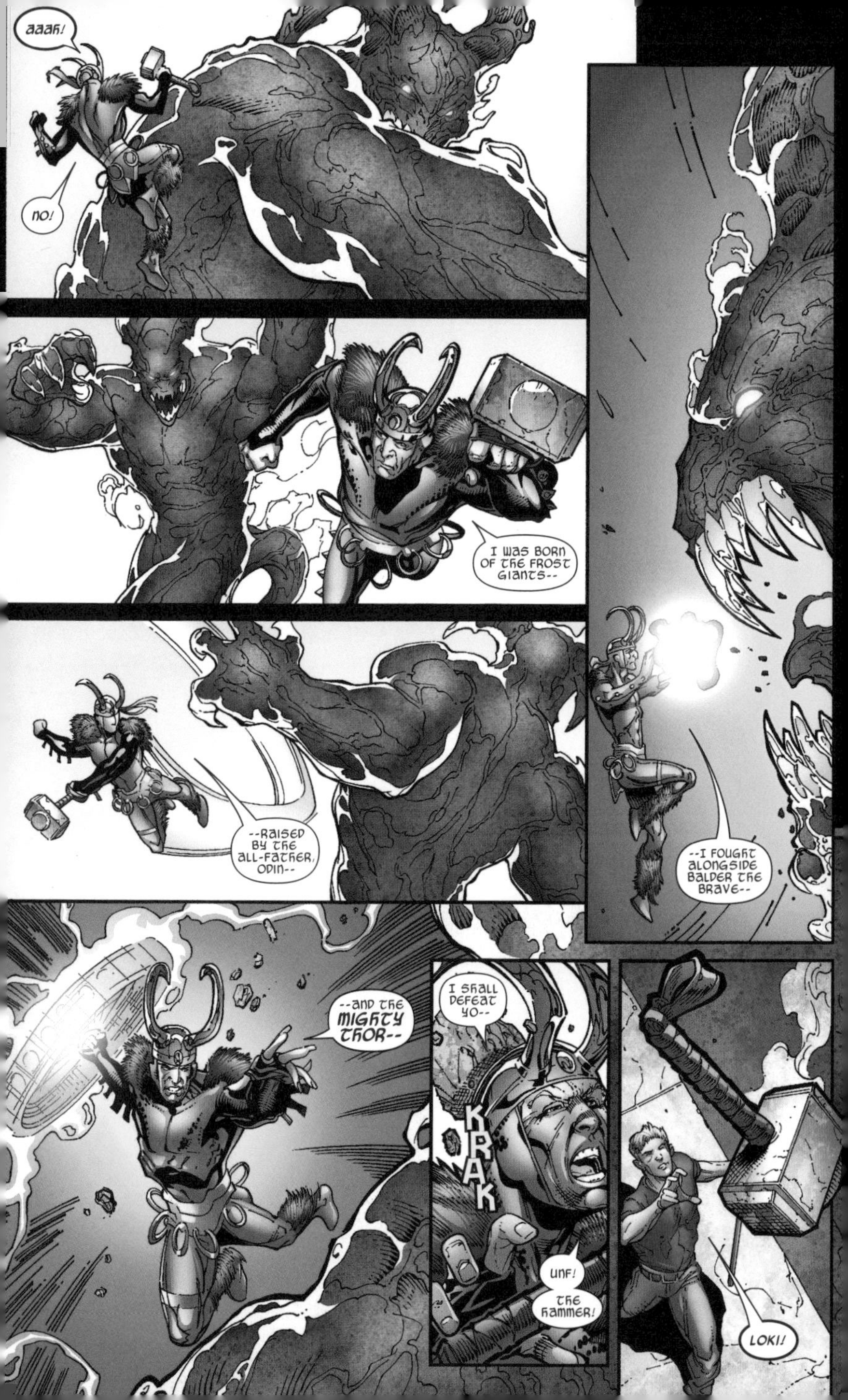
AAAH!
NO!
I WAS BORN OF THE FROST GIANTS--
--RAISED BY THE ALL-FATHER, ODIN--
--I FOUGHT ALONGSIDE BALDER THE BRAVE--
--AND THE MIGHTY THOR--
I SHALL DEFEAT YO--
KRAK
UNF!
THE HAMMER!
LOKI!

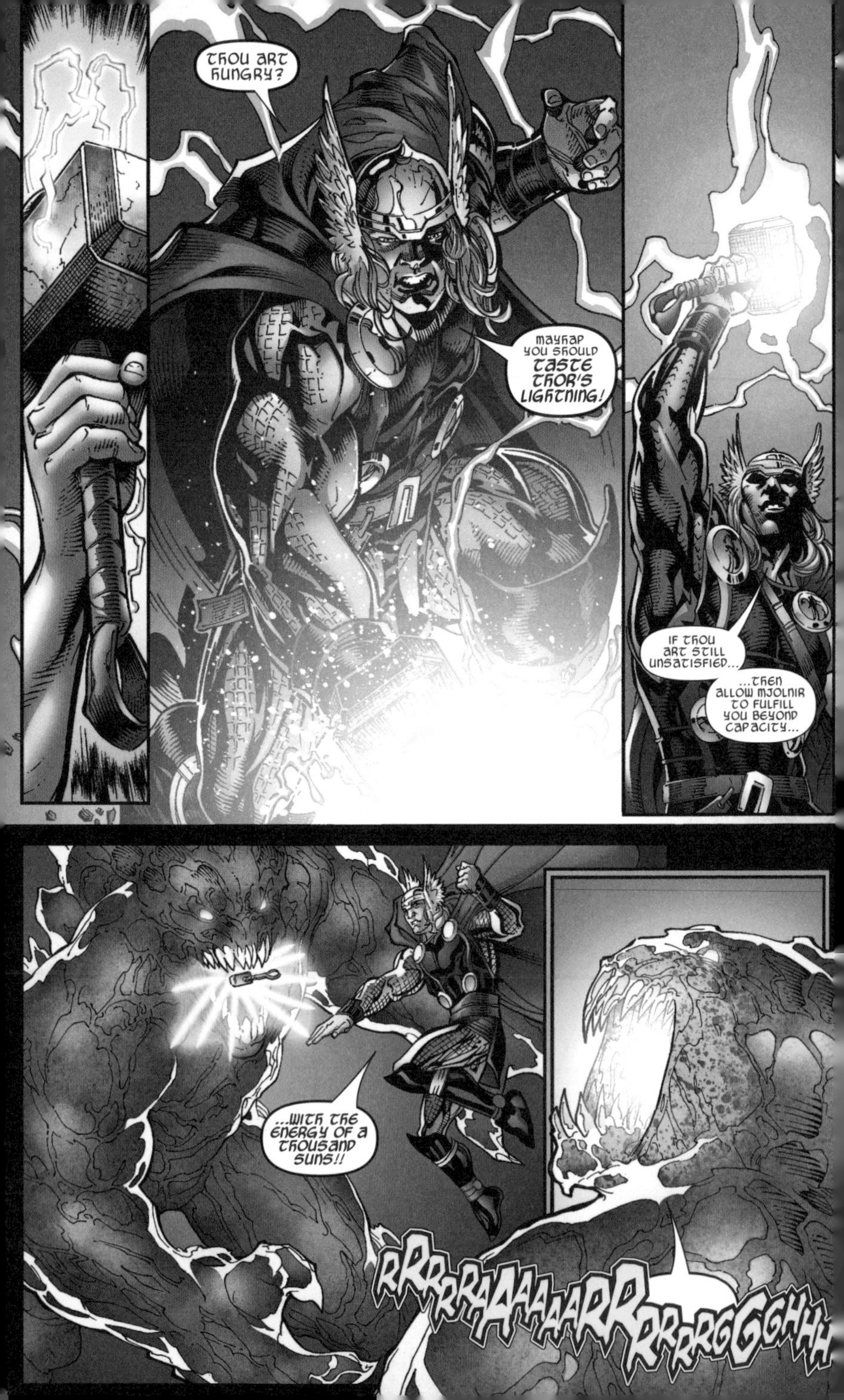
THOU ART HUNGRY?
MAYHAP YOU SHOULD TASTE THOR'S LIGHTNING!
IF THOU ART STILL UNSATISFIED...
...THEN ALLOW MJOLNIR TO FULFILL YOU BEYOND CAPACITY...
...WITH THE ENERGY OF A THOUSAND SUNS!!
RRRRRAAAAAARRRRRRGGGHHH

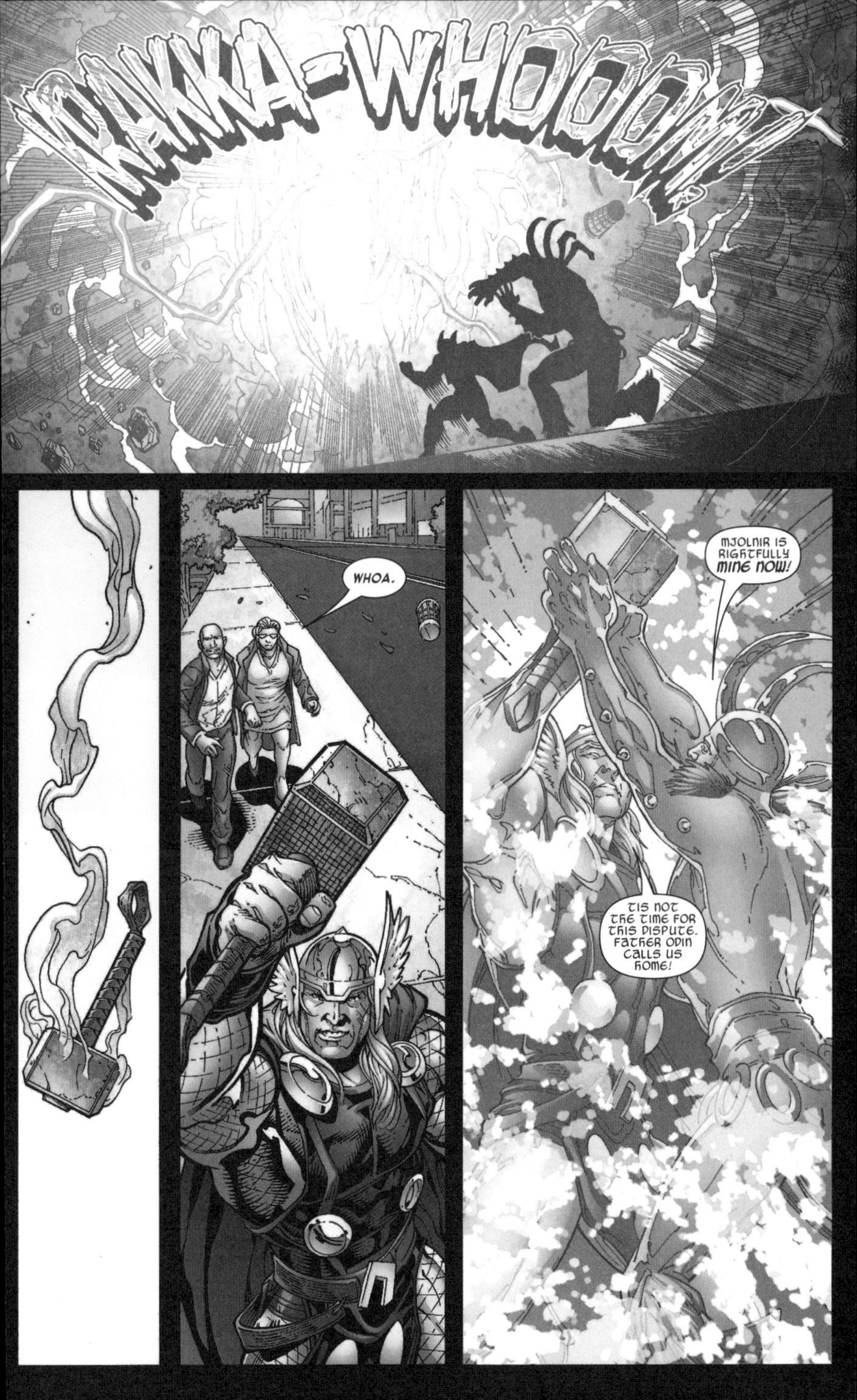
WHOA.
MJOLNIR IS RIGHTFULLY MINE NOW!
TIS NOT THE TIME FOR THIS DISPUTE. FATHER ODIN CALLS US HOME!

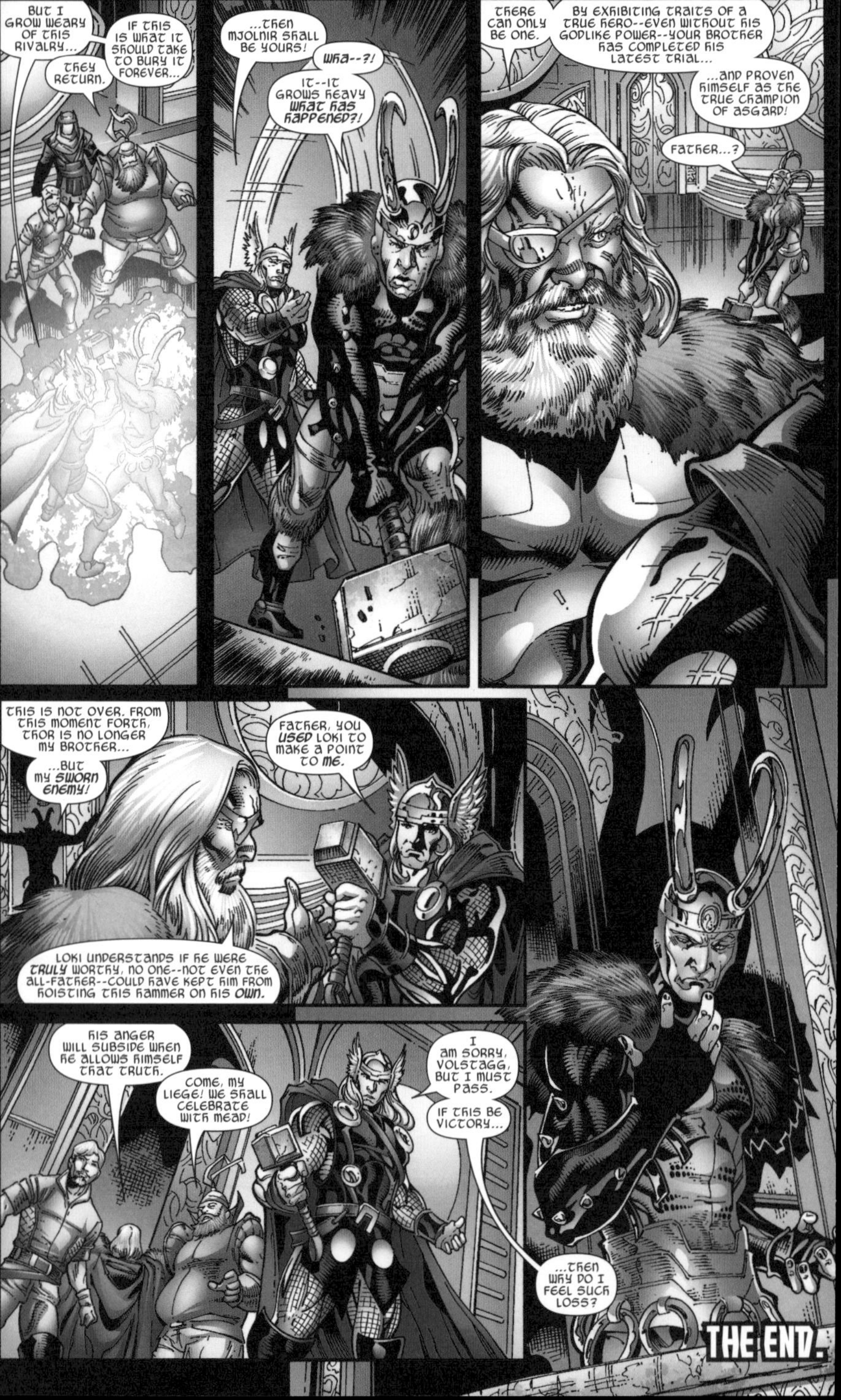

BUT I GROW WEARY OF THIS RIVALRY...
IF THIS IS WHAT IT SHOULD TAKE TO BURY IT FOREVER...
THEY RETURN.
...THEN MJOLNIR SHALL BE YOURS!
WHA--?!
IT--IT GROWS HEAVY WHAT HAS HAPPENED?!
THERE CAN ONLY BE ONE.
BY EXHIBITING TRAITS OF A TRUE HERO--EVEN WITHOUT HIS GODLIKE POWER--YOUR BROTHER HAS COMPLETED HIS LATEST TRIAL...
...AND PROVEN HIMSELF AS THE TRUE CHAMPION OF ASGARD!
FATHER...?
THIS IS NOT OVER. FROM THIS MOMENT FORTH, THOR IS NO LONGER MY BROTHER...
...BUT MY SWORN ENEMY!
FATHER, YOU USED LOKI TO MAKE A POINT TO ME.
LOKI UNDERSTANDS IF HE WERE TRULY WORTHY, NO ONE--NOT EVEN THE ALL-FATHER--COULD HAVE KEPT HIM FROM HOISTING THIS HAMMER ON HIS OWN.
HIS ANGER WILL SUBSIDE WHEN HE ALLOWS HIMSELF THAT TRUTH.
COME, MY LIEGE! WE SHALL CELEBRATE WITH MEAD!
I AM SORRY, VOLSTAGG, BUT I MUST PASS.
IF THIS BE VICTORY...
...THEN WHY DO I FEEL SUCH LOSS?
THE END.

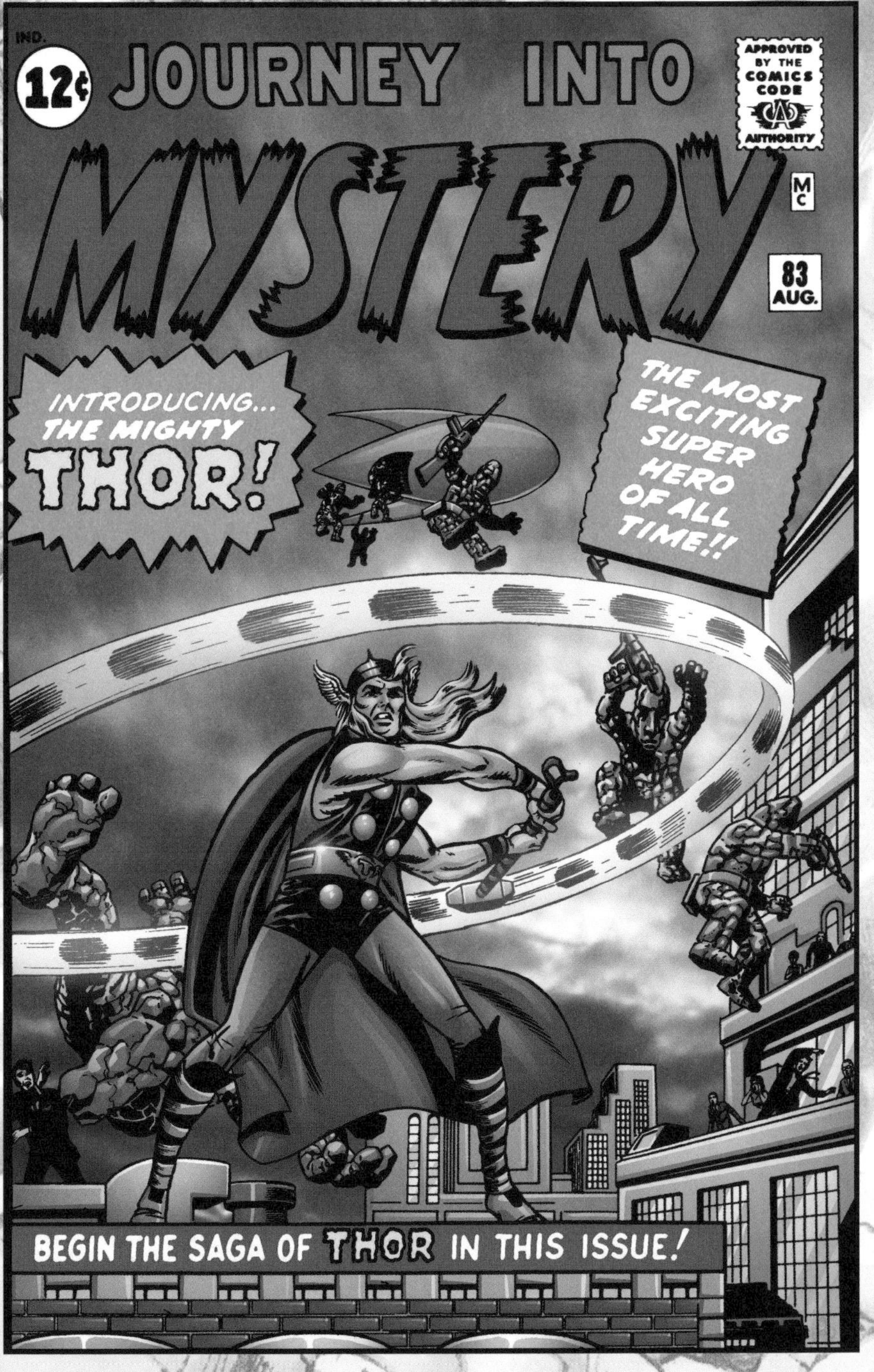
IND.
12¢
JOURNEY INTO
MYSTERY
MC
APPROVED BY THE COMICS CODE AUTHORITY
83
AUG.
INTRODUCING... THE MIGHTY THOR!
THE MOST EXCITING SUPER HERO OF ALL TIME!!
BEGIN THE SAGA OF THOR IN THIS ISSUE!

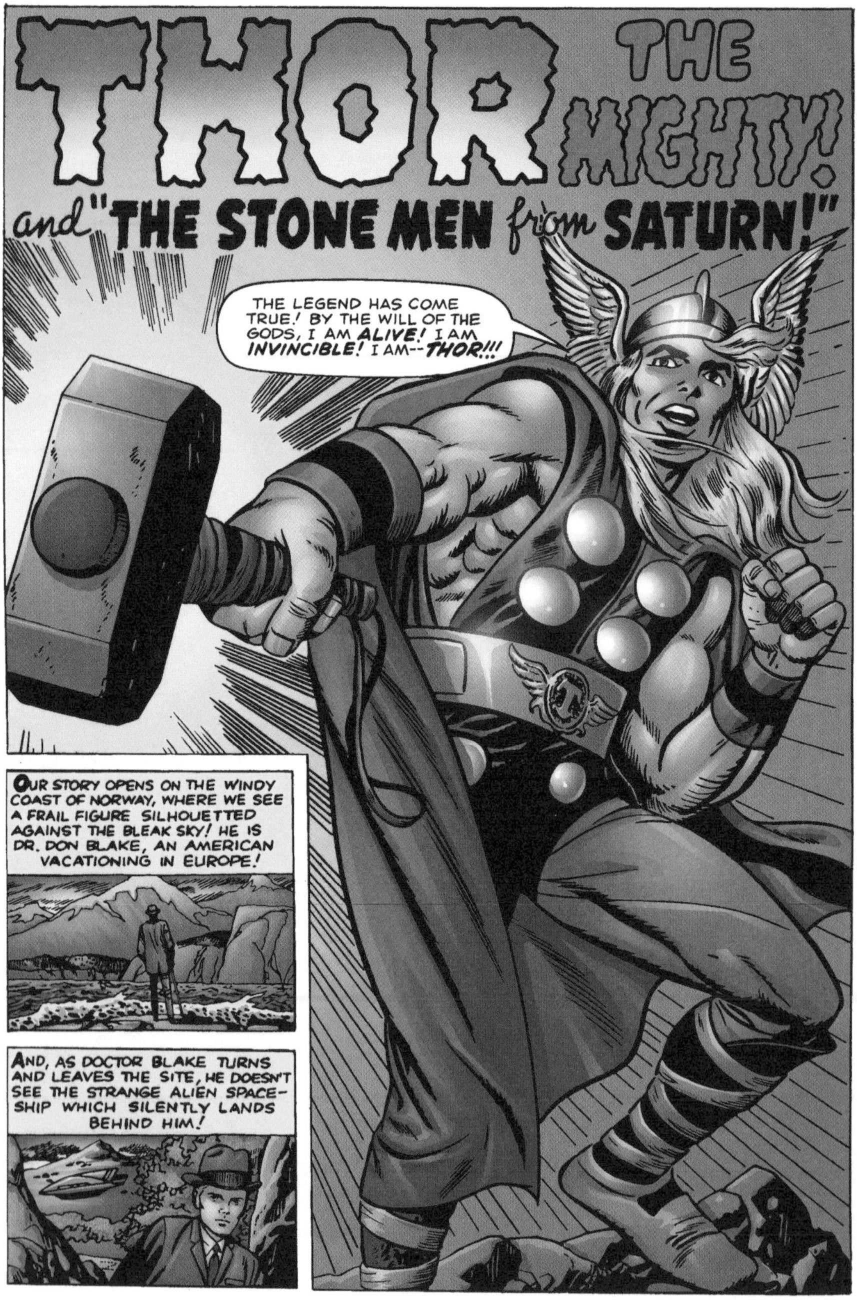
THOR THE MIGHTY!
and "THE STONE MEN from SATURN!"
THE LEGEND HAS COME TRUE! BY THE WILL OF THE GODS, I AM ALIVE! I AM INVINCIBLE! I AM--THOR!!!
OUR STORY OPENS ON THE WINDY COAST OF NORWAY, WHERE WE SEE A FRAIL FIGURE SILHOUETTED AGAINST THE BLEAK SKY! HE IS DR. DON BLAKE, AN AMERICAN VACATIONING IN EUROPE!
AND, AS DOCTOR BLAKE TURNS AND LEAVES THE SITE, HE DOESN'T SEE THE STRANGE ALIEN SPACE-SHIP WHICH SILENTLY LANDS BEHIND HIM!

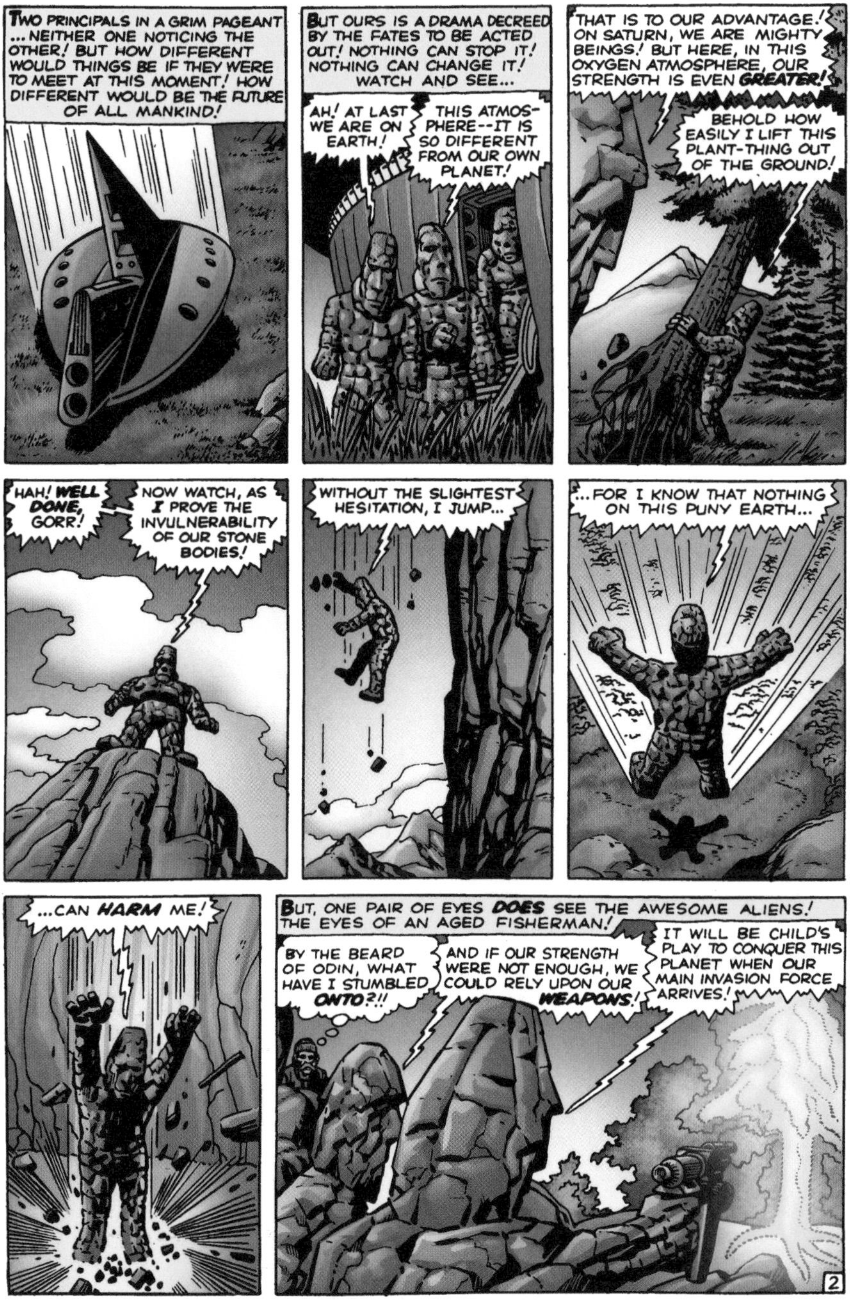

TWO PRINCIPALS IN A GRIM PAGEANT ... NEITHER ONE NOTICING THE OTHER! BUT HOW DIFFERENT WOULD THINGS BE IF THEY WERE TO MEET AT THIS MOMENT! HOW DIFFERENT WOULD BE THE FUTURE OF ALL MANKIND!
BUT OURS IS A DRAMA DECREED BY THE FATES TO BE ACTED OUT! NOTHING CAN STOP IT! NOTHING CAN CHANGE IT! WATCH AND SEE...
AH! AT LAST WE ARE ON EARTH!
THIS ATMOSPHERE--IT IS SO DIFFERENT FROM OUR OWN PLANET!
THAT IS TO OUR ADVANTAGE! ON SATURN, WE ARE MIGHTY BEINGS! BUT HERE, IN THIS OXYGEN ATMOSPHERE, OUR STRENGTH IS EVEN GREATER!
BEHOLD HOW EASILY I LIFT THIS PLANT-THING OUT OF THE GROUND!
HAH! WELL DONE, GORR!
NOW WATCH, AS I PROVE THE INVULNERABILITY OF OUR STONE BODIES!
WITHOUT THE SLIGHTEST HESITATION, I JUMP...
...FOR I KNOW THAT NOTHING ON THIS PUNY EARTH...
...CAN HARM ME!
BUT, ONE PAIR OF EYES DOES SEE THE AWESOME ALIENS! THE EYES OF AN AGED FISHERMAN!
BY THE BEARD OF ODIN, WHAT HAVE I STUMBLED ONTO?!!
AND IF OUR STRENGTH WERE NOT ENOUGH, WE COULD RELY UPON OUR WEAPONS!
IT WILL BE CHILD'S PLAY TO CONQUER THIS PLANET WHEN OUR MAIN INVASION FORCE ARRIVES!
2

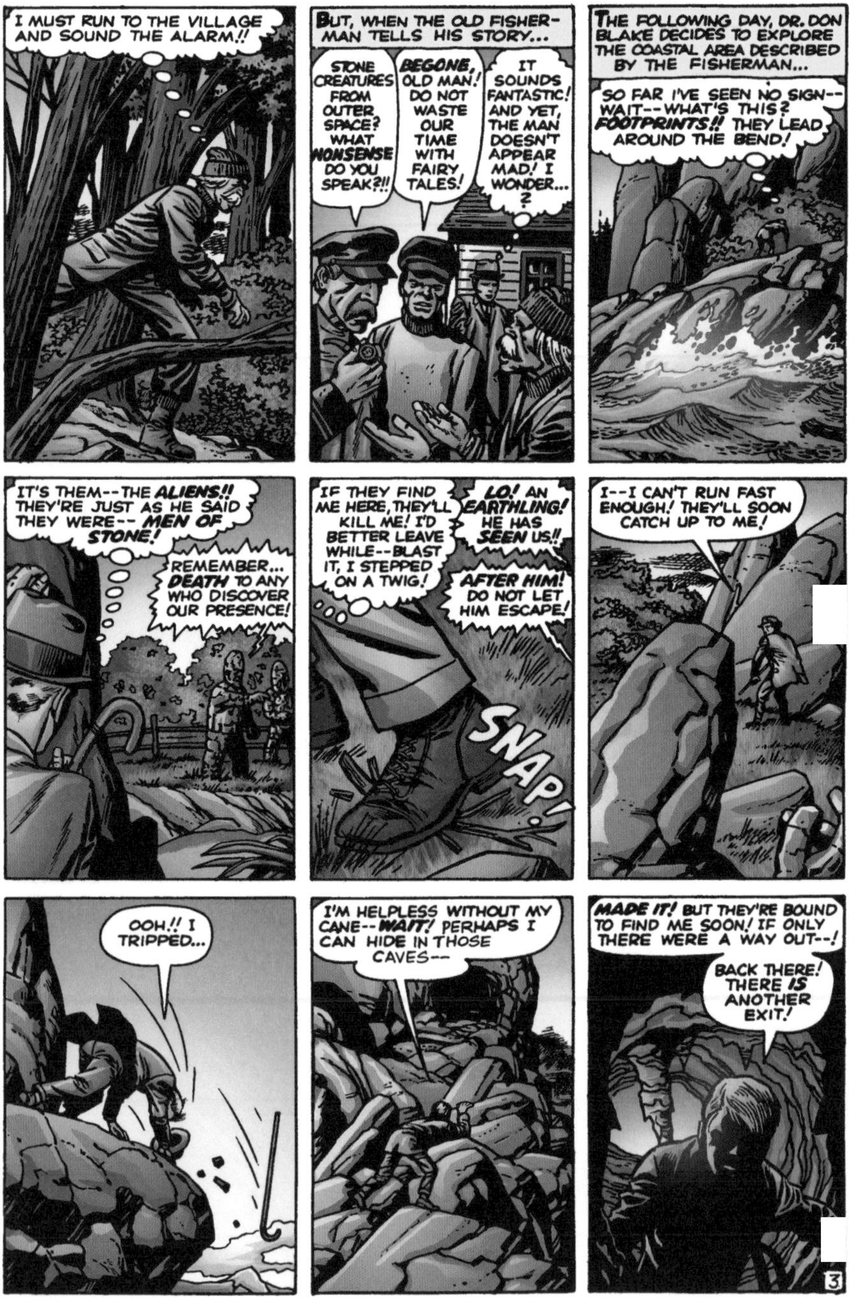

I MUST RUN TO THE VILLAGE AND SOUND THE ALARM!!
BUT, WHEN THE OLD FISHERMAN TELLS HIS STORY...
STONE CREATURES FROM OUTER SPACE? WHAT NONSENSE DO YOU SPEAK?!!
BEGONE, OLD MAN! DO NOT WASTE OUR TIME WITH FAIRY TALES!
IT SOUNDS FANTASTIC! AND YET, THE MAN DOESN'T APPEAR MAD! I WONDER...?
THE FOLLOWING DAY, DR. DON BLAKE DECIDES TO EXPLORE THE COASTAL AREA DESCRIBED BY THE FISHERMAN...
SO FAR I'VE SEEN NO SIGN--WAIT--WHAT'S THIS? FOOTPRINTS!! THEY LEAD AROUND THE BEND!
IT'S THEM--THE ALIENS!! THEY'RE JUST AS HE SAID THEY WERE--MEN OF STONE!
REMEMBER... DEATH TO ANY WHO DISCOVER OUR PRESENCE!
IF THEY FIND ME HERE, THEY'LL KILL ME! I'D BETTER LEAVE WHILE--BLAST IT, I STEPPED ON A TWIG!
LO! AN EARTHLING! HE HAS SEEN US!!
AFTER HIM! DO NOT LET HIM ESCAPE!
SNAP!
I--I CAN'T RUN FAST ENOUGH! THEY'LL SOON CATCH UP TO ME!
OOH!! I TRIPPED...
I'M HELPLESS WITHOUT MY CANE--WAIT! PERHAPS I CAN HIDE IN THOSE CAVES--
MADE IT! BUT THEY'RE BOUND TO FIND ME SOON! IF ONLY THERE WERE A WAY OUT--!
BACK THERE! THERE IS ANOTHER EXIT!

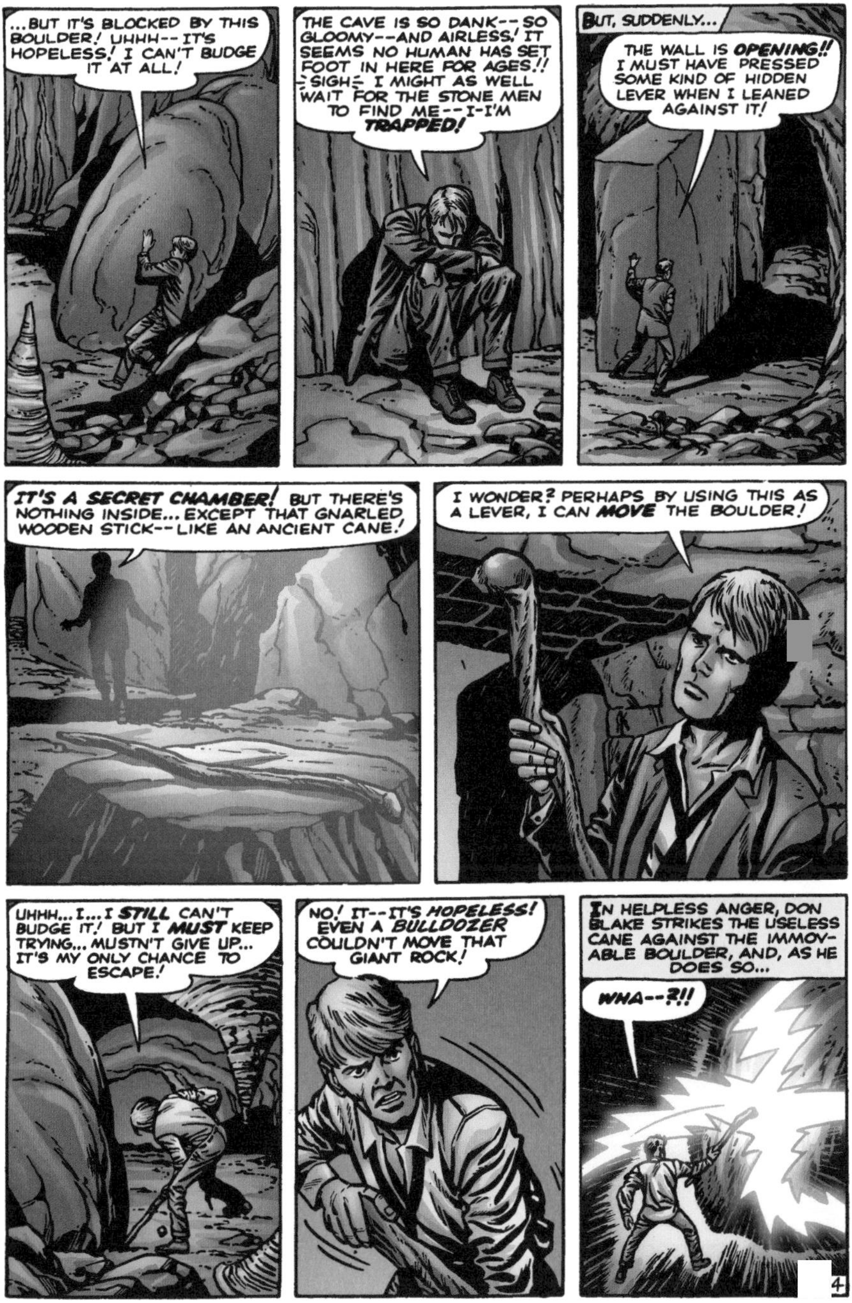
...BUT IT'S BLOCKED BY THIS BOULDER! UHHH--IT'S HOPELESS! I CAN'T BUDGE IT AT ALL!
THE CAVE IS SO DANK--SO GLOOMY--AND AIRLESS! IT SEEMS NO HUMAN HAS SET FOOT IN HERE FOR AGES!! -SIGH- I MIGHT AS WELL WAIT FOR THE STONE MEN TO FIND ME--I-I'M TRAPPED!
BUT, SUDDENLY...
THE WALL IS OPENING!! I MUST HAVE PRESSED SOME KIND OF HIDDEN LEVER WHEN I LEANED AGAINST IT!
IT'S A SECRET CHAMBER! BUT THERE'S NOTHING INSIDE... EXCEPT THAT GNARLED WOODEN STICK--LIKE AN ANCIENT CANE!
I WONDER? PERHAPS BY USING THIS AS A LEVER, I CAN MOVE THE BOULDER!
UHHH... I... I STILL CAN'T BUDGE IT! BUT I MUST KEEP TRYING... MUSTN'T GIVE UP... IT'S MY ONLY CHANCE TO ESCAPE!
NO! IT--IT'S HOPELESS! EVEN A BULLDOZER COULDN'T MOVE THAT GIANT ROCK!
IN HELPLESS ANGER, DON BLAKE STRIKES THE USELESS CANE AGAINST THE IMMOVABLE BOULDER, AND, AS HE DOES SO...
WHA--?!!
4

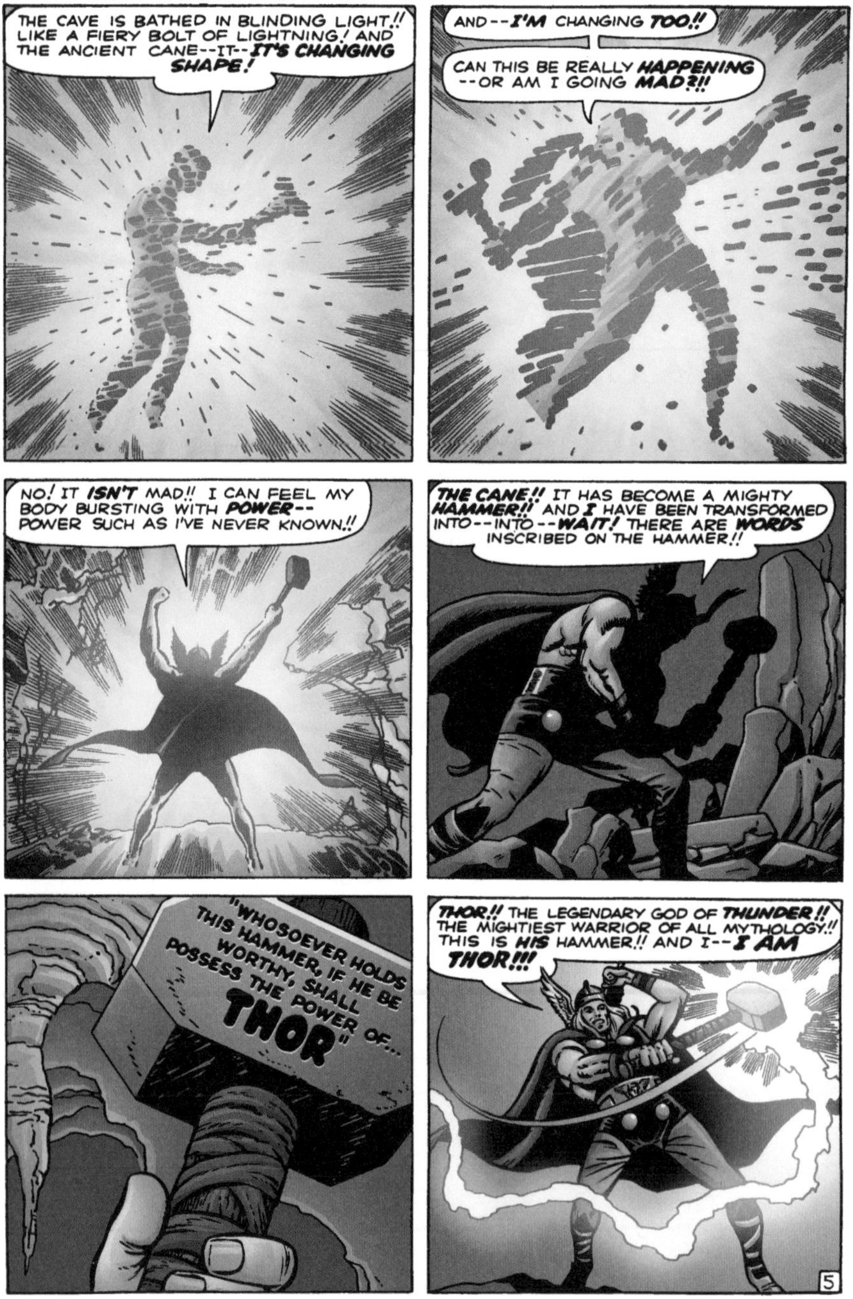
THE CAVE IS BATHED IN BLINDING LIGHT!! LIKE A FIERY BOLT OF LIGHTNING! AND THE ANCIENT CANE--IT--IT'S CHANGING SHAPE!
AND--I'M CHANGING TOO!!
CAN THIS BE REALLY HAPPENING --OR AM I GOING MAD?!!
NO! IT ISN'T MAD!! I CAN FEEL MY BODY BURSTING WITH POWER-- POWER SUCH AS I'VE NEVER KNOWN!!
THE CANE!! IT HAS BECOME A MIGHTY HAMMER!! AND I HAVE BEEN TRANSFORMED INTO--INTO--WAIT! THERE ARE WORDS INSCRIBED ON THE HAMMER!!
"WHOSOEVER HOLDS THIS HAMMER, IF HE BE WORTHY, SHALL POSSESS THE POWER OF... THOR"
THOR!! THE LEGENDARY GOD OF THUNDER!! THE MIGHTIEST WARRIOR OF ALL MYTHOLOGY!! THIS IS HIS HAMMER!! AND I--I AM THOR!!!

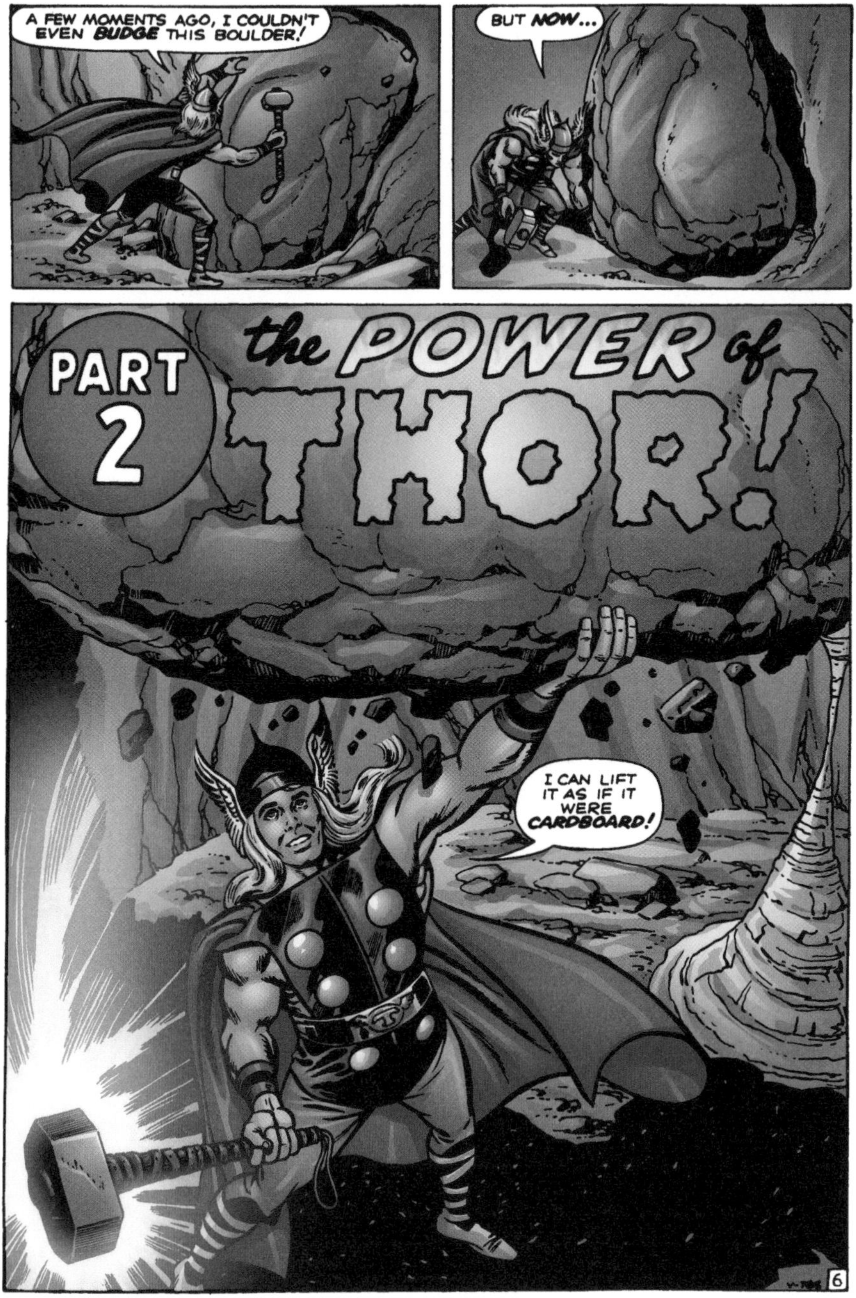
A FEW MOMENTS AGO, I COULDN'T EVEN **BUDGE** THIS BOULDER!
BUT **NOW**...
PART 2
the POWER of THOR!
I CAN LIFT IT AS IF IT WERE **CARDBOARD**!
6

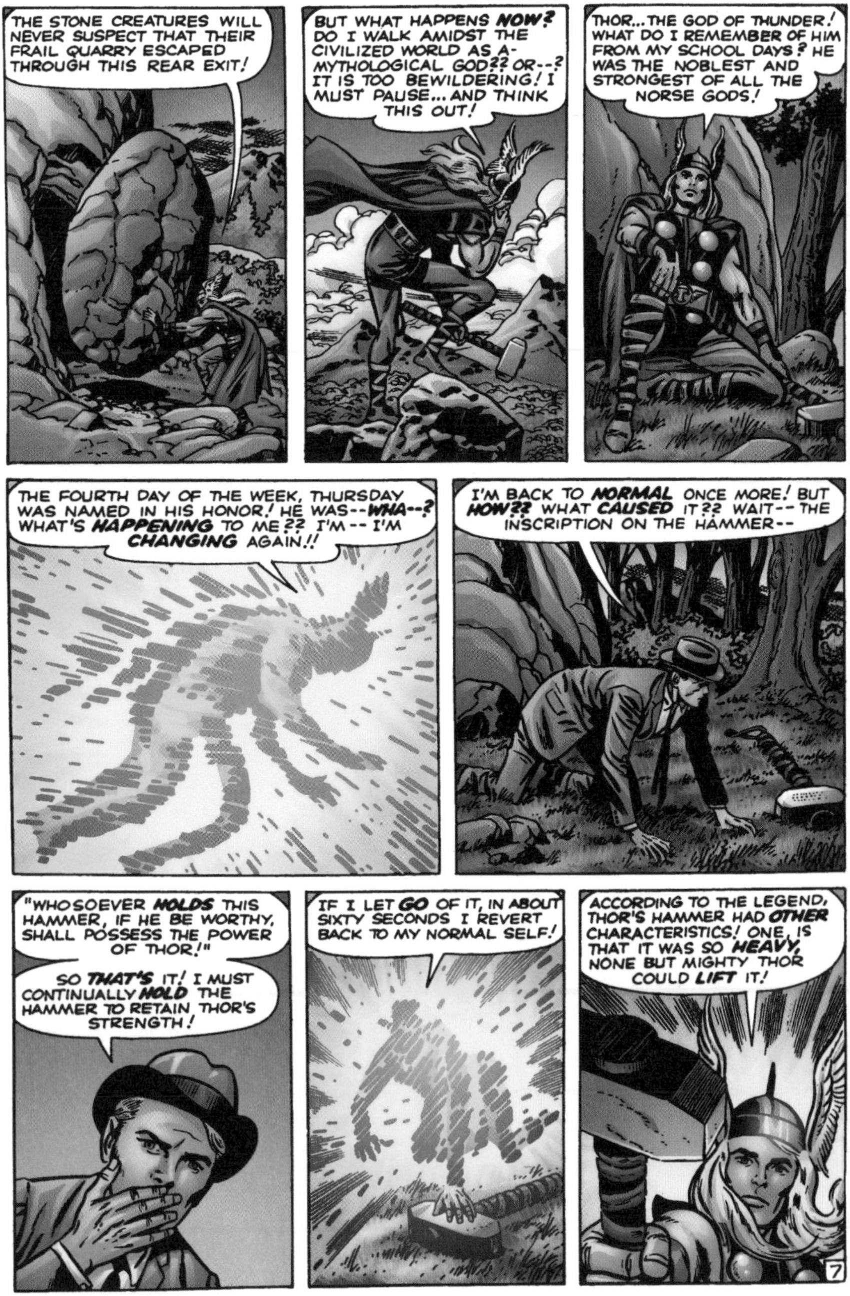
THE STONE CREATURES WILL NEVER SUSPECT THAT THEIR FRAIL QUARRY ESCAPED THROUGH THIS REAR EXIT!
BUT WHAT HAPPENS NOW? DO I WALK AMIDST THE CIVILIZED WORLD AS A MYTHOLOGICAL GOD?? OR--? IT IS TOO BEWILDERING! I MUST PAUSE... AND THINK THIS OUT!
THOR... THE GOD OF THUNDER! WHAT DO I REMEMBER OF HIM FROM MY SCHOOL DAYS? HE WAS THE NOBLEST AND STRONGEST OF ALL THE NORSE GODS!
THE FOURTH DAY OF THE WEEK, THURSDAY WAS NAMED IN HIS HONOR! HE WAS--WHA--? WHAT'S HAPPENING TO ME?? I'M -- I'M CHANGING AGAIN!!
I'M BACK TO NORMAL ONCE MORE! BUT HOW?? WHAT CAUSED IT?? WAIT-- THE INSCRIPTION ON THE HAMMER--
"WHOSOEVER HOLDS THIS HAMMER, IF HE BE WORTHY, SHALL POSSESS THE POWER OF THOR!"
SO THAT'S IT! I MUST CONTINUALLY HOLD THE HAMMER TO RETAIN THOR'S STRENGTH!
IF I LET GO OF IT, IN ABOUT SIXTY SECONDS I REVERT BACK TO MY NORMAL SELF!
ACCORDING TO THE LEGEND, THOR'S HAMMER HAD OTHER CHARACTERISTICS! ONE, IS THAT IT WAS SO HEAVY, NONE BUT MIGHTY THOR COULD LIFT IT!
7

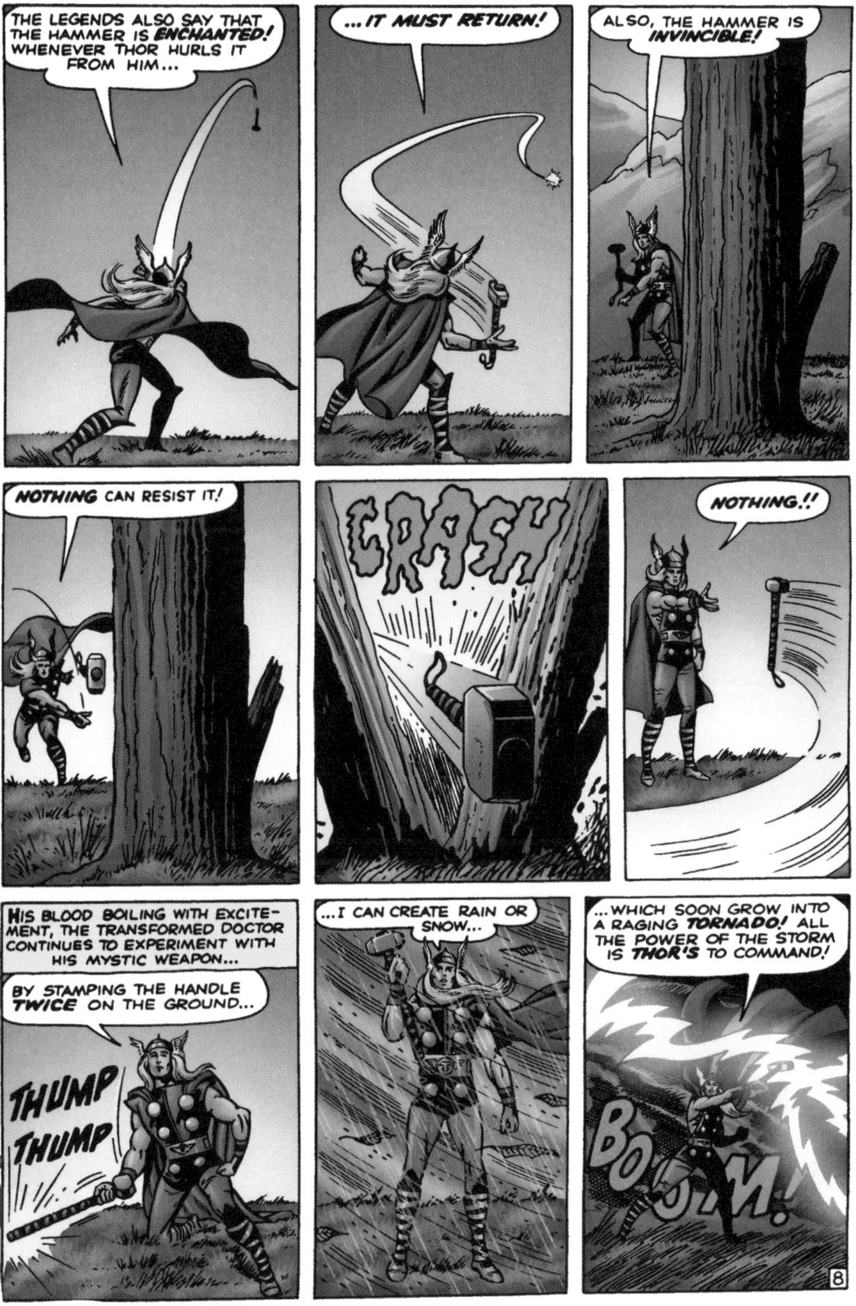
THE LEGENDS ALSO SAY THAT THE HAMMER IS ENCHANTED! WHENEVER THOR HURLS IT FROM HIM...
...IT MUST RETURN!
ALSO, THE HAMMER IS INVINCIBLE!
NOTHING CAN RESIST IT!
CRASH
NOTHING.!!
HIS BLOOD BOILING WITH EXCITEMENT, THE TRANSFORMED DOCTOR CONTINUES TO EXPERIMENT WITH HIS MYSTIC WEAPON...
BY STAMPING THE HANDLE TWICE ON THE GROUND...
THUMP
THUMP
...I CAN CREATE RAIN OR SNOW...
...WHICH SOON GROW INTO A RAGING TORNADO! ALL THE POWER OF THE STORM IS THOR'S TO COMMAND!
8

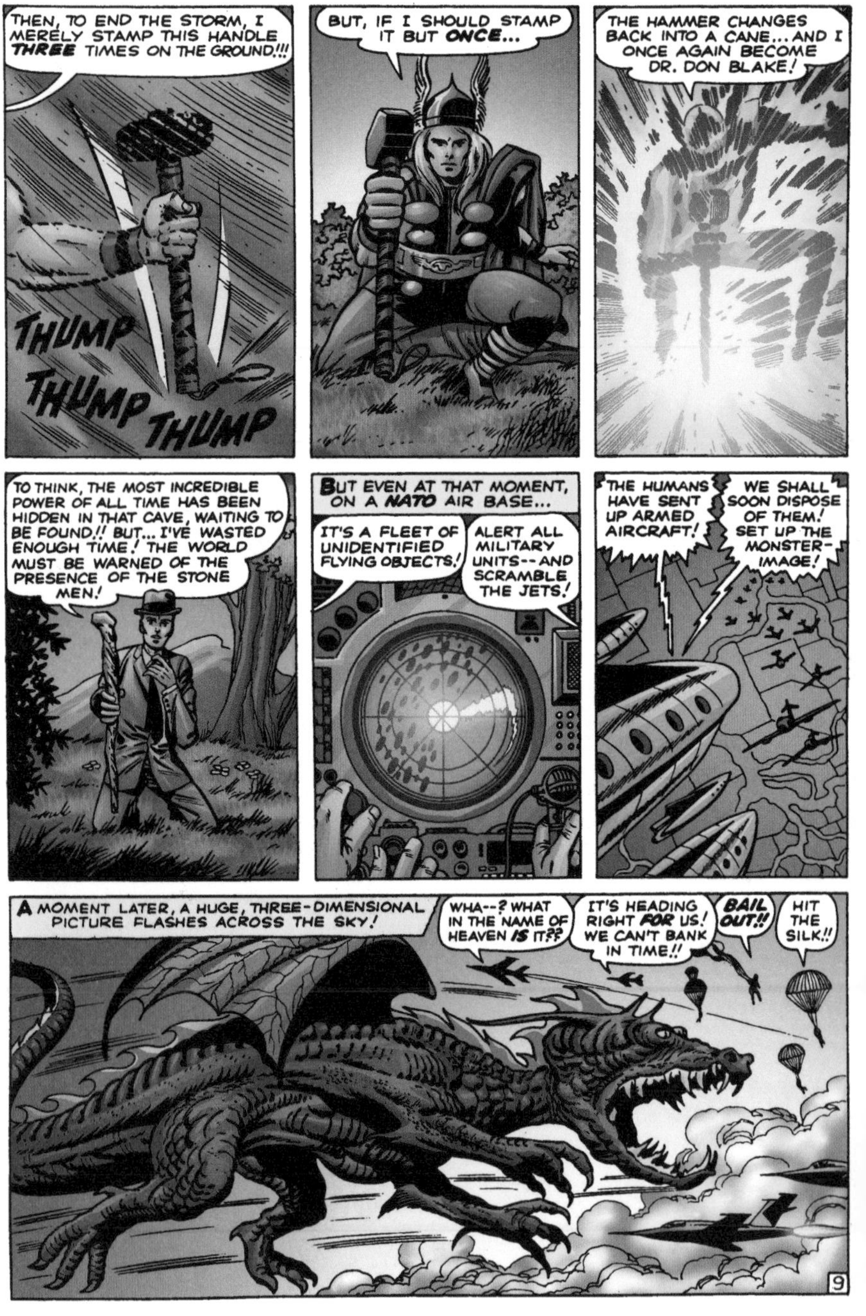
THEN, TO END THE STORM, I MERELY STAMP THIS HANDLE THREE TIMES ON THE GROUND!!!
THUMP
THUMP
THUMP
BUT, IF I SHOULD STAMP IT BUT ONCE...
THE HAMMER CHANGES BACK INTO A CANE... AND I ONCE AGAIN BECOME DR. DON BLAKE!
TO THINK, THE MOST INCREDIBLE POWER OF ALL TIME HAS BEEN HIDDEN IN THAT CAVE, WAITING TO BE FOUND!! BUT... I'VE WASTED ENOUGH TIME! THE WORLD MUST BE WARNED OF THE PRESENCE OF THE STONE MEN!
BUT EVEN AT THAT MOMENT, ON A NATO AIR BASE...
IT'S A FLEET OF UNIDENTIFIED FLYING OBJECTS!
ALERT ALL MILITARY UNITS--AND SCRAMBLE THE JETS!
THE HUMANS HAVE SENT UP ARMED AIRCRAFT!
WE SHALL SOON DISPOSE OF THEM! SET UP THE MONSTER-IMAGE!
A MOMENT LATER, A HUGE, THREE-DIMENSIONAL PICTURE FLASHES ACROSS THE SKY!
WHA--? WHAT IN THE NAME OF HEAVEN IS IT??
IT'S HEADING RIGHT FOR US! WE CAN'T BANK IN TIME!!
BAIL OUT!!
HIT THE SILK!!
9

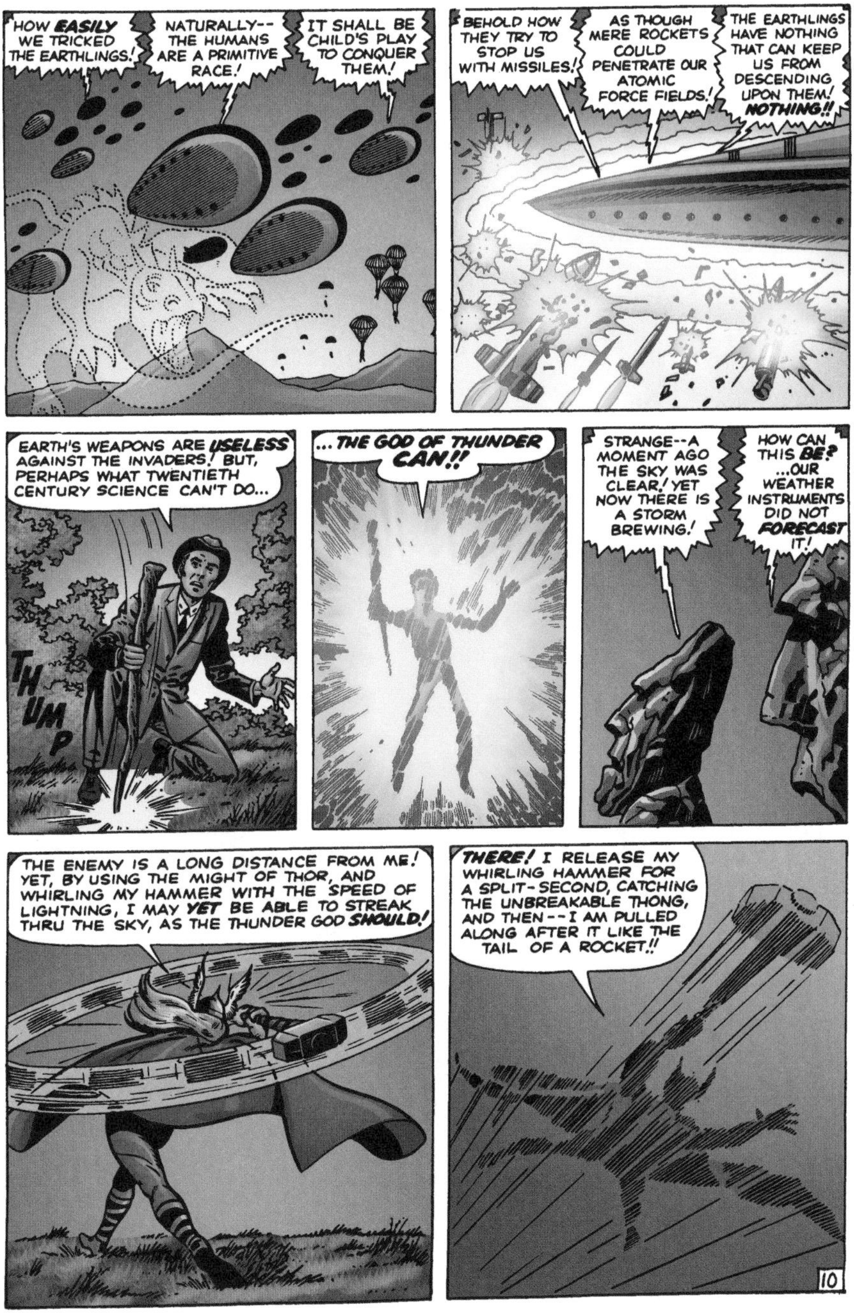
HOW EASILY WE TRICKED THE EARTHLINGS!
NATURALLY-- THE HUMANS ARE A PRIMITIVE RACE!
IT SHALL BE CHILD'S PLAY TO CONQUER THEM!
BEHOLD HOW THEY TRY TO STOP US WITH MISSILES!
AS THOUGH MERE ROCKETS COULD PENETRATE OUR ATOMIC FORCE FIELDS!
THE EARTHLINGS HAVE NOTHING THAT CAN KEEP US FROM DESCENDING UPON THEM! NOTHING!!
EARTH'S WEAPONS ARE USELESS AGAINST THE INVADERS! BUT, PERHAPS WHAT TWENTIETH CENTURY SCIENCE CAN'T DO...
THUMP
...THE GOD OF THUNDER CAN!!
STRANGE--A MOMENT AGO THE SKY WAS CLEAR! YET NOW THERE IS A STORM BREWING!
HOW CAN THIS BE? ...OUR WEATHER INSTRUMENTS DID NOT FORECAST IT!
THE ENEMY IS A LONG DISTANCE FROM ME! YET, BY USING THE MIGHT OF THOR, AND WHIRLING MY HAMMER WITH THE SPEED OF LIGHTNING, I MAY YET BE ABLE TO STREAK THRU THE SKY, AS THE THUNDER GOD SHOULD!
THERE! I RELEASE MY WHIRLING HAMMER FOR A SPLIT-SECOND, CATCHING THE UNBREAKABLE THONG, AND THEN--I AM PULLED ALONG AFTER IT LIKE THE TAIL OF A ROCKET!!
10

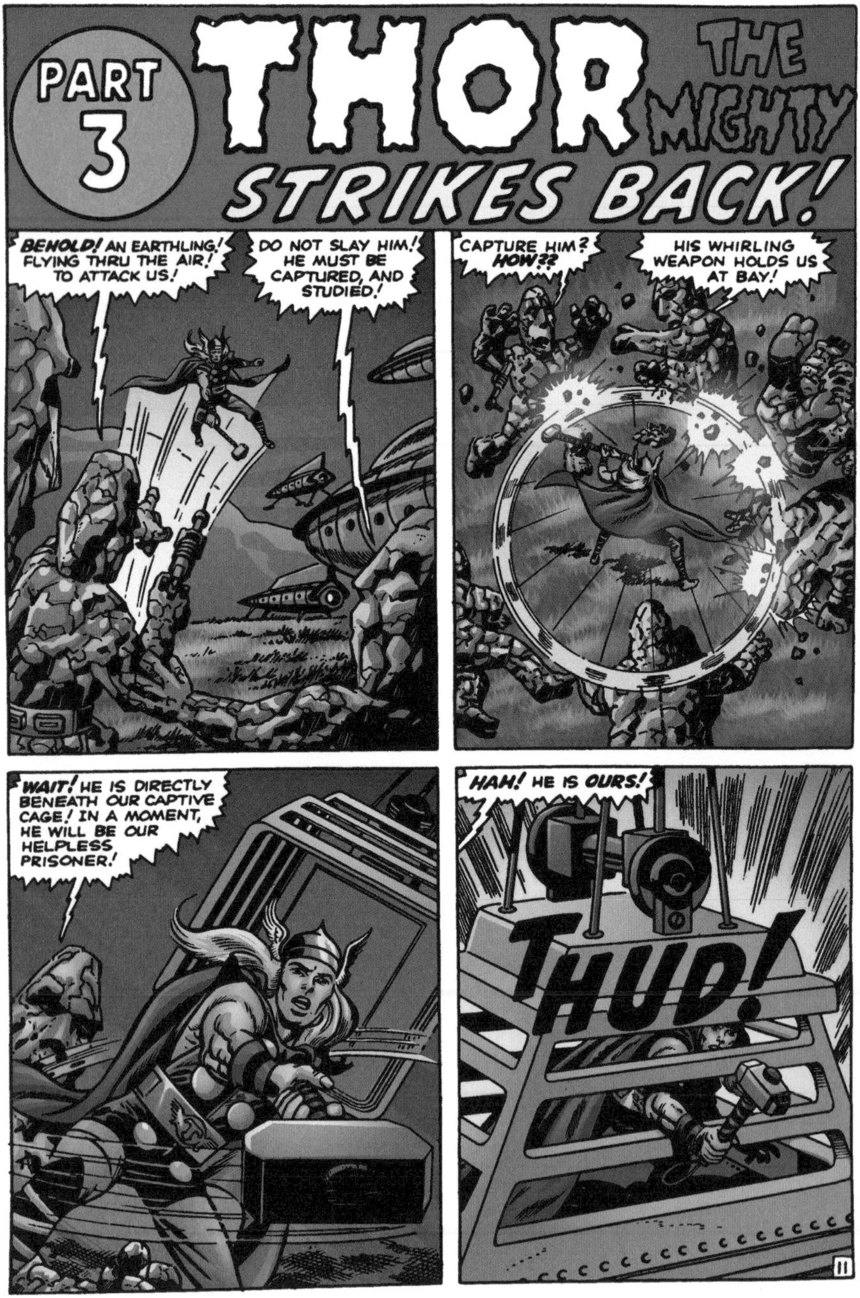
PART 3
THOR THE MIGHTY STRIKES BACK!
BEHOLD! AN EARTHLING! FLYING THRU THE AIR! TO ATTACK US!
DO NOT SLAY HIM! HE MUST BE CAPTURED, AND STUDIED!
CAPTURE HIM? HOW??
HIS WHIRLING WEAPON HOLDS US AT BAY!
WAIT! HE IS DIRECTLY BENEATH OUR CAPTIVE CAGE! IN A MOMENT, HE WILL BE OUR HELPLESS PRISONER!
HAH! HE IS OURS!
THUD!
11

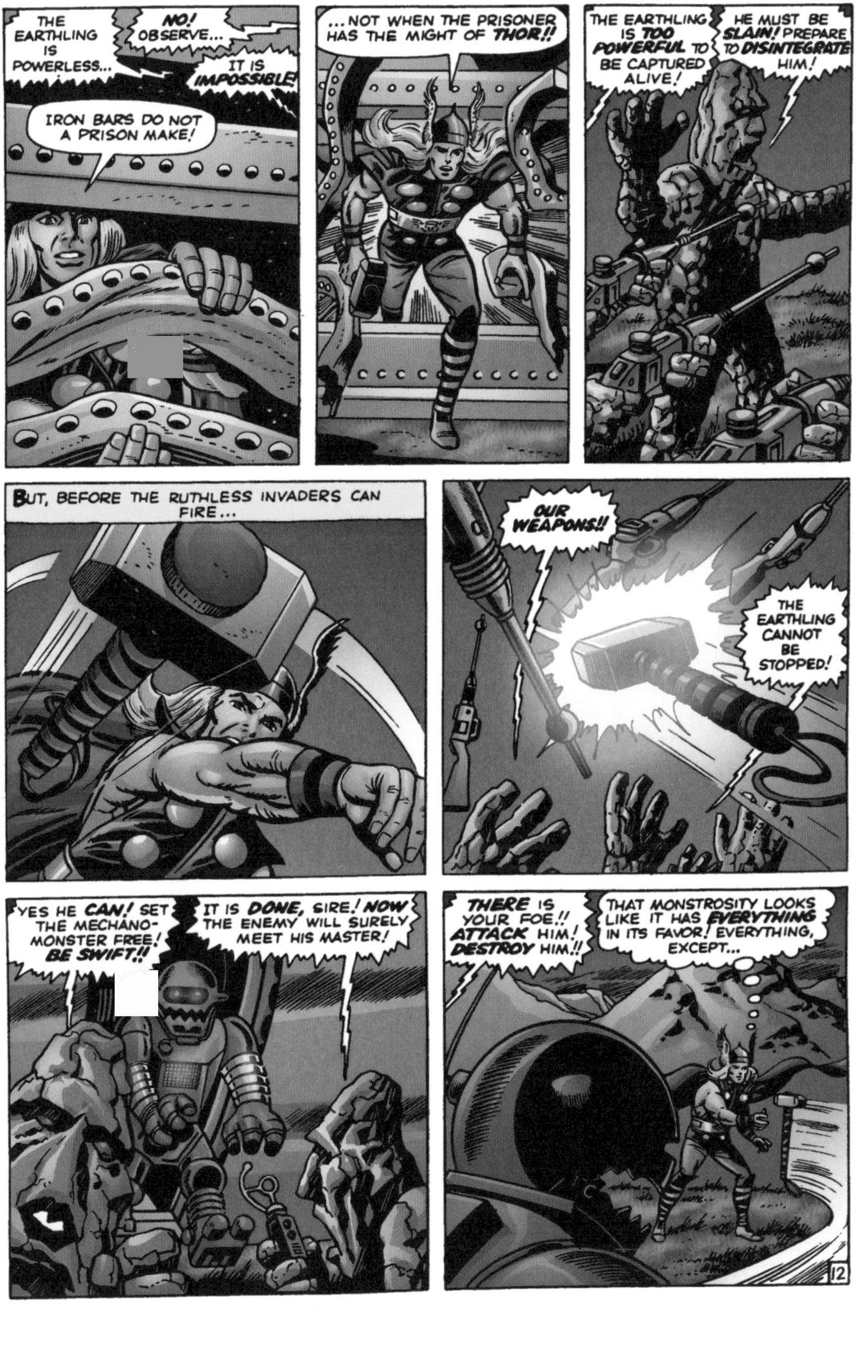
THE EARTHLING IS POWERLESS...
NO! OBSERVE...
IT IS IMPOSSIBLE!
IRON BARS DO NOT A PRISON MAKE!
...NOT WHEN THE PRISONER HAS THE MIGHT OF THOR!!
THE EARTHLING IS TOO POWERFUL TO BE CAPTURED ALIVE!
HE MUST BE SLAIN! PREPARE TO DISINTEGRATE HIM!
BUT, BEFORE THE RUTHLESS INVADERS CAN FIRE...
OUR WEAPONS!!
THE EARTHLING CANNOT BE STOPPED!
YES HE CAN! SET THE MECHANO-MONSTER FREE! BE SWIFT!!
IT IS DONE, SIRE! NOW THE ENEMY WILL SURELY MEET HIS MASTER!
THERE IS YOUR FOE!! ATTACK HIM! DESTROY HIM!!
THAT MONSTROSITY LOOKS LIKE IT HAS EVERYTHING IN ITS FAVOR! EVERYTHING, EXCEPT...
12

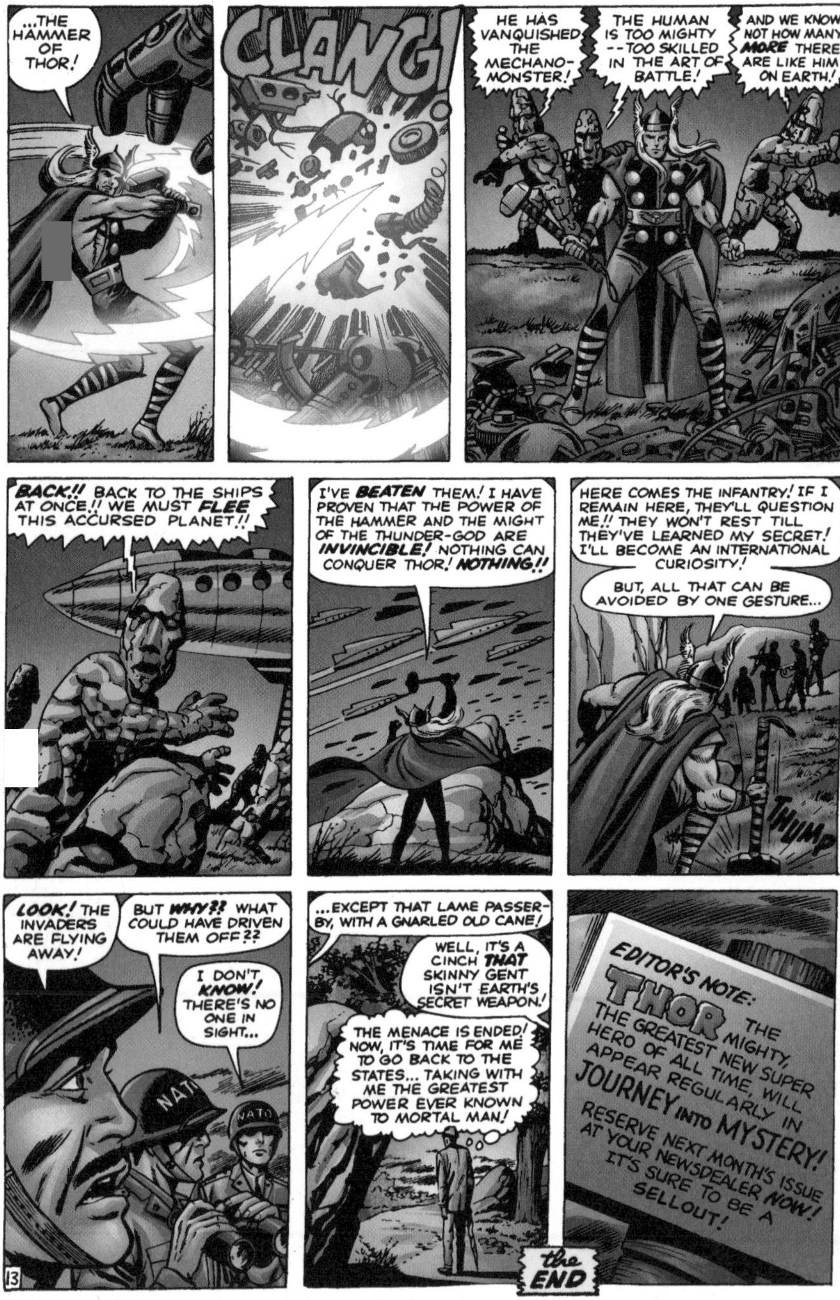

...THE HAMMER OF THOR!
CLANG!
HE HAS VANQUISHED THE MECHANO-MONSTER!
THE HUMAN IS TOO MIGHTY --TOO SKILLED IN THE ART OF BATTLE!
AND WE KNOW NOT HOW MANY MORE THERE ARE LIKE HIM ON EARTH!
BACK!! BACK TO THE SHIPS AT ONCE!! WE MUST FLEE THIS ACCURSED PLANET!!
I'VE BEATEN THEM! I HAVE PROVEN THAT THE POWER OF THE HAMMER AND THE MIGHT OF THE THUNDER-GOD ARE INVINCIBLE! NOTHING CAN CONQUER THOR! NOTHING!!
HERE COMES THE INFANTRY! IF I REMAIN HERE, THEY'LL QUESTION ME!! THEY WON'T REST TILL THEY'VE LEARNED MY SECRET! I'LL BECOME AN INTERNATIONAL CURIOSITY!
BUT, ALL THAT CAN BE AVOIDED BY ONE GESTURE...
THUMP
LOOK! THE INVADERS ARE FLYING AWAY!
BUT WHY?? WHAT COULD HAVE DRIVEN THEM OFF??
I DON'T KNOW! THERE'S NO ONE IN SIGHT...
NATO
NATO
13
...EXCEPT THAT LAME PASSER-BY, WITH A GNARLED OLD CANE!
WELL, IT'S A CINCH THAT SKINNY GENT ISN'T EARTH'S SECRET WEAPON!
THE MENACE IS ENDED! NOW, IT'S TIME FOR ME TO GO BACK TO THE STATES... TAKING WITH ME THE GREATEST POWER EVER KNOWN TO MORTAL MAN!
EDITOR'S NOTE: THOR THE MIGHTY, THE GREATEST NEW SUPER HERO OF ALL TIME, WILL APPEAR REGULARLY IN JOURNEY INTO MYSTERY! RESERVE NEXT MONTH'S ISSUE AT YOUR NEWSDEALER NOW! IT'S SURE TO BE A SELLOUT!
the END